Darwen Born, Blackburn Bred –

Growing up in the Age of Affluence

by

Paul Laxton

Published by New Generation Publishing in 2016

Copyright © Paul Laxton 2016

First Edition

The author asserts the moral right under the Copyright, Designs and Patents Act 1988 to be identified as the author of this work.

All Rights reserved. No part of this publication may be reproduced, stored in a retrieval system or transmitted, in any form or by any means without the prior consent of the author, nor be otherwise circulated in any form of binding or cover other than that which it is published and without a similar condition being imposed on the subsequent purchaser.

www.newgeneration-publishing.com

Contents

About the Author iii

Acknowledgements v

Introduction vii

Chapter One - My Little Town: Blackburn with Darwen.. 1

Chapter Two - Home, Family and Environment 34

Chapter Three - Primary School: Terror by Penguin 71

Chapter Four - Listen to the Band 91

Chapter Five - Grammar School 120

Chapter Six - The Idiot's Lantern 152

Chapter Seven - Rovers Till I Die 189

Chapter Eight - The Terrace Culture 232

Chapter Nine - The World of Work 258

Chapter Ten - Growing Away 279

About the Author

Paul Laxton was born in Darwen, Lancashire, in December 1952. He was educated at St Mary's College, then a Roman Catholic direct grant Grammar School for boys in Blackburn. In 1979 he obtained a Bachelor of Education (Upper Second Class Honours) in History and Education from the University of Keele. After teaching for five years in high schools in Kings Lynn and Newcastle-Under-Lyme, he changed career and joined the prison service as a uniformed officer in 1984. The author served at nine different jails, rising to hold posts as Deputy Governor at Dover, Ford and Lewes prisons, before retiring in 2010. An active trade unionist he served on the National Executive Committee of the Prison Governors Association from 2007 and was awarded Distinguished Life Membership on retirement. In 2013 he published his first book, "26 Years Behind Bars: The Recollections of a Prison Governor", which was crammed with fascinating anecdotes and penetrating insights into the English criminal justice system as well as exposing the suffocating nature of public sector bureaucracy. In 2014 he published his second book, "My Generation: How We Trashed Our Inheritance", a polemic charting the failures of the baby boomer generation when they reached the levers of power.

Now retired, he lives with his wife, Leonore, in West Yorkshire, spending many happy days watching horse racing and cricket as well as being active in both the Civil Service Pensioners Alliance and the Campaign for Real Ale.

Acknowledgements

My long suffering wife Leonore, for her unstinting support and quiet acceptance of my frequent and lengthy retreats to my study

My friend of thirty-seven years, Dave Robins, not just for his proofreading skills, but also for his restraining influence on my tendency to verbal excesses.

My daughter Genevieve, who when she is old and I am long gone can look at the three books on her bookshelf that provide a permanent reminder of where her father came from, what he believed in, and what he did in life.

Introduction

Like my first two books, this is not a scholarly work of history, nor is it truly a memoir or an autobiography. I am under no illusion that my life merits an autobiography in its own right; however, it is appropriate to use aspects and phases of my life to illustrate a key theme of this book: what it was like to grow up in working-class communities, in my case, Blackburn and Darwen, during the period of affluence which lasted for about thirty years – from the end of World War Two until unemployment climbed above the four per cent mark in mid-1975 – and has never been below that since. To use more meaningful figures there has never been less than one million people in the UK unemployed since that fateful year. In December 2014, 1.96 million people seeking work were unemployed, around six per cent of the labour force. William Beveridge, author of the historic report that bears his name, defined full employment as an unemployment rate of no more than three per cent…an annual figure not exceeded after 1945 until 1970. The unemployment rate is not the only measure of affluence, but I would argue that it is the most significant. Until the golden age of jobs after World War Two – apart from wartime itself – there has always been a pool of unemployed people that has kept wages down and kept those in jobs insecure. My point is that job security for a generation changed the lives and expectations of working people, and gave them industrial and political power, as well as spending power that they had never enjoyed before, and sadly have not enjoyed since. For these reasons, it was truly the age of affluence.

Forty years on we have a vast array of consumer goods, which could not have been envisaged in 1975. Tablets, smart phones and smart televisions are the latest "must have" technology that families seem to have almost regardless of the state of their finances, something which symbolises a major change in social attitudes, which could fairly be described as a culture of entitlement. If affluence is defined solely by material possessions, then we live in the most affluent age ever. The problem is that the world of the I-Phone exists alongside zero-hour contracts at work, expensive housing, and a reduction in social mobility. Properly defined, affluence is not simply about consumption. True prosperity is also about security, particularly in old age, opportunity, and the prospect that reasonable aspirations for individuals, families and communities can be realised. In that sense the period in which I grew to manhood was unique.

I was born in 1952, part of the first wave of what are referred to as "baby boomers". Our parents – who had grown up in the "hungry thirties" – no longer had to worry where the next meal was coming from, because even if the father lost his job he could walk into another one on Monday morning. Diseases that denoted an impoverished childhood, such as rickets, declined drastically. As regards opportunity and aspiration for one generation only, working-class children could access free grammar schools and, with the advent of student grants in 1962, progress to university and out into the professions, as I did. The same is not true for our children. Good schools are at a premium and the only predictable outcome of a university education for all except those whose wealthy parents can pay, is thirty years of debt as a consequence of loans and tuition fees. Affluence is also about a feeling of freedom, the shrugging off of dependence. My working-class generation was able to break free from the shackles of our often ignorant and prejudiced parents, and from the worst hypocrisies of organised religion. We were also spared compulsory military service.

This book does not claim to be a sociological tract, although it does use a technique familiar to that discipline, the perspective of the participant observer. Of necessity my perspective is limited on the one hand by the breadth of this book and on the other by the paths I took or were ordained for me. As my mother was Roman Catholic, it followed that her children were too. We were therefore part of a minority, to some extent still looked down on as the faith was associated historically with disloyalty to the crown, and sociologically with Irish Catholic migrants who were perceived as bottom of the social heap until immigrants from Pakistan arrived in the town. I was also part of the minority, around thirty per cent that attended grammar school. As a consequence, my perspective is not that of contemporaries who left school at fifteen or sixteen years old, were manual workers until their retirement, and who spent their entire lives in what is now the borough of Blackburn with Darwen. For a number of them affluence will have been cruelly curtailed by the de-industrialisation that took place in the North and Midlands in the 1980s. Others will have seen their pension schemes closed down by employers pleading poverty. Their adult experiences will be very different to the ones I describe with respect to myself in the final chapter. However, although our childhoods will have been differentiated by religion and education, there is much that we have in common through the music we loved, the football team we watched and the working-class culture that we shared. I have tried to bring that to life in this book.

The format of the book is partly chronological and partly thematic with the chapters interspersed. Chapters One and Two set the scene. Blackburn – and I include Darwen alongside Blackburn, although the two towns were not formally united for local government purposes until 1974 – is the subject of a potted history and sociology, as it is the town where I grew up. I hope that local readers who are after all my main target audience, will forgive me the inevitable errors and lapses of memory. However, the reader will not need to have grown up in Blackburn to identify with it, as in many respects it could be any industrial town or city in the North and Midlands, or for that matter any industrial area in Wales or Scotland. Blackburn is typical of the towns and cities that expanded at a rate of knots during the industrial revolution, establishing Great Britain as the workshop of the world in the nineteenth century, before being hit by the great depression in the 1930s. The need to fight a major war and the post-war government consensus on the desirability of full employment brought prosperity back to the town, but in reality decline and affluence were hitched together on an uneasy tandem during my youth.

Chapter Two discusses my family life. We are not especially interesting as a family, but I have no doubt that readers from the baby boomer generation will readily identify with the parenting, the lifestyle I describe, and how we became part of the consumer society that grew with the age of affluence, and has never left us, even in reduced circumstances. It makes sense to place this chapter before the thematic chapters on youth culture. Chapter Three is about my personal experience of a Roman Catholic primary school in the late '50s and early '60s. I have no doubt that it will resonate with readers who endured similar experiences. St Edwards RC Primary School, Darwen, was a horrendous place in that era. It was joyless, brooding and intimidating. Every day was filled with grim foreboding. Unless they are of my generation, I doubt that any of its staff will have the first idea of the kind of environment it once was and its ranking just below prisons and workhouses as a place of mortal dread. No doubt the experiences of current pupils are much more positive.

Chapter Four is devoted to the music that we listened to, which came to symbolise the accelerating progress of social change in the face of the older generations sometimes desperate and usually failing attempts to apply the brakes. The music listened to by "My Generation", also amply reflected the new affluence as the sales of vinyl records soared. Chapter Five is about grammar school, which in my case was St Mary's College, Blackburn. Unlike primary school, it appears to me that there is a great deal of writing out there about the grammar school experience. I doubt that my chapter will add anything to the sum of human knowledge, but it is at the core of the dominant theme of this book. The increased social mobility that was part of the broader affluence I have described, gave people like me a life that was a great adventure, and took some of us far from our roots. New right thinkers and certain newspapers habitually criticise those who work in the public sector on the basis that as they are paid out of taxes, they are essentially parasitic. It is a bleak view that I do not share. I spent the bulk of my life in the public sector, first in education and then, for rather longer, in the prison service. Along with policing, nursing and the probation service these are professions that historically attracted the sons and daughters of workers who aspired for something better for their children. It is no crime to choose that which at the same time appears most secure, whilst at the same time offering an opportunity to put something back into society. Sadly, as we have seen even police officers and nurses have been made compulsorily redundant, and the probation service has been virtually dismembered.

Chapter Six is another one about culture, in this case the television. My parent's generation were brought up with the radio, or wireless, to give its usual name at the time, and the cinema, always assuming they could afford to go. We were the first television generation, all two channels of it in glorious black and white. No matter how primitive it seems, in retrospect the development of television ranks behind only the development of the contraceptive pill in terms of its impact on society in the thirty years after World War Two. Chapter Seven is devoted to my beloved Blackburn Rovers. The names of the players may mean little to the modern reader, but the dire straits clubs have found themselves in as a consequence of useless boards of directors, either hiring equally useless managers or alternatively preventing good managers from doing their job, will be familiar to almost all football supporters of whatever generation following clubs both big and small. It is fashionable to describe modern footballers as mercenary overpaid prima donnas, but we should be under no illusion that the very less well paid players of the past were necessarily any more likely to put in a proper shift on a Saturday afternoon. In this chapter Blackburn Rovers are also a prism through which to view the past. The same applies to Chapter Eight, which looks at the early days of the modern terrace culture, which was created by young working-class people. Unfortunately, alongside the singing, the humour and the comradeship grew acts of hooligan violence, which culminated in the Heysel Stadium disaster in 1985. The terrace culture as we knew it was spawned by affluence.

The final two chapters hang together. Chapter Nine – The World of Work, is about my experience as a fully-fledged member of the blue collar working class, before returning to education. My initial decision to opt out of higher education gave me around three years' worth of authentic personal experience of the shop and factory floor, the regular domain of working-class people, long enough for me to understand it, write about it meaningfully, and to realise that my education had given me the opportunity to have a career rather than simply a job. The final chapter is about finding a career, and in the end there were two, and the process of growing away from my roots that accompanied it. Retirement has been secured by a public sector final salary pension, which according to the Daily Mail is the ultimate symbol of affluence in twenty-first century Britain.

I apologise in advance to readers for any errors of fact which are impossible to eradicate entirely with the passage of time when the memory is the sole source of information. However I make no apology for the judgements made and the opinions expressed.

Chapter One

My Little Town: Blackburn with Darwen

"I read the news today, Oh boy, 4000 holes in Blackburn, Lancashire."

As I'm sure even younger readers know that is a line from "A Day in the Life", a track from the classic Beatles album: "Sgt. Pepper's Lonely Hearts Club Band", credited to Lennon and McCartney but in fact largely written by John Lennon. Unlike the USA where numerous towns and cities are immortalised in songs, there are very few English towns and cities that find their way into the British charts apart from London. Unlike Durham, Winchester, Finchley, Portsmouth and Liverpool, Blackburn did not get a name check in the title, but the song in which it features although never released as a single is considerably more feted than "Durham Town" by Roger Whittaker (1969 No12), "Winchester Cathedral" by the New Vaudeville Band (1966 No5, and USA No1), "Finchley Central", also by the New Vaudeville Band (1967 No11), and "Portsmouth" by Mike Oldfield (1976 No3), which as an instrumental should perhaps not be included. Furthermore, I would imagine the citizens of Liverpool still cringe at the tuneless despoiling of their city in Little Jimmy Osmond's gruesome "Long Haired Lover From Liverpool" (1972 No 1). Half a million people really did buy that rubbish, but amazingly you can't find anyone who will admit that it was once part of their vinyl collection. Chart anoraks could doubtlessly find a few others by poring over close on one hundred pages of lists of songs going back to the 1950s but I doubt they will discover anything that is genuinely iconic. Back in the summer of 1967 the teenage population of Blackburn was thrilled to have our town mentioned in a song by the Beatles, the greatest band in the world, and still unsurpassable half a century later. Looking back it was probably the closest Blackburn ever came to being part of the "swinging sixties". In the 1980s, "4000 Holes" was appropriated as the title of a Blackburn Rovers fanzine, which served to demonstrate a generation on the lasting impact of that fleeting mention. Our neighbours and rivals in Burnley would probably call it "4000 shitholes".

So why the 4000 holes? Well, apparently earlier in 1967 Blackburn council had surveyed the number of potholes in the town's roads that were in need of repair. The council really did count them all and also concluded that it could not afford to repair them, hardly a source of local pride. The subsequent appearance of a random minor news item in a Beatles song was probably a result of its appeal to Lennon's well-developed eye for the absurd. Had he lived Lennon would have no doubt found it equally absurd that his throwaway line would have inspired a Blackburn Rovers fanzine more than fifteen years after the song was written. In the 1980s the town was in dire straits and 4000 holes was probably an underestimate. Gallows humour was a pre-requisite of keeping your sanity if you were one of Blackburn's unemployed during the rapid rundown of industry that occurred in the first half of a decade that ranks only behind the 1930s for the despair and dereliction that it brought to Britain's traditional manufacturing centres. Gallows humour was also a pre-requisite of supporting Blackburn Rovers back in the 1980s as the club endured five agonising near misses in campaigns for promotion to the old first division from which it had been relegated as long ago as 1966. Back in 1966, the year before council employees counted the potholes, Blackburn was in the early stages of a wholesale redevelopment of the town centre, which included the controversial demolition of some much loved structures, the culverting of the River Blakewater, and the building of a new market and shopping complexes that would showcase architectural modernity. The 1960s was a decade of optimism and the demolition and building program would demonstrate both the town's ambition and its ability to respond to the needs of an affluent consumer society. A mere twenty years later the shopping centre was a highly visible, shabby and dated symbol of decline and decay, which mercifully has at least been partially reversed though unemployment remains higher than the national average. The twenty-first century regeneration of the town centre is almost complete, with just the new bus station waiting to open at the time of writing. I have to say that physically separating the bus station from its traditional boulevard home outside the railway station seems to me to be a very strange decision.

There had been a time when the people of Blackburn had no need of self-deprecating humour when Blackburn's (and much of Lancashire's) prosperity rested on the cotton trade. That prosperity funded the traditional Victorian symbols of success: mighty stone buildings, sweeping public parks, and an ornate railway station, which told the visitor everything he needed to know about the status of this once unremarkable market town. The cotton trade in Blackburn can be traced back to around 1650 when it was a domestic industry manufacturing fustian. In 1764 James Hargreaves invented the Spinning Jenny. In 1769 Richard Arkwright patented the Water Frame and ten years later Samuel Crompton, who spent part of his life in Darwen, invented the Spinning Mule, although he could not afford to patent the machine. These three inventions transformed cotton spinning. Arkwright himself is regarded as the father of the factory system. His water powered mill at Cromford in Derbyshire was the first to house the complete process from receiving the raw material to turning out the finished product and began operation in 1771. Arkwright's workers were employees not contractors and the working day was governed by the clock rather than the hours of daylight. Blackburn was not far behind and the factory system took off from about 1775.

Cotton Weaving, however, remained at least partially a domestic industry for another half century until the invention of a reliable power loom. Edmund Cartwright had built the first power loom in 1784 and the gradual spread of powered looms had provoked sporadic outbursts of loom breaking by handloom weavers faced with either destitution or entering the factory, which peaked between 1811 and 1813. So serious were the outbreaks of violence in Lancashire, the West Riding of Yorkshire and Nottinghamshire that the army had to be called in to suppress the movement. Following show trials at York in January 1813, seventeen men were publicly hanged before the authorities decided that was sufficient to deter further outbreaks. Not until 1841 was there a fully automated and reliable power loom courtesy of William Kenworthy and James Bullough of Blackburn. With this the gradual extinction of hand loom weavers was swiftly concluded. From then on the expansion of weaving was now extremely rapid and was given further impetus by the co-terminus development of the railway system. Blackburn became a weaving town. Between 1850 and 1870, sixty-eight weaving mills were built and also four combined weaving and spinning mills. Between 1870 and 1890, a further eighteen mills were built. By 1899 there were 129 cotton mills in Blackburn.

Unlike heavy industries, such as mining and engineering, the textile industry employed large numbers of women and children as well as men. The 1851 census showed that forty-nine per cent of employees in textiles were female. In 1899 the school leaving age was raised to thirteen but twelve-year-old children were allowed under local by-laws to become "half timers", spending half of the day in the factory and half in school until 1922 when the school leaving age was raised to fourteen under the 1918 Education Act. Both my grandmothers born in 1900 and 1901 respectively were half timers. They were lucky compared to earlier generations. Until the 1819 Factory Act forbade children under nine from working in cotton mills, even four-year- old children could be found working in factories. Six-day working was still the norm but a compulsory cessation of work at 2pm on a Saturday had been in force since the 1850 Factory Act. Once a 1pm finish became the norm, then workers effectively had a Saturday half-day. Textile workers also had an annual week's holiday, known as "wakes week", which from 1914 was the third week in July for Blackburn workers, and in 1906 agreement was reached that gave textile workers twelve days annual holiday per year including bank holidays, raised to fifteen in 1915. However, these were unpaid and workers had to wait until the 1938 Holidays with Pay Act before employers were compelled to grant a week's paid holiday. The modern entitlement is four weeks plus eight statutory bank holidays, making a minimum of twenty-eight days. When I joined the workforce in 1971, the minimum was two "wakes" weeks, plus six statutory bank holidays. New Year's Day did not join the official roster until 1974 and the Mayday holiday, the most recent to be added, not until 1978. The Darwen fortnight commenced a week before Blackburn. As a railwayman, my father rarely got his summer fortnight coinciding with wakes weeks and I can remember his holiday falling in May in 1960 when we went for a week's holiday in the Isle of Wight. Now he would be fined. With the dramatic decline of manufacturing in the 1980s and the growing expectations of worker flexibility in an employment market that favoured employers, the wakes closedown of industrial towns and cities swiftly became a relic of the past.

After World War One there was a short boom. The slump came in 1921 when Lancashire found itself hamstrung by import tariffs in India, which had taken advantage of the war to develop its own market, one that it was now determined to protect. One third of looms lay idle and it was all downhill from there. Any improvements in trade were short lived. During the General Strike (1926) production at half of the town's mills was suspended because of a lack of fuel. There was another slump in 1928 and the following year 40,000 workers went on strike for a week in a bid to overturn twelve per cent pay cuts proposed by the mill owners. Between 1923 and 1929, twenty-eight mills closed down permanently. With the great crash of 1929, things got even worse. One hundred mills were idle in 1930 and 21,000 people were unemployed. Between 1930 and 1934, a further twenty-six mills closed permanently. At the peak of the Great Depression in 1932, 30,000 people were unemployed, thirty-seven and a half per cent of the working population. Blackburn was paying dearly for its lack of industrial diversification.

Neighbouring Darwen had a visit from future Indian leader Mohandas Ghandi in 1931, who came to see for himself the suffering inflicted on the town from India's boycott of British goods as it sought independence from the British Empire. Ghandi's view was that unemployed weavers were well off compared to India's poor. Whilst that is undoubtedly true the destitution and despair amongst the unemployed cannot be underestimated. It is vividly described in the autobiographical works of William Woodruff (1916–2008) "The Road to Nab End" and "Beyond Nab End". Nab End is simply the end of the line, the place where all hope is gone. The welfare state was rudimentary. The benefits available were below subsistence level and there was the hated means test whereby the wages from a boy's paper round would be deducted from his father's dole money. Working people were hit not just in their pocket but in their pride. Nothing would have delighted them more for work to be available, instead they were treated as scroungers. The principle of less eligibility reigned supreme. The workhouse had gone but pauperisation of those who could not support themselves was still official policy. The childhood memories of the 1930s were seared into the minds of my parent's generation and affected their attitudes to life for decades afterwards. My grandparent's generation (if not my maternal grandmother) and those of my parent's generation who had reached the age of twenty-one took their revenge on the Tories at the ballot box in 1945 and the post-war settlement lasted until Mrs Thatcher came to power in 1979.

The decline of the cotton trade continued after World War Two. At the start of the 1950s, just fifty mills remained and twenty-five per cent of the town's working population depended on textiles for employment compared to a peak of sixty per cent thirty years previously. By 1960, just thirty of those mills were left although still sufficiently numerous for mill chimneys to be a feature of the town. I am just about old enough to remember a mill town as it was before the Clean Air Act of 1956 was fully implemented. I can remember the black smoke belching from the chimney of Ewood Mill. I can also remember a weather phenomenon that for us is just part of history, although sadly not if you live in an industrial city in China – smog. Smog is a portmanteau of two words: smoke and fog. It is visible air pollution and derived from coal and industrial emissions reacting with typical winter fog. Just about every house in the densely packed working-class districts burned coal. It remains prevalent in China because the Chinese burn coal on an industrial scale. The dirt stuck to everything and the gradual implementation of the Clean Air Act transformed the respiratory health of working people. The omnipresent grime gave rise to a rhyme published in the Darwen News on 9 March 1878:

"Between two hillsides bleak and barren, lies lovely little dirty Darren."

The phrase "Dirty Darren" was still in use during my childhood, and I often wondered where it came from. In practice Darwen was no dirtier than anywhere else where there was large scale industrial production.

During 1964 a further four mills closed although one of them, Pioneer Mill, became Netlon, a company manufacturing high tensile mesh. By the beginning of 1975 there were just 6,000 textile workers in the town. Albion Mill close to where I grew up closed that year. In 1976 there were just 2,100 looms operating compared to just under 80,000 in 1907. By 1984 there were just four mills left. By 2005 it was all over. The last mill closed and the industry that had made the town great was officially dead. Just one mill survives in neighbouring Burnley, or at least it did in 2011.

Industrial diversification had begun slowly in the town. Scapa Dryers opened in 1927 but the real boost came in the late 1930s as the spectre of another war loomed. The Royal Ordnance Factory (known locally as the Fuse factory because it made fuses for explosives) employing around 2,500 workers opened, as did a Gas Mask factory. Phillips opened a factory in the Little Harwood district, which provided another 4,000 plus jobs. Blackburn was back at work and during the war unemployment was zero. Post-war industry easily re-absorbed its fighting men back into the workplace as twenty-five years of peacetime full employment began. The cotton trade was not missed as prosperity and economic security was available from jobs in both the public and private sector. Major employers included Northrop, Bancrofts, Mullards which had gone into partnership with Phillips, the aforementioned Scapa Dryers and R.O.F., Walkersteel and three breweries. In the 1950s, Northrop, which made automated looms mainly for the overseas market, employed 3,000 workers. At its peak Mullards, which made valves and televisions, employed 7,500 workers. Walkers, run by brothers Fred and Jack developed from a sheet metal business into the largest steel stockholders in the UK. The move to a fifty-five acre site at Guide in 1970 symbolised the firm's rise to pre-eminence as one Blackburn's most important businesses. When the company was sold to British Steel in 1989 for £330 million, it employed 3,400 workers over sixty sites. Jack Walker used his retirement to bankroll his beloved home town club, Blackburn Rovers, and was rewarded with the Premier League title in 1995. He died in 2000 but the Walker trust continued to put money into the club until 2008. In life and in death over twenty years Jack Walker is reckoned to have put around one hundred million pounds of his fortune into Blackburn Rovers. Brother Fred died in 2012. Jack Walker never even joined the club's board, but Bill Bancroft of the aforementioned Bancroft's did become Chairman in 1970, and can be credited with the stabilisation and slow revival of the club after the disastrous stewardship of the 1960s. Chapter Seven deals with this period in the club's history in detail.

Over the border in Darwen workers enjoyed similar employment opportunities. The town's largest employer was Crown Paints with over 1,000 employees, known to my parent's generation as Walpamur, before becoming part of the Reeds group in the 1960s, although it has since became an independent company again. The company originated from the firm founded by the Potter brothers in Darwen who developed and patented the first calico printing machine adapted for wallpaper in 1839. With a major wallpaper business in the town it was no surprise to find a number of paper mills. I worked at Hollins Paper Mill three summers in a row during my student days. Textiles retained a presence with the iconic India Mill. When the mill chimney was built in 1867, it was the tallest and most expensive chimney in the UK at 330 feet tall. The chimney is now a grade two listed building and is without a doubt the town's most important historic structure dominating the town's skyline. Darwen has another iconic landmark, the Jubilee Tower, built on the moors high above Sunnyhurst wood in 1897 to celebrate Queen Victoria's sixty years on the throne. Coal mining had once had a presence in Darwen but the last pit closed in 1963.

Affluence and prosperity are relative concepts. Blackburn and Darwen workers were certainly better paid than they had been but incomes were low compared to the south-east and to other industrial areas with powerful trade unions that could drive up wages above inflation year on year. London print workers in Fleet Street were the aristocracy of the working class until their power was broken in the 1980s. Car workers in places such as

Coventry, Oxford, Luton and Liverpool were another group that did well. The feel good factor began to dissipate slowly from about 1971 onwards. In that year local unemployment figures showed there to be 1,149 in the dole queue. Compared to the 1930s, this was insignificant but it was a harbinger of what was to come. The era of full employment was over. Slowly but surely prosperity slipped away. In 1971 the General Post Office left Darwen Street, which was bad news for the businesses there as footfall was badly hit. In 1972 Johnny Forbes Gents' Outfitters closed. It was not a major employer but it was a well-known and well-established business within the town. In 1974 the third phase of the town's redevelopment was put on hold although it eventually went ahead three years later. Two mills closed in 1975 with the loss of over 2,000 jobs. In 1976 local unemployment reached six and a half per cent, one per cent above the national average. In 1978 there was a real body blow when Whitbread, which had taken over the former Dutton's brewery in 1964, closed it down. The building was demolished in 1986 and the following year a Morrison's supermarket opened on the site. This is a classic example of how seemingly secure, reasonably well-paid jobs for working men were replaced (eventually) by low paid and often part-time jobs for a mainly female workforce. The takeover of small brewers by what were then the "big six" and subsequent closure of local breweries despite promises not to do so was one of the least appealing features of the brewing trade in that period. The same would happen again in 1990 when Scottish and Newcastle Brewery closed down Matthew Brown, three years after the takeover.

Looking back there is no doubt that the decision to make my future elsewhere was the right one. Of the four siblings only my brother remained in the town. He left school aged sixteen in 1978 and was fortunate enough to get a job at Mercedes-Benz where he remained for twenty-three years. He was one of the lucky ones but those who remained in their jobs often found pay packets depressed as employers gained the upper hand. My father remained on the railway finishing his time at Preston in 1989. Nevertheless, he had dodged the bullet three times as Lower Darwen, Accrington and finally Blackburn sheds closed down. Lower Darwen had closed in the early 1960s, but the closures of Accrington and Blackburn were part of the slippery slope that became apparent in the 1970s. Fortunately for him there were those content to accept voluntary redundancy and take their chance elsewhere. The outlook for unemployed men in their fifties was decidedly grim as a combination of the government's deflationary policies and a culture of complacency in Britain's boardrooms that had developed in the good times, took their toll on traditional industry. In the early 1980s the R.O.F. made 414 redundancies and there were 400 job losses at Mullards, which eventually went into administration in 2009. It was even grimmer for school leavers. By 1981 four-fifths of school leavers had no job. By 1982, 8,000 people were on the unemployment register. In 1985, one-third of unemployed workers had been out of work for more than twelve months. Twelve per cent of those unemployed had had no work for three years. It was no consolation to the town's unemployed that things were nowhere near as bad as in 1932. The unemployed still felt humiliated and worse still were demonised by ignorant ministers, one in particular who thought that it was funny to mock the unemployed by singing his own lyrics to Gilbert and Sullivan operettas at a Tory party conference. In 1988 the town lost its branch of Woolworths.

Revival was a slow process as unemployment fell slowly from its mid-eighties peak. Some things would never return. The dog track had closed in 1984 and in the same year Blackburn was reduced to one cinema as increasing ownership of video recorders reduced cinema footfall even further. In the 1950s there had been fourteen. The Odeon Cinema, the town's largest, had played host to the Rolling Stones on 5th March, 1964. Sadly, I was not there. There is still only one cinema but it is a state of the art modern multiplex.

Although it created relatively few jobs it was the town's football club that gave Blackburn back its pride and swagger, winning the Premier League title ahead of the of Manchester United, the country's biggest and most famous club, in a duel that went to the last day of the 1994–95 season. I have told the story of the club from 1960 to 1980 in Chapter Seven. The revival of the club is down to one man, the aforementioned Jack Walker and dates from 1987 when he personally subsidised the wages of high profile new players, Steve Archibald and Ossie Ardiles. As well as continuing to put up funds for transfer fees and wages, Mr Walker also donated the steel for the new roof for the refurbished Riverside End. In the summer of 1991 the football world sniggered as press stories circulated that the club were trying to sign no less a player than Gary Lineker. The player was similarly amused but the sniggers stopped abruptly when the legendary former Liverpool star, Kenny Dalglish, signed on the dotted line as the new manager. All of a sudden big name players were more than willing to come to Blackburn, and to put up with clearing dog turds from Pleasington playing fields before training could commence. In due course Jack Walker would provide a new state of the art training facility at Brockhall, and he would also provide the cash for the complete rebuilding of Ewood Park, which also involved purchasing a factory and a large number of terraced homes at above market value to persuade the owners to sell. Thankfully, the council were more than happy to accommodate Jack Walker, a complete contrast to the blinkered local authorities that came close to destroying clubs such as Charlton and Wimbledon. Between 1992 and 1994 the other three sides of the ground were completely rebuilt, and a dated ground with less than 4,000 seats in a capacity of 21,000 was transformed into a modern all seated stadium holding over 31,000 spectators. Fittingly Manchester United were the first opponents after the rebuild was completed. Jack Walker got his reward in 1994–95 when little Blackburn Rovers won the Premier League. Only supporters of Burnley and Manchester United were seriously ungenerous about the achievement.

Just like the day President Kennedy was assassinated, any Rovers' fan old enough to remember can tell you where he or she was on Sunday 14 May, 1995, when the title was clinched despite losing 1-2 at Anfield to Liverpool. The lucky ones – 3,000 or so – were actually at the match. As the game was televised live only on Sky Sports, a subscription channel, the rest of the town apart from the lucky few who had Sky Sports, had to either go to a pub that subscribed, or just like the Coronation in 1953, find a friend or relative to allow you to join them in their sitting room. In my case I travelled over from Huddersfield where I lived and watched the game at my brother's home in Darwen, along with our father and my brother's father-in-law, who generously donated copious quantities of his home brewed beer to the cause. Only the fact that I had to travel back across the Pennines for work the following day prevented me from getting absolutely rat-arsed. I hasten to add that I was not driving, and travelled by train. Most other supporters celebrated long into the night and many only worried about work long enough to call in sick. Nevertheless, I would venture to suggest that once the hangovers had subsided the feel good factor actually benefitted productivity.

Of course it could not last. Kenny Dalglish promptly decided he did not want to be manager anymore, and a year later Alan Shearer decided he did not want to play for Blackburn any more. The Premier League brand grew rapidly in size and importance and clubs like Blackburn very soon found that to compete they had to offer wages out of line with the club's income, and did not always get the required commitment in return. Rovers were relegated in 1998–99, but were back within two seasons under Graeme Souness, and followed up by winning the League Cup in 2001–02. By then we all knew that cup success and a maximum sixth place was the summit of realistic ambition. The people of the town were happy just to be there. The fans would always have the memory and the club's name would forever be on the trophy, something clubs as big as Liverpool, Everton, and Tottenham Hotspur have yet to achieve. Jack Walker died in 2000 and left money in trust to support what of necessity were more modest ambitions. By 2008 the money was running out and in 2010 the club was purchased by Venky's, an Indian firm specialising in the production of poultry. As we all know relegation followed in 2012, and there are few signs of a return. For older fans like me there is a sense of deja-vu, a modern reworking of the club's demise half a century ago. As has been said Chapter Seven provides a detailed analysis of the club's travails in the 1960s and 1970s.

Returning to the narrative, in 1994 The Blackburn to Clitheroe line re-opened for passengers. It had closed in 1962, just prior to the infamous report by Doctor Beeching, which led to the slashing of Britain's railway network. Unfortunately, the section from Clitheroe to Hellifield, which joins the iconic Leeds to Carlisle line a few miles south of Settle, is still only used for passenger services when trains need to be diverted. In 1997 Blackburn finally got its motorway link and the following year the town got back its independence from Lancashire County Council. Modern Blackburn is still well short of full employment. Figures obtained for 2013 show that only 70.1 per cent of the working age population were in employment compared to a national average of 77.4 per cent. In 2015 the Wensley Fold district of Blackburn was rated the nineteenth most deprived in the country. Post-war affluence is a folk memory for those struggling to get by on a mixture of benefits and insecure part-time work when it is available.

Since 1998 the modern borough has been known officially as Blackburn with Darwen. This is as it should be as the two towns are very much intertwined. The small town of Darwen lies to the south-east of Blackburn and at the 2011 census boasted 28,046 souls compared to Blackburn's 105,085. "Darreners" as they are known were mightily miffed when in 1974 their proud little town was swallowed up by Blackburn as part of the major local government shake up that came into force that year. Darwen like Blackburn owed its nineteenth century growth and prosperity to the cotton trade, and can trace the ebb and flow of its fortunes culminating in the great depression of the 1930s to the same overdependence on the industry in the Victorian era. The absence of a decent academic history of Darwen makes it impossible for me to make it an equal partner in this chapter, but it will be or will have been referenced where appropriate as it will at intervals elsewhere in the narrative of this book. Its social and economic history of the cotton era may be largely unwritten, but it is pretty much a mirror image of its larger neighbour.

Although I grew up in the Ewood district of Blackburn about half a mile from the boundary between the two towns, I was, like my father, actually born in the now defunct Bull Hill maternity hospital, Darwen, so I can claim if I wish to be a "Darrener", as can my brother and one of my two sisters. I cannot be certain why I was born in Bull Hill rather than Blackburn's Queens's Park Hospital. It is possible that it was because Queen's Park was once the town's workhouse and therefore carried a residual stigma but the more likely explanation is that we were registered as a family with a medical practice in Darwen, presumably dating from when my parents set up the marital home there in 1947 prior to moving across the town boundary a year or so later. I went to a Roman Catholic primary school in Darwen as did all of my siblings but Catholic "Darreners" who passed the 11 plus examination made the reverse journey into Blackburn for grammar school education as did many adult commuters for their employment. The work journey was not just one way. My mother, one of my sisters and a close friend all did stints with what was then Darwen's largest employer,

Crown Paints. I also worked for a period at another major Darwen employer, India Mill. Originally known as the Darwen Spinning Company Ltd., it was the single most important textile enterprise in Darwen and its machinery ran from 1871 until the mill's closure in 1991. The grand five-storey mill, a grade two listed building now survives as a conference centre.

Darwen residents who love their football support Blackburn Rovers, not Bolton Wanderers. Blackburn's most celebrated footballer, Bryan Douglas, lives in retirement in Darwen, and his close friend and former England captain, the late Ronnie Clayton, ran a newsagents in the town during his playing days. Busloads of Darreners came into Blackburn on Saturday to crawl round the pubs, visit the Mecca dance hall (in my time renamed the Golden Palms), and also the Cavendish nightclub. As well as work, leisure and education, parliamentary politics also crossed town boundaries. Darwen was not large enough for a parliamentary constituency of its own so as well as the surrounding rural districts it also took in chunks of Blackburn including Ewood where I grew up, Mill Hill where my grandmother lived, and Lower Darwen, which despite its name, was actually in Blackburn.

The first parish church in Blackburn can be traced back to 596, the early Anglo-Saxon era of our history. The present structure which stands behind the Blackburn Boulevard dates back to 1826, on the site of the medieval church. In 1926 the church was given cathedral status and Blackburn got an Anglican Bishop. The current Bishop is the ninth incumbent. However, along with Bury St Edmunds and Guildford, Blackburn shares the unwanted distinction of boasting a cathedral without holding city status. Bizarrely neighbouring Preston, a town of similar size to Blackburn, which does not have a cathedral and comes under the diocese of Blackburn, was granted city status in 2002, becoming England's fiftieth city in the fiftieth year of the reign of Elizabeth the Second. However

I should add that the requirement of an Anglican cathedral in order to obtain city status was dropped as long ago as 1889, so we cannot blame the apparent snub on the perceived secularity of Tony Blair's government.

Blackburn, then spelt in old English as "Blaechbourne", appears in the Domesday Book as a royal manor. It simply means black or clear water, bourne (burn) simply being another word for water. Blackburn therefore derives its name from the River Blakewater on which the town stands. The River Darwen, which flows through my home district of Ewood and joins with the Blakewater in Witton Country Park, gives its name to the neighbouring small town of Darwen. The Darwen/Blakewater ultimately becomes a tributary of the rather better known River Ribble. For another five centuries Blackburn remained largely anonymous. It was noted as a market town in the reign of Elizabeth the First and was given permission to establish a grammar school known to all locals as QEGS, full title Queen Elizabeth's Grammar School. Blackburn had also gained the right to hold annual fairs. Along with the grammar school, an annual Easter fair survives to this day. Interestingly, Blackburn was also noted as a centre of Catholic recusancy. A recusant was a person who refused to attend Anglican services on a Sunday, an offence punishable by heavy fines during the reign of Elizabeth when "Popish" recusants as they were known, were regarded as potential plotters against the crown seeking to restore the hegemony of the Catholic church, which had been brutally shattered by her father, Henry the Eighth. Full legal disabilities against Catholics were not removed until 1829. Local Catholicism would get a major shot in the arm from Irish migration subsequent to the potato famine of the 1840s, which forced large numbers of Irish families to abandon the country of their birth. It would get another smaller one from Polish ex-servicemen, who stayed on in the UK after the end of World War Two.

In 1780 the population of Blackburn was estimated at around 8,000. The first official census in 1801 recorded the population as 11,980. In the next thirty years thanks to the fast growing cotton trade the population increased nearly two and a half times to 27,091. In 1901 Blackburn's population peaked at 127,626. The growth was extraordinary and it was a similar story in neighbouring towns. The daddy of them all was Manchester, known as "cottonopolis". From a population of around 10,000 (a substantial town) at the start of the eighteenth century, it had grown to 186,000 by 1851. The population of the city of Manchester (not to be confused with the conurbation we know as Greater Manchester) peaked at 766,311 in 1931. Manchester achieved city status in 1853, the first new city for 300 years. As has been said Blackburn has never been able to match that particular feat but along with Manchester it did achieve parliamentary representation in 1832, electing two MPs until 1955, and was granted borough status in 1851. Historically, borough status was very important as local government developed under Plantagenet rule as the charters issued by the King gave towns privileges and independence from the local Lord as well as the right to send two burgesses to the House of Commons when parliament was summoned. Citizens of boroughs were free men, not serfs.

    The 1888 Local Government Act confirmed Blackburn's independence as one of what were under the act designated as county boroughs. This independence from Lancashire County Council, which included its own borough police force, lasted until 1974 and its loss was keenly felt by local people as the town became essentially subordinate to county hall in Preston. Blackburn's borough councillors were re-designated as district councillors, a status not surprisingly perceived as significantly inferior to the status of borough councillor, given that district councillors once sat on what were called urban and rural district councils (UDCs and RDCs), which in reality were not much more than glorified parish councils. Bigger towns and cities than Blackburn lost their independence as a result of restructuring. Stoke-On-Trent, a city with two and half times Blackburn's population, found itself subordinate to Staffordshire County Council. Neighbouring Darwen was designated a non-county borough in the 1880s as part of local government reorganisation and got a town council for the first time, but subordinate to Lancashire County Council. Under re-organisation it was subsumed into Blackburn in 1974, re-appearing as part of the new unitary authority, independent of Lancashire County Council, of Blackburn with Darwen in 1998.

Under this new structure Darwen eventually got back its own subordinate council in 2009. Darwen got its own parliamentary constituency in 1885, retaining it until 1983 when it joined with Rossendale to form the constituency of Rossendale with Darwen. On the face of it, this is nonsense, joined with Blackburn for local government purposes, but not for parliamentary representation. However, once the population of Blackburn had declined to the point at which there was no overspill electorate to export to a neighbouring constituency, the fate of Darwen was sealed. By 1971 the population of Blackburn had fallen to 101,000, the lowest figure since 1881 when its 104,000 inhabitants saw the town rank at number twenty in the population charts for UK towns and cities. It was inevitable that the next boundary commission would take note. However, the most recent parliamentary boundary commission re-detached the Fernhurst ward where I grew up from Blackburn, once again linking it with Darwen in the slightly re-drawn Rossendale and Darwen constituency in time for the 2010 General Election.

In my lifetime (I was born in December 1952), Blackburn has elected exclusively Labour MPs. In 1945 Labour regained Blackburn, then a dual member constituency, from the Conservatives. Subsequent to a boundary commission report dual member constituencies were abolished and Blackburn was divided into separate East and West constituencies. Barbara Castle, first elected in 1945, won the East division for Labour and Ralph

Assheton the West Constituency for the Conservatives at the 1950 election. At the next election in November 1951, both retained their seats and this marked the last occasion that a Blackburn parliamentary constituency elected a Conservative MP. Another boundary commission reduced Blackburn to one seat, which Mrs Castle held by less than 400 votes against a popular local Conservative councillor, Tom Marsden, in 1955. Blackburn should have fallen to the Conservatives in 1959 on the national swing, but Mrs Castle actually increased her majority against a new Tory candidate. By the time Tom Marsden was reinstated as Conservative candidate in 1966, the chance was gone. Barbara Castle (1945–79) was never again seriously challenged and her successors Jack Straw (1979–2015) and Kate Hollern (2015–) have never looked remotely in danger of being unseated. The decline of working-class conservatism, often described as the deference vote, coupled with a solidly Muslim population that has risen steadily since the first Asian migrants came in the 1950s to around twenty-five per cent of the town's population, has ensured that the Conservatives and all other parties are firmly locked out. At the time of writing (December 2015) it is now almost inconceivable that Labour can lose Blackburn and it is to be hoped that Kate Hollern can match the eminence of her two predecessors who both held high office in Labour governments. Mrs Castle, given the soubriquet of The Red Queen by her official posthumous biographer, was once tipped as Britain's first woman Prime Minister. That did not happen but until her eminence was eclipsed by Mrs Thatcher, Barbara Castle was far and away the best known, and most successful in career terms, female politician in the UK.

However, Darwen, whatever else it had in common with Blackburn, did not share its larger neighbour's political preferences. In its ninety-eight-year history, the Darwen constituency resolutely refused to elect a Labour MP, not even in the Labour landslide of 1945. The closest Labour came was in 1966 when the Conservative majority was reduced to 1,735 votes. Sadly for Labour needing only a 1.9 per cent swing to take the seat in 1970, there was a late almost undetected swing to the Conservatives, which saw the Labour majority of ninety-six turned into a Tory majority of thirty-six, propelling Edward Heath into Downing Street and taking Darwen well out of Labour's reach. The Liberal party did occasionally challenge Conservative hegemony winning Darwen for the last time in 1931 when Sir Herbert Samuel became the local MP. He lost in 1935 and the Conservatives retained the seat until abolition in 1983. However, despite not contesting the seat in 1955 and 1959 the Liberal Party maintained a significant following in Darwen. My old Biology teacher, Tony Cooper, contested Darwen in four successive elections between 1970 and 1979, on each occasion comfortably out-polling the party's national performance. His 15,060 votes in February 1974 represented 26.4 per cent of the turnout, the Liberal party's best performance in the seat since 1935. The real difference between the Blackburn and Darwen constituencies was the latter's rural hinterland, predominately Conservative and amounting to around forty per cent of the electorate. The ability of the Conservatives to take up to one third of manual working-class votes ensured that the seat remained beyond Labour's grasp.

My maternal grandmother, Irish by descent and Roman Catholic by faith, was one of those working-class Tories, which was decidedly atypical for that particular combination. She was not a fan of the Conservative MP since 1951, Charles (from 1981 Sir Charles) Fletcher-Cooke. Oddly enough Fletcher-Cooke had stood for Labour in 1945 but switched allegiances. There was a minor scandal involving him in 1963 when he was forced to resign as a junior Home Office minister subsequent to an approved school absconder dressed in a dinner jacket being caught driving Fletcher-Cooke's car apparently with permission, but without a valid driving licence or insurance. Fletcher-Cooke claimed that his actions were well intentioned but misguided and arose out of his desire to provide after care to young delinquents. My grandmother believed that Fletcher-Cooke's interest in young delinquents had rather more to do with what she saw as his sexual proclivities at a time when homosexuality was illegal and a matter for condemnation by our self-appointed guardians in politics and the press. The dissolution of his eight-year marriage in 1967 – coincidentally the year homosexuality between consenting adults was legalised – served only to harden her opinion but it did not mean the loss of her vote. All that can be said is that if there was a secret then Fletcher-Cooke took it with him to the grave. A barrister by profession, he achieved some eminence when piloting the 1961 Suicide Act, which finally decriminalised suicide, on to the statute book. He died in 2001 at the age of eighty-six.

My own parents were Labour voters at General Elections, although my mother did confess to voting Conservative in 1959, often dubbed the "You've never had it so good" election thanks to Prime Minister Harold Macmillan telling the public that they had indeed never had it so good. Job security, miniscule unemployment, a massive public housing programme, the development of the NHS, and the increasing availability of consumer goods all signalled a prosperity that actually reached down to ordinary working people for the first time. Whether the Conservatives deserved the credit they got for it at the ballot box was another matter, but then working-class Conservatism had long preceded the affluent society. After the passing of the 1867 Reform Act had enfranchised the skilled working class, the Tories moved swiftly and decisively to garner the vote. At national level Disraeli's government (1874–80) enacted significant social reform and promoted patriotism via the expanding Victorian Empire. At local level networks of Conservative clubs sprang up which can be found to this day in the northern industrial towns and cities. The Liberals rather sourly took the view that the Conservatives, in hock with the breweries, were buying up working-class votes with a more sophisticated version of "treating" that existed in the days before the secret ballot. None of this prevented Liberal clubs with liquor licences from being set up in opposition. My memory, which could be wrong, tells me that Darwen still had three Conservative clubs when I was a young man, and just the one Liberal club. Including the cricket club Darwen in 2015 still has seven social clubs.

Thus the Conservatives were well established when the Labour party came along at the beginning of the twentieth century to challenge the old order. Working-class Tory MPs were almost as rare as rocking horse manure but that was far from the case as regards local councillors. In our own ward one of the Conservative councillors was a railway colleague of my father's, Stan Woods, who lived in a corner terrace in Finsbury Place close to our home. I do not know whether or not my parents voted for Stan Woods at local elections but I do know that on social matters there was little difference between Labour and Conservative working men. They supported the death penalty for murderers, were opposed to the legalisation of homosexuality, and took a dim view of women who gave birth out of wedlock. Fifty years on only religious fanatics would want to go back to a society where gays lived in fear of being exposed and illegitimacy was a stigma carried by innocent children. The working class has likewise moved on, and rather more than its detractors amongst the metropolitan elite would have us believe.

Relatively few people now call for the return of the death penalty even when the most atrocious crimes are committed, but back in 1948 there was widespread relief in the town when the murderer of a child being treated in Queen's Park Hospital was apprehended, convicted and hanged. The case made the national headlines as it was the first time ever that mass fingerprinting had taken place when the entire adult male population of Blackburn was asked to co-operate with the police so that the murderer, whom police were confident was a local man, could be brought to book. Peter Griffiths was eventually tracked down as police caught up with those who for whatever reason had not made themselves available. There was no petition for a reprieve and as far as the good people of Blackburn were concerned Griffiths' date with the hangman constituted justice for the murdered three-year-old June Devaney and her family. Respectable working-class people may no longer support the death penalty in numbers but tend to be much tougher in their attitude to crime simply because they are most likely to be affected by it. Try being one of the few people living on a sink estate with a steady job and see how often your home gets burgled.

The typical Blackburn Labour voter in my youth was every bit as patriotic as his Conservative counterpart. Working people had borne the brunt of the war against Hitler and imperial Japan. Without the commitment of the bulk of the population to the Second World War, Churchill's leadership skills would have been unavailing. However, pride in our native land was not accompanied by aggressive nationalism and crude chauvinism. Working people had much to be proud of but once the war was over Germany was quickly forgiven. Witness the remarkable acceptance of Bert Trautmann, German paratrooper, veteran of the Russian front, and British prisoner of war when, having elected to stay on in England, he emerged as first choice goalkeeper for Manchester City, and became a soccer hero when in 1956 he defied a broken neck to help Manchester City win one of the most remarkable FA Cup finals ever staged. It is a reminder of the remarkable capacity of competitive sport to break down barriers and dissipate hatred and prejudice, although it would take rather longer for black footballers to be accepted despite being British born. British ex-servicemen of my father's generation were less forgiving of Japan and the main reason for this was that the experience of the typical prisoner of war of any nationality at the hands of the Japanese was to be treated as almost sub human whereas the Nazi's reserved that fate for Jews, Slavs and Gypsies. A British servicemen captured by the Germans was far more likely to survive incarceration than one captured by Japan. Despite the holocaust of which most Britons were ignorant until the end of the War, the German soldier was respected as a brave patriot simply doing his duty, rather than being perceived as a brainwashed barbarian. Of course it would be ridiculous to deny the presence of a racist subtext as regards the Japanese imperial army, but it is difficult for any generation to feel anything other than negativity for those who so flagrantly disregarded the Geneva Convention.

My parent's generation were brought up with the empire. Their school text books, which we frequently inherited, showed large chunks of Africa and Asia coloured red, which signified British rule. Some of these territories were autonomous dominions of the crown, independent in all but name, and it has to be said mainly white. Most of the remainder were still referred to as colonies, and only in 1966 did the cabinet post of Secretary of State for the Colonies disappear when it became part of the Commonwealth Office reflecting the rapid move to independence and therefore equal status alongside Britain for the former colonies. Britain began disengaging from the empire in fairly short order after World War Two. Building the New Jerusalem at home was not compatible with the expense of maintaining an empire nor was it compatible with the American view of the new world order. Labour was happy to shed the "white man's burden", the Conservatives rather less so and its backwoodsmen caused considerable problems for more liberally minded reforming Tory Colonial Secretaries of State such as Iain McLeod and Reginald Maudling, who took a more jaundiced view of the small ruling elites of white settlers in Eastern and Southern Africa. I can only tell it as I remember it and my memory of how the empire was viewed by our parent's generation had very little to do with celebrating martial vigour, conquest for the sake of it, and total subjection of the natives, but rather it was about pride in our civilisation, the values that we exported, and the improvement of the condition of the people in the colonies. The Victorians exuded moral purpose. Whether or not Britain was a largely benevolent imperial power is of course debated by historians, although I doubt it is debated by Indian widows spared being pushed on to their husband's funeral pyre by a colonial administration determined to stamp out the practice of "suttee", widow burning for those unfamiliar with the term. The citizens of Blackburn most certainly had no doubt.

All this was pretty academic until immigration from the colonies began after the War bringing the empire to Britain. It accelerated in the 1950s when the UK found itself with a Labour shortage, rather than the surplus much loved by employers who could then depress wages. The first migrants were from the West Indies; black, Christian and English speaking. Their experience was not a happy one as they discovered they were not welcome in what they considered to be the mother country. It must have come as terrible shock to people who saw themselves unequivocally as British. The bulk of migrants to Blackburn were from the Indian sub-continent, brown skinned Asians, mainly Muslim, and non-English speaking. The local townspeople referred to the incomers as "Pakis", although many were actually Muslim citizens of India rather than of Pakistan. They did not necessarily share the rose tinted vision of England brought by West Indian migrants, which was perhaps just as well. For some citizens of Blackburn it was as though an alien spaceship had landed. Ridiculous stories suggesting that they ate dog food circulated around the town. It took the opening of the first curry houses in Blackburn to put that one to bed. According to trip advisor there are now 187 of them, not quite as numerous as the holes, but more numerous than the number of pubs selling cask ale, eighty-six according to the East Lancashire branch of the Campaign for Real Ale (CAMRA).

Nevertheless, the Asian community soon established itself as those men who stuck it out sent for their wives and children or started families in England. I cannot remember seeing many Asian women in the 1960s but those that were seen did not wear full face veils and certainly not the Burqa. Islam itself was also invisible as Mosques were contained in private houses until the new community had the wealth and confidence to build their own complete with distinctive minarets. Their most visible presence in the workplace was in the declining cotton industry and on the buses. Wages in the cotton industry were low and in an era of full employment the Blackburn worker could and did take his National Insurance card elsewhere. Back in the 1960s, buses still had conductors to take the fares leaving the driver to do just that. It's fair to say that Asian bus conductors were not always well treated by a minority of passengers who abused them and refused to pay the fare. There is an early episode of Coronation Street in which the inspector summarily sacks a Pakistani bus conductor subsequent to a dispute with a passenger about a fare even though it was manifestly clear that the passenger had not paid. I would assume that the episode was based on a real life occurrence. My one particular memory of Pakistani bus crew is one particular conductor whose face was dreadfully pitted by smallpox scars. This loathsome disease was still endemic in the Indian sub-continent in the early 1960s, and in 1961–62 there were two separate outbreaks in Bradford and South Wales attributable to migrants having flown into the UK whilst incubating the infection. One died and one survived. Nineteen people died in South Wales, a mortality rate of around forty per cent. In Bradford seven of the fourteen confirmed cases succumbed. Additionally, three children died as a result of post-vaccination reactions. Bradford was close enough for people to be seriously worried but the two outbreaks were successfully contained. It was not a good time to be a migrant from the Indian sub-continent in Britain as feelings ran very high in the affected and neighbouring areas.

Over two generations the Asian community in Blackburn has grown to around a quarter of the total population. The community is heavily concentrated in the north-east of the town. A 2007 BBC Panorama programme found that the white British community (69.1 per cent according to the 2011 census) and the Asian community were living parallel and segregated lives. The officially sanctioned British form of apartheid is multiculturalism, which actively discourages integration. It is not comparable with the oppressive racist interpretation that disfigured South Africa, as in the de-industrialised areas of the UK, it is a story of two under privileged communities both of who feel that life has sold them short. Multiculturalism works against cultural cohesion by emphasising the ways in which communities differ at the expense of what they have in common and does not help those, principally women, who feel stifled by the patriarchal mores of their own community. White Guardian reading feminism does not speak effectively for these women because respect for another community's culture is deemed more important. This is moral relativism at its most intellectually bankrupt.

Educationally, no social group underachieves more than the white working class. Asian migrants value education for their children rather more, but are understandably frustrated when the only jobs apparently open to school leavers are waiting on in curry houses, and driving taxis when they are older. Back in the 1960s the indigenous working class believed strongly that the newcomers were a threat to their jobs. Of course in times of plenty this was not true. As far as the newcomers were concerned the open racism was unpleasant, but mattered less when work was plentiful. As the work dried up these things began to bite. Blackburn witnessed one of the earliest manifestations of far right success in elections. National Front candidate, John Kingsley Read polled just under five per cent of the votes in each of the two elections of 1974, hardly a success, but as he was the party's leader, he got publicity out of all proportion to his real importance. Read who died in 1985, split from the National Front in 1976 and formed the National Party, winning two council seats in Blackburn, which brought shame on the town. Once chairman of Blackburn Young Conservatives, Read departed mainstream politics when Edward Heath admitted the Ugandan Asian refugees in 1972. Read's use of the crudest racist expressions spat with real venom would not now be tolerated, but the 1970s were a different world. The latest manifestation of the fascist right, the British National Party (BNP) has been at least partly neutered by laws to deal with incitement to racial hatred, which they know will be enforced. Blackburn did not suffer riots in 2001, unlike Burnley, Oldham and Bradford, but there was renewed far right activity. The BNP actually saved its deposit at the 2005 election.

Muslim population figures for a sample of Blackburn's council wards taken from the 2011 census are illuminating:

Fernhurst	1.7%
Ewood	3.4%
Mill Hill	5.4%
Roe Lee	20.4%
Beardwood	31.2%
Little Harwood	51.9%
Corporation Park	62.6%
Audley	68.7%
Shear Brow	77.7%
Bastwell	85.3%

Bastwell, the most Muslim ward of all boasts less than ten per cent of the population identifying itself as white British. The Muslim population of the UK is just under five per cent of the population, in Blackburn it is more than five times that. The Beardwood/Lammack ward, is the closest to reflecting the ethnic and religious mix of the town, but is not genuinely representative of the social mix, being home to more than its fair share of Blackburn's middle class. The Muslim population of the ward quadrupled between the 2001 and 2011 censuses, suggesting that the phenomenon known as "white flight" was taking place, probably in the parts of the ward closest to existing Asian majority areas. Fernhurst, Ewood, and Mill Hill are the whitest wards within the old town boundary but districts such as Shadsworth and Higher Croft (not detailed above) with large estates of social housing as opposed to the terraces of Fernhurst, Ewood and Mill Hill, are almost as white. No longer living in the town, I cannot give a detailed social commentary or history, but the sample figures do support the one of the premises of the Panorama programme. Population trends suggest that the Asian ghettoes will grow even more monolithic and that few Muslims will try their luck in the south-west of the town. That people choose to live amongst those they perceive as their own comes as no surprise but it does not necessarily indicate that the two communities live lives of constant suspicion and sullen hostility. Local politicians and faith leaders work hard to promote tolerance, understanding, and the feeling of belonging to a broader community. My old school, a wholly mixed sixth form college since the last selective intake of boys sat its "O" levels in 1980, retains its Roman Catholic ethos but twenty-eight per cent of its students are from ethnic minorities according to a 2008 Ofsted report. The vast majority of the ethnic minority intake are Muslim and clearly their parents are more than happy to patronise the college, which does not accept the wearing of face veils. So clearly tolerance and compromise are alive and well in Blackburn, and two major arrests for suspected terrorist involvement are no more representative of the Muslim community than the BNP are of the indigenous one.

Postscript:

As well as the aforementioned Jack Walker Blackburn is the birthplace of a number of people who have achieved fame in their chosen field.

William Woodruff, author, historian and modest war hero. I have referred to his two autobiographical books earlier in the chapter. Woodruff died in Florida in 2008 at the age of ninety-two and is arguably Blackburn's most eminent son.

Alfred Wainwright, lifelong Blackburn Rovers fan, probably Blackburn's best known former citizen although he moved from the town to Kendal in 1941. He was a fell walker, guidebook author and illustrator famed for his seven volume "Pictorial Guide to the Lakeland Fells". Wainwright devised the 192-mile footpath coast-to-coast footpath from west to east across northern England, which remains popular today. He died in 1991 at the age of eighty-four having become a TV personality in the last few years of his life.

Carl Fogarty, former 500 cc world motorcycle champion.

Bryan Douglas, (1934-) was probably the most naturally talented player ever to where the iconic blue and white halved shirt. Douglas played thirty-six times for England including the 1958 and 1962 World Cup final stages in Sweden and Chile respectively.

Lionel Morton of the Four Pennies. Blackburn's very own chart topping group at the height of the beat boom, although only Morton was actually born in the town. Juliet, co-written by Morton and two other members of the band topped the charts in 1964.

Russell Harty, 1970s and 1980s TV presenter of chat shows and arts programmes. He previously taught English and Drama at Giggleswick School. Harty died in 1988 at the relatively young age of fifty-three from liver failure.

Thespians are very well represented.

Ian McShane. Best known for the title role in the long running series, Lovejoy, where he played an antiques dealer.

Kathleen Harrison. She died in 2005 at the venerable age of 102. Despite being brought up to speak with flat vowels of the north, she is principally remembered for cockney speaking roles in The Huggetts and the title role in Mrs Thursday, in which the erstwhile cleaner is bequeathed the company where she works. Kathleen Harrison is guaranteed to be on your screens every Christmas when the original version of Dickens "A Christmas Carol" gets its annual airing on one of the terrestrial channels. She played Scrooge's cleaner, the redoubtable Mrs Dilber.

Former Coronation Street actress, Wendi Peters.

Steve Pemberton, perhaps best known for his role as Mick Garvey in the comedy, Benidorm.

Anthony Valentine. Best known for his sinister roles as Toby Meres in the TV series "Callan" (1967–72) and as Major Mohn in "Colditz", which ran from 1972 to 1974. Callan and Colditz will be fondly remembered by older readers. One of his last TV roles was a short stint in Coronation Street (2009–10). Anthony Valentine died on 2 December 2015, just days before I wrote this section, at the age of seventy-six.

Famous "Darreners" do not include any actors but they do include two sportsmen of real renown, even if their names mean nothing to all but our oldest citizens and devious quizmasters.

Dick Burton (1907–74) was British Open Golf champion in 1939. As a consequence of the War and the subsequent suspension of the competition, he held the title for a record seven years.

Sam Wadsworth (1896–1971) was a professional footballer. Wadsworth captained Huddersfield Town to three successive league championships 1923–24, 1924–25, and 1925–26. He also captained England. Wadsworth joined the army when the Great War broke out in August

1914, shortly before his eighteenth birthday and before he could make his first team debut for Blackburn Rovers, whom he had joined from Darwen. Badly wounded in the War, Rovers gave him a free transfer on his return. He joined Huddersfield after a stint at Nelson. Wadsworth won an FA Cup winners medal in 1921–22 knocking out Blackburn Rovers on the way, but did not play in Town's defeat against Blackburn in the 1928 final. Perhaps the most remarkable feature of Wadsworth's career was that he did two stints as manager of PSV Eindhoven in the Dutch League, one before and one after the Second World War, coaching PSV to the championship play-offs in 1951, which they duly won, a year after winning the Dutch equivalent of the FA Cup. Wadsworth was a true pioneer. If anyone can find an English manager/head coach working abroad before Wadsworth, please let me know. It could be a long search.

Chapter Two

Home, Family and Environment

My late father, Eric Laxton, was born in Darwen, Lancashire, a small town to the south of its larger neighbour, Blackburn, in July 1924. In 1931 Darwen would achieve momentary fame when the visit of Mohandas Gandhi, the leader of the Indian independence movement, whose visit to the town to see for himself the hardships being suffered by workers in the cotton mills as a consequence of the movement's boycott of British goods, was captured on the newsreels of the day. The mills have gone although the distinctive steep sloping terraces remain. Darwen is pronounced "Darren" in Lancashire dialect and its inhabitants are known as "darreners". My father was a dialect speaker although not with the fluency of his mother. To him Darwen was almost always "Darren", and only given its correct appellation in conversation with someone perceived to be further up the social scale.

The village of Tockholes on the edge of Darwen was where my father grew up in one of a row of seventeenth-century silk weaver's cottages, which these days are much sought after residences. The road is known as Silk Hall. His father James Arthur Laxton was a train driver and his mother Maud (nee Bradshaw) was a cotton weaver. A younger brother, Allan, came along in 1927 and at the time of writing is still very much alive and living with his daughter in Essex. My grandfather died of pneumonia in 1929, leaving behind a widow with two small boys. There was no help from the state but somehow my grandmother stayed in regular work throughout the depression and downright penury was avoided. Fortunately, her late husband's mother and sister were able to assist with childcare and conveniently the local elementary school was across the road from Great Grandma's home and round the corner from the bus stop to Tockholes. Nevertheless, there were clearly occasions when arrangements could not be made. There is a family photograph of my father and uncle as small boys outside their home, which was cut off by a snowstorm that also prevented their mother from getting home from her work in the mill. My grandmother eventually remarried and outlived her second husband also before dying of lung cancer in 1966 at the age of sixty-five. She had never smoked in her life but the dust from more than fifty years of work in the cotton mills did its lethal work. Great Grandma lived on increasingly blind, deaf and housebound until 1970 when she died at the great age of ninety.

My late mother Margaret Laxton (nee Swan) was born in Blackpool in 1926, the eldest of three children. This town has spawned some famous sons and daughters. Among their number are comedy actor Ricky Tomlinson, singer Coleen Nolan of the Nolan sisters, Cynthia Lennon, first wife of Beatle John Lennon, and Graham Nash, founder member of the Hollies. George Carman QC who died in 2001 and was the leading barrister of his day was also born in Blackpool. Although Stanley Matthews was not born in Blackpool (he was born in Stoke-On-Trent), his name is forever linked with Blackpool because the famous FA Cup final of 1953 where Matthews finally got his winner's medal at the age of thirty-eight after being on the losing side in two previous finals. In 1965 Matthews became the first footballer to be knighted. Unlike Darwen, Blackpool needs no introduction to the reader.

My maternal grandfather worked in the hotel trade in Blackpool. Tragically, he was killed when he hit his head after a fall from his bicycle, also in 1929. My grandmother was left a widow with two small daughters and a son growing inside her. She moved back to Blackburn where her Irish born father rented a small two-bedroom terraced home. Unfortunately, my maternal great grandfather decided that three children were too much of a handful so my mother and her sister, Joan, found themselves in the care of the nuns at Nazareth house where they remained until my mother was ten when he finally relented. He died not long after. Primrose Terrace remained my grandmother's home until 1971 when she moved into sheltered accommodation for just a few months before a terminal diagnosis brought her into our home. The bereavement and much reduced circumstances affected my grandmother's health adversely, not a good place to be in the hungry thirties with only the most basic welfare provision and the indignities of the means test to endure in order to obtain assistance that was actively begrudged by the authorities to claimants, despite the terrifying level of unemployment. I know my grandmother worked during the War but I have no memory of her working when I was a child. The founding of the NHS was a godsend to her as the numerous tablets that she took for her heart condition could never have been afforded before. Somewhat improbably she lived to be seventy, also dying of cancer rather than the heart condition or any other of her numerous ailments.

My paternal grandmother was a shrewd woman who was determined that her sons would not be killed in the War. Using the family connection with the railway, she succeeded in getting both my father and my uncle on to the railway, which was a reserved occupation, when they reached their seventeenth birthdays. Whereas Uncle Allan would leave the railway a few years after the War ended, my father remained for the rest of his working life, working his way up to driver and finishing his time driving intercity trains on the northern section of the West Coast mainline. My father's forty-eight-year career almost ended in tragedy. Around six months before he was due to retire in the summer of 1989, he briefly dozed off in the cab and his intercity express hurtled past a red signal. Had he not woken up in time the express would have crashed into a stationary train on the Ribblehead viaduct and numerous fatalities, inevitably including my father, would have resulted. As an accident it had the potential to rival the Tay Bridge disaster in notoriety. In the end it was another near miss of the kind the public never get to hear about. Although The Sun did pick up the story it was relegated to a few lines in the middle of the paper. As we know many Sun readers skip from page three straight to the sports pages. The truth was that my father had fallen asleep momentarily but also that equipment designed to stop the train in the event of driver incapacitation also failed. A deal was done whereby my father in return for his silence remained at home on full pay for the remaining six months until his sixty-fifth birthday. It was not the way he would have chosen to finish.

My father's fourteenth birthday actually fell in the last week of the summer term in 1938. He began work the following week still wearing short trousers under his overalls. My mother likewise left school at fourteen years old. The school leaving age was not raised to fifteen until 1948. A child's meagre wages were an eagerly anticipated event in northern working-class households where budgets were desperately tight, even for those in work. Of course, if the parents were out of work then state assistance was promptly reduced by the amount of the young person's wage. That kind of means testing was very cruel and hit families in their pride as well as their pocket. Nevertheless, starting work at fourteen was an advance on the regime endured by my grandparent's generation who became "half timers" at the age of thirteen, splitting the day between work and school for the final year of education. The vast majority of working-class children spent their entire scholastic lives undergoing what was known as elementary education under the same roof. Secondary education provided in the great public schools and in grammar schools was largely the province of the upper and middle classes respectively. Even when a free place at the local grammar school was won in the competitive 11 plus examination, which my grandparent's generation referred to as "the scholarship", the daunting cost of school uniform and sports kit was beyond the means of working-class families. My father's younger brother Allan was the first member of the Laxton family to win a grammar school place, but he did not go on to take his school certificate (the predecessor of GCE O levels), and like my parents his schooling finished at the age of fourteen. His eldest son, Nigel, would fare rather better at the same Darwen Grammar School and go on to university. Whether my grandmother paid the fine for withdrawing her son from the grammar school before the age of sixteen, I do not know.

My mother also failed the 11 plus, which she had been expected to pass. Shortly after her death in 2013 my youngest sister handed me a copy of some of her papers, which included submissions for the writing class she attended in the early years of her retirement. In one of those short essays she describes how she began menstruating during the examination. This was an era when children grew up in ignorance and long before schools took responsibility for sex education. I had often wondered why my mother failed the 11 plus, now I knew. In the end it would have been academic as it would have been financially impossible for her to go to grammar school, but I have no doubt she would have loved to have been able to say that she passed the examination. Her destiny therefore was factory or shop work as a prelude to marriage and the life of a housewife. However, my mother was determined to have an office job and she succeeded in moving from the factory floor at Newman's slipper factory and never returned, in due course getting her shorthand and typing qualifications in those far off days before computers transformed office life.

Although not a superstitious person my mother was told by a fortune teller that she would marry a man in uniform. Given that this was towards the end of the War ended this was hardly a revelation! My father did wear a uniform, that of a railway fireman. They married in February 1947 and honeymooned in Felixstowe, of all places. Married life began in a small terraced house in Darwen, which they purchased via a mortgage. The following year they made the decision to sell the home and instead rent a semi-detached farm cottage in the Ewood district of Blackburn, about half a mile from the boundary with Darwen and close to the Blackburn Rovers football stadium. The rent was low and included free milk, there was a large piece of land rather than a tiny back yard, and it was a short walk to my father's place of work at Lower Darwen locomotive shed. The Fernhurst pub, which became my father's second home, was closer still. It had two other advantages; first, it had three bedrooms which made it more suitable as a family home, and second, apart from the farmhouse there were no immediate neighbours. Although the nearest terraced street was only fifty yards away and the main A666 only one hundred yards away, it came with the seclusion that my mother craved. She had a lifelong dislike of nosey neighbours and petty working-class snobbery. This way no one knew that my mother did not scrub the front doorstep. My parents would come to regret renting, but not the house in which they lived and would be the family home until my mother, by now a widow, sold up in 2003. That they were able to buy was down to one piece of luck and one radical Prime Minister. Following the death of the farmer in 1966, his widow sold the farm and farm cottage to the council. As council tenants my parents were able to make use of Mrs Thatcher's right to buy legislation (although they did not reward her with their vote), to become homeowners again after a thirty-five-year hiatus.

As we know nothing is more influential than our childhood on the adults we become. For my parent's generation there was another powerful influence that mercifully succeeding generations have not had to endure: World War Two. However, while we would not have to endure the physical reality of war, there were times when it felt that it was rammed down our throats, so powerful was its influence on my parent's generation, and also on my grandparent's generation whose lives had been touched by two global conflicts. The British film industry was equally obsessed and it took two decades before the endless stream of formulaic movies featuring stiff upper lipped British heroes finally petered out. Although rationing finally ceased in 1954, it hung like a pall over our family mealtimes. "We fought a (or two) World War(s) for you" was the familiar battle cry of the older generations when they discovered as Bob Dylan put it, that "…your sons and your daughters are beyond your command."

My parents had tough childhoods, my mother especially so. My father's family were Methodists and his mother had all the virtues and vices of protestant non-conformity. Working-class Methodists were fiercely proud, independent and emotionally reticent people. They believed in hard work, honesty and thrift. Alcohol was not compatible with these virtues, and staunch Methodists were confirmed teetotallers, who often went as far as making a written declaration of their intent to forego alcohol, known as signing the pledge. My father signed the pledge as a teenager, but it was not one that he kept. Respectable people maintained themselves and their families; charity was for the feckless and indigent. To be out of work was a social disgrace even when it was no fault of your own. "Them that don't work, don't eat," was drummed into them. My paternal grandmother and her ilk would never have dreamed of stealing and would rather have gone hungry than accept what they perceived as charity. It is an attitude that it is still alive amongst some of the poorest pensioners, who resolutely refuse to claim pension credit because they see it as a stigma rather than an entitlement. I think it is fair to say that it is an attitude that will die with them. Sexual propriety was a given and very strictly defined. It was for married heterosexuals only. Anything else was sinful and likely to lead to eternal damnation. Methodists prided themselves on being god fearing.

The downside of Methodism and other non-conformist sects that derived from the puritan rather than the Anglican tradition was just as prominent. The staunchest practitioners were often narrow- minded, judgemental and censorious. It was a black and white world which left no room for nuance or ambiguity. Shades of grey were for the sky. It was not just that Methodists abhorred swearing, drinking and fornication. At its worst, frequently manifested, secular Methodism was a joyless repressive creed which frowned on pleasure, laughter and general frivolity. Like Ulster Presbyterians they sought to close children's play areas on Sundays. In the district where I grew up worshippers at Lower Darwen Congregationalist Church would emerge from services on a Sunday afternoon, approach the playing fields and inform us that there were "no games on Sundays". In those far off days of fifty years ago, children still feared adults and feared the police even more, so we did not tell them to "fuck off", as would happen now. Instead, we simply waited for them to go before we came back. That way honour was satisfied. Respectability was a cardinal virtue. One of the pleasures of smug self-defined respectability is finding social inferiors to look down upon. Nowhere was the class system more alive than amongst the working classes where the gradations were far more subtle than the conventional notions of the time of three social classes immortalised in the classic sketch starring John Cleese, Ronnie Barker and Ronnie Corbett.

My paternal grandmother epitomised the best and worst of the Methodist tradition. She was totally honest, driven by the work ethic, and obsessively thrifty. Widowhood did not prevent her from becoming a homeowner. There were no treats or money slipped surreptitiously into a child's hand when the parents weren't watching from this silver haired grandmother. If she mentioned money at all it was to ask how much we had saved. I never heard her swear and I do not recall ever seeing her touch alcohol. She looked down on both her son's wives. As I have said my mother was of Irish extraction. My maternal grandmother was born Catherine Murphy, unmistakeably Irish Catholic. Grandma Swan was therefore socially inferior on two counts being both Irish and a papist. However, she regarded the Irish family next door to her as social inferiors because they were recent migrants who still spoke with Irish accents. In the language of the time they were still bog Irish. Grandma Swan also liked a drink, patronised street bookies before betting shops were legalised in 1961, and had spent chunks of her life in receipt of the meagre welfare available. In short she was well below the salt. Anti-Irish and Anti-Catholic prejudices would gradually be replaced in '50s and '60s by prejudice against immigrants with black and brown skins. My own mother would eventually crack under the strain of her mother-in-law's snobbery and prejudice and throw a bowl of water over her in exasperation. It was a tale still repeated long after my paternal grandmother was dead.

Uncle Allan's wife, Clara, who preferred to be known as Clare, also suffered at the hands my grandmother's prejudices. Her family background was deemed inferior and so was her morals. Clara's future mother-in-law suspected (rightly I understand) that her son and his girlfriend were engaged in pre-marital sex, then a major taboo. Pre-marital chastity is now a quaint historical custom in our culture. Rather than risk the stigma of illegitimacy in the family, they were rushed to the altar. As it happens, she need not have worried. Aunt Clara did not get pregnant for another sixteen years. After several years of childlessness they decided to adopt, which further appalled my grandmother, concerned that bad blood might be introduced into the family as adopted children were normally the product of sexual relationships between unmarried and therefore immoral people. The word "bastard" was the second worst insult in the dictionary (only bad bastard was worse), and bastardy was the protestant non-conformist equivalent of Catholic original sin, in that illegitimate children bore the sinfulness of their parents, and could pass it down the generations.

Religious intolerance was not the sole province of protestant non-conformity. Protestants had learned all about religious intolerance from that great authority on the subject, the Roman Catholic Church. Mixed marriages were frowned up by the Catholic Church and protestant future spouses were required to agree that the children of such a union would be brought up in the Catholic faith. In this way our fate at the hands of the Sisters of the Passion described in Chapter Three, was sealed. It is no wonder that my paternal grandmother warned her eldest son that "the father (i.e. the priest) would take the children away". My father was also expected to attend instruction about the Catholic faith so that he could support my mother in our religious upbringing. As it turned out the priest at St Peters, Blackburn, Father Flannery, whom my Dad nicknamed Father Flowerpot, was not a religious proselytiser and preferred to discuss the fortunes of the town's football club. My grandmother was not overtly religious but she deferred automatically as many Irish Catholics did to the authority of the parish priest and the nuns beneath him who ran the local Catholic primary school. The Catholic Church was patriarchal and women were expected to defer to men and it was instilled via the dominance of the parish priest. As children we would learn just how deeply this was subconsciously ingrained within our mother's psyche. Irish parish priests in England sought as much as possible to replicate the iron grip that they had on the rural peasant populations of what in 1949 would become the Republic of Ireland. Primary schools were a critical tool in maintaining this hegemony. However, when one leaves out the arcane doctrinal differences, there was little difference between the faiths when it came to child rearing and a woman's place within the home. Culture, tradition and religion reinforced each other as they continue to do in Islam today.

Few people under fifty years old will have any real comprehension of just how powerful this cocktail was in ruling our young lives and was only weakening its grip gradually and reluctantly as the first wave of baby boomers reached adulthood. It is almost impossible to convey the subdued almost brooding atmosphere of an English Sunday in the late '50s and early '60s, even allowing for the fact that motoring was a minority pursuit and therefore there was much less traffic noise. The first and most obvious difference was in the frequency of religious observance. My mother ceased to attend Mass for reasons she would never discuss but would pack us off without fail on a Sunday morning, until I rebelled at the age of fourteen or fifteen and simply refused to go anymore. I had not expected my defiance to get a result. As I recall we usually attended 10.15 Mass and were home for 11.15. My Church of England friends had to attend Sunday school after their service so I would normally not see them until after lunch when finally it was possible to go out and play with other children. For the Methodists and Congregationalists the football game was short as there were both afternoon and evening services for them to attend. As Catholics the nuns expected our attendance at Benediction on Sunday afternoons, but they were to be disappointed. Unlike missing Mass it was not a mortal sin, in fact it wasn't even a small sin, so the nuns contented themselves with periodic tirades at morning assembly about our irreligious behaviour. However, the advantages we enjoyed over protestant children in terms of Sunday observance were reversed when it came to the kind of religious force-feeding we endured Monday to Friday, of which more in the next chapter. If we were not able to play out Sunday was incredibly miserable. When we could play outside exuberance was frowned upon. Children were not welcome in the streets on Sundays and as I have said not always welcome where there were open spaces. In Northern Ireland the gates to children's playgrounds were physically padlocked.

Sunday observance also manifested itself in the very restricted shopping opportunities available. The Shops Act of 1950 consolidated various pieces of legislation that restricted Sunday trading. Hours were limited and although fresh food could be sold tinned food could not. The paper shop opened in the morning only, and Off Licences were only permitted to open for the sale of alcohol for the same hours as public houses. Different rules pertained for private clubs and for restaurants, such as they were, and for seaside shops in the summer. Competitive sport was not played on Sundays as it was illegal to charge for admission. The opening hours for pubs in England were restricted to two hours at lunchtime and three and half hours in the evening. If we thought that was grim for drinkers, in Scotland and Wales it was a whole lot grimmer. From 1853 to 1962 pub doors were firmly shut in Scotland on a Sunday. Off Licences were not open until 1994. In Wales all pubs closed on a Sunday from 1881 to 1961. Even after 1961, counties in Wales could and did close pubs to drinkers via a system of local option in plebiscites held every seven years. Not until 1996 was Wales completely wet on a Sunday and local option was not formally abolished until 2003. There were, of course, ways round the system as I discovered when staying in Aberystwyth in the mid-seventies. You could sit down and have a beer with your fish and chips in a sea front restaurant. Equally, you could drink all day in your hotel. A group of us took the piss out of system by drinking brown ale with our cornflakes at breakfast in the hotel. None of this was much use in a northern working-class town that was not a holiday destination where few people could afford restaurant meals. The middle classes who might patronise restaurants were not the target. It was about keeping the working classes on whose toil the wealth of the nation rested, sober and industrious.

It is indisputably so that Britain was more religious, more disciplined and more deferential during my childhood and adolescence. Nevertheless, the veneer of respectability and outward emotional reticence often concealed more than it revealed. It would be absurd to pretend that people did not fornicate, that some men did not beat their wives, and that there was not child abuse in the home, the school, and as we have discovered, in the care system and the approved schools for young delinquents. Divorce was not merely expensive but a massive social stigma on a par with illegitimacy. Until I divorced for the first time in 1992, Great Uncle Bert, then long deceased, had become the family pariah living in exile in faraway Crewe, after not one but two divorces. Three years later, I would equal his record. To this day we remain the family's only divorcees. For the vast majority of working-class people it was no more possible to simply flounce out of a relationship because of a spouse's adultery than it was for a persistent wife beater to be reported and face justice. The police did not get involved in what were called domestics, not unless someone was killed. Even after the children were long grown up, couples lived together in mutual loathing until death finally brought relief to the survivor. These were different times, not necessarily happier ones. As we would discover, children had no voice. Those who suffered physical or sexual abuse whether in outwardly respectable or wholly disreputable families had no one to complain to and no one who would believe them if they did.

Looking back it feels like a world in which so much was forbidden. Adults were as infantilised as children. As with the House of Commons behind the billycocks and the watch chains of the local worthies lurked hypocrisy – "do as I say not as I do" – never more absurd than when it was clearly visible. One of the pleasures of being a local councillor was being appointed to the Watch Committee. This august body had the great responsibility of determining whether films, particularly those given an "X" certificate, could be shown in the town's cinemas. Few things were more absurd than its members (all male) pulling up their collars and shuffling into a cinema for a private viewing of a sexually explicit (by the standards of the time) film, and then having enjoyed the pleasure of naked female flesh announcing that the film was too filthy to be shown to the people of the town. In this respect they were no better than the dirty raincoat brigade, who attended showings of naturist films, which for some strange reason where considered to be asexual. For film directors this was just a way of filming naked women without attracting too much criticism.

My parent's harsh upbringings and their wartime experience manifested themselves particularly at the dining table. We ate cheap cuts of meat so mince and stewing beef were dietary staples. My father ate tripe and onions, pig's trotters, and a broth made from a sheep's head with the brains on a side plate. Eventually, we got a cat and he consented to give her the brains. I'm not quite sure when he gave up these dishes but he was certainly still eating them when I left home to start teacher training in 1974. Mercifully he did not inflict these dishes on us but we were expected to eat everything and if we were still hungry we should go to the breadbin. Indeed, my father wiped his plate with a slice of bread throughout my childhood. I would go so far as to say that the "no waste" rule was almost an obsession with my father and directly related to both his childhood and wartime experiences. Any complaint by us about lumpy mashed potatoes was met with the solemn intonation: "Waste not, want not, sayeth the Lord." My mother's mashed potatoes were always lumpy and to this day I will not have mash on my plate. Roast potatoes were served only once a week at weekends, and other than that only at Christmas with that once a year treat, the turkey. It was a relief to have new potatoes in summer except that we then lost the treat of roast potatoes at weekend. Chips were permitted only once and occasionally twice a week. Mother's rule was one potato each so portions were small. When we complained at only having six chips, we were solemnly informed that eating too many chips gave you a square arse. The same kind of rationing persisted on the weekly visit to Grandma Swan when we had fish and chips from the chip shop when three portions fed four people. My parents and grandparents could not emancipate themselves from the ingrained parsimony of their youth.

My mother worked for very little of my childhood. She was able to return to work on a part-time basis when my sister Andrea started school in 1960. The birth of my brother James in October 1961 saw her return to the role of full-time housewife. Another sister, Madeline, was born in January 1965. I was born in December 1952, but my mother had had a previous pregnancy, which resulted in the birth of a stillborn son. My mother's life was therefore dominated by regular child birth, as it was for many working-class women. She did not return permanently to the workplace until 1973, initially on a part-time basis. The contraceptive pill was not available (initially to married women only) until 1964, too late for my mother even assuming that her Roman Catholic scruples would have allowed her to use it. The Catholic Church was firmly against artificial methods of birth control and remains so to this day. It is no coincidence that the largest families in our neighbourhood were Roman Catholic. My mother's sister Joan who had three children did break the church's taboo on the pill with tragic consequences, dying in 1969 around a year after emigrating to Canada with her family, of a complication caused by what was still a fairly experimental drug. For much of my childhood therefore, my father was the sole earner. My youngest sister's experience was of rather greater affluence as she grew older with two earners in the house and two older siblings having fled the nest. Indeed when she went up to University in 1983 my parents were assessed as having to pay a contribution to her student grant.

There were times when my mother resented her role as a housewife, although for the most part she accepted as her lot in life. In reality there was no alternative to getting on with it and her dreams would have to be realised through her children. Working-class women had to be very good at budgeting otherwise there would be times when families could not eat. My father was a traditional dominant working-class male who did not divulge the details of his wage packet, and regarded men who handed over their wage packets unopened to their wives on payday as borderline homosexual. This sort of working-class norm only broke down gradually. The traditional distinction between those who had what was called staff status and were paid monthly into their bank, and those who were paid weekly in cash had to wait for the unlikely figure of Margaret Thatcher for reform. In the prison service where I worked from 1984 to 2010, uniformed grades could elect to be paid weekly in cash until 1987. My mother, therefore, was given her budget and my father came and went as he pleased. As payday approached there was a noticeable change in what was on offer. I can't describe it as a menu, since the only option was take it or leave it. By Wednesday there were no fresh vegetables on the menu for which I was grateful since I could not stand cabbage and the only other alternative tended to be carrots. I never saw broccoli or green beans on a plate until I was 21 although at school we did have turnips mixed with carrots. At least in summer there were garden peas. The familiar Wednesday meal was meat and potato pie made with stewing beef in a pot garnished with a pastry crust. However, the upside of Wednesday was that if my mother had the energy it was baking day, which equalled apple pie for pudding and, if we were really lucky, my mother would make ginger cake. Either made a welcome change from puddings such as semolina, tapioca and rice in the days when this was a dessert with skin on the top rather than something eaten with chicken tikka masala. Cake in the tin was also welcome as the one solitary packet of chocolate digestives permitted every week in the family budget was gone by Saturday night. Thursday's meal was often a stew made simply with potatoes and mincemeat as the sole ingredients, particularly if my father was on a late shift and had not brought home his pay. It was not unusual for our bus fares to and from school to be the only cash left in my mother's purse on a Thursday morning.

Until I went to Grammar School in 1964 we came home for lunch, except that as a working-class family we called it dinner. Our evening meal was called tea, usually eaten about five o'clock. This was the most unexciting meal of the day and when the budget was running low something as unappetising as a tongue sandwich might be all that was available. Liver was another staple item in our diet. These days I cannot claim to know anyone who eats offal such as tripe, liver or ox tongue. Fish fingers appeared in our diet in the early '60s and sometimes my mother would make her own fishcakes. One of the benefits of going to Grammar School was that my parents moved the midday meal to teatime. It guaranteed me two hot meals a day, a real bonus. More to the point, we got chips twice a week at school. On the other three days there was no escape from the dreaded mashed potato. I can remember sausages, sausage pie and fish fingers (always on a Friday as we were a Catholic school) being served every single week without fail. However, I was luckier than my sister. I had largely dodged school meals at primary school but as a consequence of me moving up to Grammar School, she endured two years of school meals at St Edward's, where instead of fish on a Friday, they served the dreaded cheese pie. Anyone not eating their food was forced to sit and stare at it until the end of the lunch break.

The world before microwaves, freezers and ready meals may sound rather harsh. Preparing ingredients and baking would not suit the modern working mother. Our childhood diet may sound dull but is it any less dull than the diets of many families at the lower end of the social scale today. The obese child, now a common sight, was a rarity in my childhood, and this was not because we were kept short. Carbohydrates in the form of potatoes were a major part of our diet, but we ate very little processed food, much less sugar, and took rather more exercise. Of course as children we always wanted more. Children by their very nature do not do deferred gratification. It is something that is enforced by parents. My father would remind us regularly that "the eyes are greedier than the belly". Talking at the table was also discouraged. My father had another slogan: "Let your meat stop your mouth," which is perhaps a little more polite than "shut your cakehole". I should explain that holes featured prominently in our father's vocabulary. As well as a cakehole, there was an ear-hole, an arse-hole and even a neck-hole. Mercifully there was one related expression he did not use, or if he did I never heard it. We took all meals at the table. I knew of no families who did not and had they done so, they would not have been considered to be respectable. It was simply inconceivable that a family would not have a kitchen table, usually one with drop leaves that could be pushed into a corner. Oddly enough in later life after we had all fled the nest my parents joined the ranks of those who balanced their plates on their knees whilst watching the television.

When it came to home comforts things were steadily improving during my childhood. We were fortunate in some respects to live in a farm cottage as it had more space and there was land on which to play football and cricket. My parents often had to tolerate large numbers of small boys at the back of our house during school holidays and summer evenings, but at least they knew where I was and could call me in very swiftly. The back-to-back slum property is not a strong memory of my childhood, although I can just about remember where they stood in our neighbourhood and can recall that they were demolished in the mid-fifties. In the industrial north they had once been the norm for housing unskilled and/or the worst paid workers and their families. Back-to-back does what it says on the tin, therefore the occupant's tiny home only had a front out on to the street, the back of the house being a party wall. Not only were there no bathrooms, there were no toilets. A privy in a courtyard between blocks of back-to-back housing would be shared by a number of families and as it did not flush the contents were emptied weekly by a council night sanitation team known as "midnight men". The demolition of these slums was a priority for post-war governments and the vast majority had gone by the early '70s, although some remain in use in Leeds, thankfully with flush toilets and therefore minus the communal privy. The last back-to-back homes were built in the same city in 1909 and to this day they are not a permitted design under building regulations. The traditional terraced home where most of our neighbours lived are sometimes erroneously referred to as "back-to-backs". This is inaccurate as these homes have front and back elevations overlooking small individual yards with a narrow cobbled street or just a cinder track between the rows of houses. Some of the streets were extremely long. These homes were often small but did have their own flush toilet, albeit outside in the yard. In the winter when the water in the cistern froze it would be necessary to take a bowl of water to flush away the contents. To avoid having to go out during the night, the inhabitants used chamber pots – as indeed did we – and slopped out in the morning.

Both my grandmothers lived in mid-terrace homes built at the beginning of the twentieth century. My paternal grandmother's home was a step up from the weaver's cottage and was a slightly grander affair given the small kitchen, known as a scullery, was separate from what was known as the living room. There was also a hall. The house had a rarely used front parlour, kept for "best" and also for when a resident died. In 1936 it was estimated that around about ninety per cent of deceased persons were laid out in the home and remained there until being buried, the working class equivalent of lying in state. As a practice it has largely fallen into disfavour with the estimated figure now being less than ten per cent of deaths. Upstairs were three rooms, one of which my grandmother had converted into a bathroom, which as a family we were allowed to borrow occasionally on a Sunday, not at this time having one of our own.

My maternal grandmother lived in the same terraced home in the Mill Hill district of Blackburn for over forty years. The house had no hall so you walked straight into the parlour and it was without a bathroom until the day it was demolished. At the back of the house there was a kitchen with one easy chair in a corner and next to it a fold away dining table. As I recall the stand chairs in the parlour doubled as dining chairs. In another corner of the kitchen was a sink where one person had just enough room between it and the gas oven to wash or fill a kettle, which was boiled on a gas ring. In another corner next to the back door was a door that led upstairs to two sparsely furnished bedrooms. There was a fireplace in the kitchen between my grandmother's easy chair and the kitchen sink. On the opposite wall close to the door from the parlour there was an alcove. This proved a godsend as it was an ideal place for the television. When not in her bedroom this small space was my grandmother's world. In it she washed, cooked, rolled her tobacco into thin cigarettes, kept warm, entertained visitors and watched TV. Outside was a yard with the two outbuildings; one a coal shed, the other a lavatory. Whether you had a smarter terrace with a hall or a walk in terrace this was an almost unvarying pattern in Northern England. Not until I lived in Stoke-on-Trent in the 1980s did I come across traditional terraced homes with gardens, and they were very few in number. There was room for a washing line and if you were lucky there might be a view other than the back of the terraces opposite. My maternal grandmother's home backed on to St Peter's School where both she and my mother were educated separated from the school fence only by a cinder track. Inside the fence was a raised bank, which obscured the view of the schoolyard. These days it would be seen as anti-paedophile measure. Mill Hill and the adjoining Griffin district were among Blackburn's tougher areas.

Ewood where I grew up was not considered to be a tough district. In the subtle gradations of working-class life, Ewood was that one step further up the respectability ladder, an all-important virtue when I was growing up. However, Ewood became a tough place on a Saturday afternoon from the mid-sixties onwards when the young men of Blackburn came together to support Blackburn Rovers and to confront those visiting fans foolish enough to advertise their presence. Looking back it seems amazing that there were so many small shops. In the days before the supermarkets established their grip it seemed like every corner property on Bolton Road in the Ewood district housed a shop, and not just the corners. Quite how Ewood supported three bakers I will never know but when I was very young it did. I can only just remember Harry Connolly's which closed in the late '50s, but Kings survived until the late '60s. There was also another short-lived baking and confectionery business in Ewood, run by ex-Rovers footballer Bill Eckersley, which sadly did not prosper and closed down. There were even two wool shops such was the popularity, and for some the necessity, of home knitting. The knitting machine, now consigned to history, was as important a labour saving device as the washing machine during my childhood. As family errand boy I did not have the luxury of collecting everything from a one-stop minimarket. I was given a list that would see me calling at Chesterton's corner shop, the Co-op and King's before arriving at Leaver's to collect fresh bread. During wakes weeks it would also be necessary to call in at Wooller's, the cobblers, which doubled as the newsagents when the paper shop closed for the holiday. The Co-op, which traced its history back to the first Co-op, opened in Toad Lane, Rochdale in 1844, was probably the most important shop in the district, and many similar ones throughout Northern England. The Co-op delivered our weekly order and paid an annual dividend much prized by working-class families at Christmas time. I can still remember our divi number – sixteen twelve – which I had to give without fail every time a purchase was made. Every penny of the dividend was precious. I can't remember when the Ewood Co-op closed, but I don't believe it survived the 1970s.

For many years there has not been a single shop between my parent's former home and Leaver's, which survives as a family business to this day. Leaver's – a quality bakers and confectioners – was the pie shop of choice for Blackburn Rovers footballers until modern nutrition put paid to the traditional lunch dutifully collected by the apprentices and delivered to the first team dressing room at the end of morning training. In those far off days fully fledged professionals only trained in the morning. At the age of sixteen visiting Leaver's was a mixed blessing. I rather fancied Janet Leaver who was the same age as me and worked in the family shop on a Saturday, but it never felt quite right to be asking her out when doing my mother's errands. For all I know she may have felt equally un-cool in a white coat serving bread and cakes to pensioners and schoolboys. One of the two newsagents, the Barbers and the Fish and Chip shop survive to this day as does Ewood Working Men's club and the sub post office. The two butchers' shops, the two wool shops, the fresh fish shop, the renowned ice cream shop, Ewood dairy, and Thompson's pet shop are long gone, as is the treasure trove that was Alicia's, a specialist sweet shop. The supermarket and the motor car, that most visible symbol of rising affluence, had put the skids under corner shops while I was still a young man.

My parents may not have believed they were prosperous but like other comparable families there began the steady accumulation of consumer goods and gradual home improvement. My father prioritised personal transport even while my mother continued to use a wash board, dolly tub and mangle to do the weekly wash. It would be fair to say that my father had little concept of a woman's work. If he can be excused at all it would be because that for many years he was a locomotive fireman, one of the most physically demanding jobs anywhere that a man could be expected to carry out. The mangle belatedly disappeared from the Retail Price Index in 1962, by which time the majority of families owned (usually on hire purchase) a washing machine, in these early days usually a twin tub whereby the washing machine and dryer were in separate compartments. We graduated from a twin tub in 1972 when my father purchased for her an upmarket German model, called a Lavalux, which carried out both functions in one container. It was such an efficient piece of equipment that my father refused to replace it for twenty years.

I cannot recall how soon my father purchased his first car but I do remember him having a van which advertised Norlax Delivery Service. My father and his brother-in-law, (uncle) Bill Norris, set up a small business delivering paraffin to homes in the local area. They acquired a large 500 gallon tank that was filled periodically by the wholesalers, which stood on a mound by the garage. As most families including our own did not have central heating in the late '50s, paraffin heaters were very popular in winter for heating up bedrooms before the occupants retired for the night, and in aspirational families for heating up parlours so that school age children had a quiet place to do homework. Although we had three rooms other than the main living room which contained fireplaces, my father would very rarely permit the burning of coal anywhere but the main room. Christmas was the obvious exception. Even if I did have permission for a fire in the bedroom I would be expected to make it and clean up the fireplace after the fire was out. This was an offer I normally refused and instead settled for the paraffin heater.

At the time of writing Bill is a hale and hearty octogenarian living in retirement in Canada. He soon tired of the paraffin business and my father carried on alone for a number of years until dwindling demand made it uneconomic. The van, however, for a time doubled as the family car. There were no windows and only two seats, and no benches in the back. My sister and I perched on the wheel arches and found ourselves in orbit when the van hit a bump in the road. Greater comfort was not long delayed.

In 1960 my father purchased a 1953 registered Lanchester Fourteen. The Lanchester had been manufactured by Daimler since 1931 and the last Lanchesters rolled off the production line in 1955. As I have said the car preceded the washing machine and it was both my father's pride and joy and the envy of his friends. He kept the car on the road until 1976 when he replaced it with another luxury model, a Jaguar Mark 2. In fact, the Lanchester remained mothballed in a barn for twenty years until he was forced to sell it after his second stroke. He never realised his dream to put it back on the road. My father also acquired a 50cc motorcycle after he transferred to the sheds at Accrington in the early '60s. In a spell when he had little overtime a moped was considerably more economic. However, my father put a more powerful engine in the bike while still licensing it as a moped, which of course was illegal.

In the fullness of time our home would be upgraded. The fridge, the freezer, the bathroom and finally the central heating became part of our lives. Our first television preceded all of them. We got that in 1957. I can date it by the fact that I can recall viewing "Watch with Mother" in the summer before I started school and being singularly miffed that I could no longer watch this programme except during school holidays. I shall say more about the television in Chapter Seven. The central heating came last in 1972. My parents held the view that heating the whole house was an unnecessary luxury. As a railway fireman my father was an expert at making roaring fires, which was fine for the living room but did little for the rest of the house. I don't recall with any certainty the reason they changed their minds. My paternal grandmother lived with us over the winter of 1971–72 finally succumbing to cancer in March. Her bed was in the "walk in" downstairs front room. There was no hall and no porch and without a fire it was desperately cold. It goes without saying that there was no double glazing. The window frames were made of soft wood and were not in the best of condition.

My best guess is that it was her stay that changed their minds. However, like most homes erected before modern building regulations the cart was put before the horse. Central heating was very welcome but it did nothing to eliminate drafts and one can only guess how much was wasted because of poor insulation.

As children we were expected to know our place. The pecking order in terms of the fire illustrated perfectly where we stood, or in this case sat. My parents had their own armchairs closest to the fire. As children when both of our parents were at home, we had two choices: the settee or the floor. At one side of the fire was a large airing cupboard with another cupboard below. On the other side in a recessed corner was a door to what we called the front room, although the living room (not lounge, much too posh for us) was also on the front. Opposite to that was a door to the kitchen, which was freezing in winter and the television stood in the remaining corner. Therefore in order for family viewing to take place the settee had to be on the party wall with the kitchen rather than facing the fire. If you were sat on the end of the settee you were therefore furthest away from the fire and closest to the draught that whistled under the door from the kitchen.

My parents would not have known what to make of TV series like "Outnumbered", where the hapless middle-class parents are given the run around on a daily basis by their three children. They are utterly spoilt, know it all, and the household totally revolves around their needs. The programme is a comedy and gives an exaggerated picture in order to get laughs, but scriptwriters could not possibly come up with a sitcom like this were there not a basis in fact. All the classic sitcoms are grounded in reality. Our parents would not have recognised this world. My father was giving to chanting doggerel about our place and how we should be treated: "Spare the rod and spoil the child," was one I heard from his mother, although in reality my father usually only had to raise his voice, which he did frequently. His other favourite again acquired from his own mother was: "Children should be seen and not heard." We were neither expected nor permitted to join in conversations between adults, nor were we allowed to chat amongst ourselves whilst adults were talking. When conversing with an adult we were not permitted to argue. "Don't argue with your elders," was another mantra chanted at home. Thus our parents were always right even when they were wrong. The same applied to adults outside the family. Thus, if a neighbour complained about one of us being cheeky or climbing over someone's back yard to retrieve a ball, then their complaint was always upheld, even if I had actually been doing my homework at the time. Try telling a child now that life isn't fair, get used to it, and you can expect them to be calling Child Line on their mobile phones. Harshness was considered character building. In many respects manliness was defined by fatherhood and heading your own household. Fathers were not gentle people. In working-class households where I grew up, fathers did not want their boys to grow up as sissies. Mums were not allowed to be too protective and an excess of sympathy shown after a minor cut or injury was sustained was frowned upon. Pain had to be born stoically.

The telephone came with the van we had before the car. I cannot describe it as a luxury because it was necessary for the paraffin business. In the late '50s calls still had to be put through an operator. I remember getting into trouble for asking the operator to call a number in a neighbouring town and when put through asking the person on the other end if he wanted to buy an elephant. I could only imagine that my Indian accent was unconvincing. Why the Indian accent? Well, Peter Sellers in a duet with Sophia Loren had a comedy record in the charts towards the end of 1960 titled, "Goodness Gracious Me" in which he sung in a mock Indian accent. What I did not know was that the recipient could ask the operator to trace the caller's number and refer the matter to my father. After a bawling out and the loss of a week's pocket money I was not minded to do it again. I would be in my teens before I no longer needed permission to use the phone. Thankfully by then it was no longer necessary to go through an operator.

My father could not have recited all of the Ten Commandments but he was an expert on the fourth one: "Honour thy father and thy mother," and he let us know that at regular intervals. Unlike the fictional family in "Outnumbered", a father's word was law, and it was the same in the houses of all my friends. Even where the husband was henpecked and had to ask permission to go to the pub, his word was final where the children were concerned. Autocratic fatherhood was further enhanced by the experience of compulsory military service during the War. Even if the man had never risen above the lowest rank of private soldier, he felt entitled to treat his home like a barrack room in which he was the one giving the orders. Our fathers may have fought for democracy but it did not extend to the family home. As I have said my father was in a reserved occupation, but that did not prevent him from telling us that something was an order, not that we were ever in any doubt. There was no question of being paid for doing any household jobs. We were simply expected to do them. At one time we were actually given a list of our daily duties. I ran errands and my sister did the teatime washing up for as long as we were at school. Indeed, the eldest of my two sisters was lumbered with compulsory washing up beyond leaving school until such a time as our youngest sibling could be entrusted with that chore. Although my father would usually make the fire, he would expect me to go outside on a winter's evening at intervals to get a shovel full of coal. Not until I left home did that job pass to my brother.

Although I have painted a picture of working-class life as a patriarchy ruled by tyrannical men, working-class women should not be seen as a species of doormats. The dynamic was always more complex than that. As I have said, working-class women were incredible money managers. It was instilled into them by their own mothers who had experienced the hungry '30s. Wives no longer needed the pawnbroker but folk memories were long. My grandmother's generation also carried another folk memory; that of husbands drinking away their wages at the pub on payday, eventually arriving home intoxicated with empty pockets. I do not know how prevalent this sort of behaviour was, but I do recall my own grandmother, who was born in 1901, telling me that her father went straight home from work on payday, wage packet intact, unlike some of her friends' fathers. I also recall reading somewhere about Lloyd George excoriating the practice of treating, i.e. buying beer in rounds. Not unexpectedly, this increases both consumption and expense. Pubs were open all day during my grandmother's childhood, and this would only cease when Lloyd George restricted licensing hours in 1915 when working-class drinking habits were adversely affecting the war effort in the munitions factories. Whether these folk memories helped create the stereotypical British battle-axe complete with curlers, rolling pin and withering put downs of male inadequacy I do not know. What I do know is that patriarchy could be and was restricted by strong women whose humble homes were never less than immaculate. The men may have thought they were in charge, but in the home the reality could be very different. A man's role was to earn and provide. A woman's role was to run home and family. A man may preside, but the wife would rule. He may have got his dinner on the table when he walked through the door from work, but he had no say in what went on the plate.

Bedtimes were another example of how strict rules were imposed. Our parents did not differentiate between term time and school holiday time. They wanted us "up the wooden hill" as my described father described it, so that they could have some free time of their own, even if that was simply my father going to the pub and my mother reading a book or working on her knitting machine. There was no question of refusing to go bed, coming down for a glass of water, or chatting with my sister in the neighbouring bedroom. The slightest hint of noise would have my father opening the stairs door and roaring, "Get asleep or I'll tan your arse." Sleep did not always come immediately but silence did. As a father myself one strict rule I did impose was appropriate bedtimes. Children need sleep and adults need respite from children.

Clothes and haircuts were other subjects of differentiation and discipline. Boys wore short trousers for school and other formal occasions until they were at least twelve years of age. I graduated into long trousers when I began my second year at Grammar School, but a good number of my class remained in shorts for another year. My father insisted on short hair which kept me out of trouble at Grammar School where the strap was used as a punishment for having hair excessively long. From the modern perspective it is hard to understand how the length of male hair became the defining symbol of the intergenerational conflict that gathered pace from about 1963 onwards. Girls on the other hand were expected to wear their hair long. Trousers were still frowned upon for adult women and only in the late 1970s would they be permitted in some schools and then usually as a privilege for older pupils. Even as late as the first decade of this century some secondary schools continued to forbid girls to wear trousers as my daughter would discover. Just as long hair became a symbol of the battle between the generations, trousers became a symbol of the struggle for female equality in hitherto male dominated professions.

Children were at the foot of the pecking order. They were there to be brought up and didn't acquire any rights until they were twenty-one years of age, the "swinging sixties" notwithstanding. They were a London metropolitan phenomenon. Children had no status until they went out to work and contributed to the family exchequer. One of the first visible symbols of adulthood was being permitted to smoke cigarettes at home. It was not unusual for both parents to smoke and permission for children to smoke in the home usually came with starting work. Although my father was a smoker until he gave up in 1972, I was not permitted to smoke in the house until I was seventeen (and still at school), having started at just short of fifteen. Sensibly I gave up in 1980. My mother never smoked at all and neither did my paternal grandmother, although it did not prevent her from dying of lung cancer just five years after completing a working life as a weaver in a cotton mill. There were no blurred lines between children and adults. My neighbour's fourteen-year-old boy addresses me by my first name and has done so since we first moved here five years ago. It is the most natural thing in the world to his generation. We were expected to address all adults formally. When I got a summer job in a local factory at the age of sixteen it came as a considerable surprise to me when the foreman told me to call him Roy rather than the formal Mr Pickup that I assumed was the norm. Deference was a habit to be ingrained from an early age. It was part of growing up in a society where the older generation had been expected to know their place and sought to ensure that we grew up with a similar view of the world. They would be disappointed as the pace of social change accelerated.

I can only recall two pieces of advice from my father (as opposed to instructions of which there were many) and both were very pithy. The first was "never let your prick rule your head", which even some Catholic priests have difficulty with never mind hormonal young men, and the second was "never trust a teetotaller". Whether I was expected to take it literally I very much doubt. What it did symbolise was the importance of alcohol in working-class communities, not just as a recreational pursuit but as a symbol of manhood. The message was that real men drank alcohol. I can recall at an interval of some fifty years an episode of Coronation Street in which one character basically says to another, "You don't smoke, you don't drink, what sort of a man are you?" These were the messages we imbibed and they were very much reinforced in the home. My father worked on the railway and although I am sure that there must have been some teetotallers among the workforce, he was very much part of and at home with the drinking culture. On a Sunday if he was not working, like all the other working men he wore a suit to go to the pub. Officially Sunday lunchtime drinking lasted only from midday until 2pm, but my father could always find an establishment that discreetly ignored licensing hours. We just had our lunch without him.

Our generation simply followed suit although we drew the line at wearing a suit on Sunday and were rather less skilled in finding an afterhours drink. There was the "Top Hat Club" (known locally as the "Top Twat"), later renamed as the "Talk of the Town", but there was an admission fee and drinks prices were extortionate. Presumably that funded the strippers that gave the club its nickname. In the summer there was Darwen Cricket club, which was rather more convivial, not just for the sunshine but also because there was no need to watch your back. Underage drinking was condoned as a period where an apprenticeship was served before graduating to the big league where you were expected to buy your round and show that you could take a drink. The ability to drink large amounts of alcohol and emerge standing was much admired. Being sick was permitted provided you carried on drinking. I had the misfortune to be the son of a father who was top dog in the bar and therefore be judged by his standards. He could drink any man under the table, except perhaps Great Uncle Reginald, who worked even harder and played even harder than my own father, if that were possible.

There is no necessary connection between alcohol and affluence for the generations represented by my father and great uncle. Although it is true that post-war wages rose faster than the price of alcohol, thus making it more affordable, there was competition for the extra pounds in the working man's pocket. Cars were an exciting toy that came within the reach of working people in the 1950s along with labour saving gadgets like washing machines, which were naturally much appreciated by the wives. The television, either rented or bought on hire purchase, was the absolute must have new toy. Young people shared in that affluence, the word teenager entered the lexicon, and the availability of comparatively well paid unskilled work boosted their purchasing power. As with adults there was competition for the teenage pound. Nevertheless, there was enough left over to spend in the pub.

I had my first (illegal) pint in Bolton in a pub called the Waggon and Horses on the way to a football match at the age of fifteen. A few weeks later on Easter Monday, 1968, I got drunk for the first time in Blackpool. The purpose of the visit was to watch the Rovers play. I don't remember too much about the day, but for some strange reason I do remember tripping on the stairs going into a pub called the Gaslight Bar and crashing through the doors, which were like those you see in the saloons in the American western TV series that were so popular when I was a child. Dignified it was not and I did not attempt to get served. I was never once refused a drink under age, but being able to grow what were then fashionable sideburns at the age of fifteen was clearly a factor in my favour. At the age of sixteen I was drinking in the town at weekends. The Dolphin and the Uncle Tom's Cabin, both long since demolished, were places with a reputation for serving underage drinkers. The only dangerous time of the year was January when the annual report of the Licensing Justices came out and there would be a short purge, but I can honestly say I never saw a policeman enter a pub in uniform until I was well past eighteen. The general rule of underage drinking was "be quiet and don't upset the locals". Even so there were some tough pubs that it paid to avoid, old enough or not.

Older residents will recall the Dun Horse, to this day one of only two pubs where I have seen price tags on the heels of the local prostitutes. Pubs like the Legs O'Man, The Swan and The Sun were not places for the faint hearted. The Harrisons on Bolton Road had probably the best jukebox in town with an array of late '50s and early '60s classics, but it did not pay to upset the former Teddy Boys who just loved this pub. One of our favourite pub crawl routes after I left school began at The Adelphi next to the railway station and continued via Darwen Street up Bolton Road to the football ground. My apologies if I have missed any out but the route would take us via The Stokers, The Duke of York (just next to Darwen Street Bridge), The Brewers, The Harrisons, The Commercial, The Horse Load, The Infirmary, The Aqueduct and finally if you could make it that far, The Albion. That is ten pubs and only the most serious drinkers could manage a pint in each. It is hard to believe that there are now only two pubs after the Adelphi on the walking route to Ewood Park. However, my own immediate local The Fernhurst, just to the south of the ground remains open as does the Fox and Hounds behind what used to be the match day coach park.

The first environment I explored outside the home was the neighbouring Fernhurst Hall Farm. Mr and Mrs Nightingale were the owners, and our home had originally been a tied cottage for a farm labourer. My parents were simply tenants although my father always assisted with haymaking as it brought in extra money. As I recall they had a large family with five children, four of them adults and one in secondary school at the time of my earliest memory. Bill Nightingale was the gruff family patriarch and we never called him anything other than Mr Nightingale. For me as a small boy the farm almost became a playground. On none school days I could be found assisting with the herding of the cattle back to the shippan for milking. The birth of calves was not a mystery as I witnessed that occurrence live out in the field on more than one occasion. However, Mr Nightingale used artificial insemination with his cattle so I never got to see the bull servicing members of the herd, which was perhaps as well. I'm sure the nuns would have been very unhappy about that kind of thing appearing in a child's exercise book.

From the age of about ten I was allowed to enter the stalls and un-tether the cows so that they could return to pasture. There was an element of danger to this as cows are nervous creatures with a powerful kick. They also had horns. A modern farmer allowing a ten-year-old boy such close proximity to cattle would expect to pay a crippling fine under Health and Safety law, and if any injuries were sustained he would expect to be on the receiving end of a law suit for a minimum five figure sum. The barn was an exciting place to play with bales of hay to climb up and leap from. I can remember dragging heavy bales of hay on balmy July evenings during haymaking. Living next door to the farm obviated the need for milk deliveries. My mother just sent me next door to the dairy with a quart jug. After morning milking and mucking out, Mr Nightingale would deliver milk by horse and cart. Sadly he was seriously injured in a road accident whilst on his round and only had a short retirement before his death in 1966. The farm was sold to the council and the new tenant farmer promptly fenced off most of the land outside the back of our house. At a stroke in the autumn of 1966 we lost our football field and cricket pitch.

Fortunately, there were other places to go. The playing fields at Lower Darwen were only a short walk away. Another popular spot was St Bartholomew's school yard close to Ewood Park where most of the local children began their school career. The yard was a perfect length for football although the outside toilets were a partial obstruction. Chipping the ball over the toilets for a team mate to run on to was a skill that had to be acquired. At one end of the yard was St Bartholomew's Anglican Church, separated from the school by a footpath. To protect the church was high fencing which was ideal as the ball could not be lost at that end nor could we break any expensive windows. The gates were the goal. At the other end there was a five-foot wall with a painted goal in the middle. One side of the pitch was classrooms and the other side a low wall with short railings. Years later a high fence was built all the way round the schoolyard, presumably built to keep paedophiles out rather than prevent small boys from playing football after school. The school itself was demolished in 2013.

Another spot for both football and cricket was the car park behind Kidder Street. The front aspects of Kidder Street's terraced homes looked out on to the back wall of the Blackburn End of the ground. They were demolished when Ewood Park was rebuilt between 1992 and 1994. The cinder car park was known to the local boys as "Little Wembley". The only thing it had in common with Wembley was that there were real goalposts. The backs of the houses on Nuttall Street and Kidder Street were protected by high fencing and on other side was a factory. The only place a ball could be lost was at the bottom end where only a low fence separated the car park from the murky shallows of the River Darwen. Nevertheless, it took a very wayward shot to lose the ball and it is was a big hit for six for small boys playing tennis ball cricket in the summer. Other places I can remember playing football were in a yard by Albion Mill and the playing fields at Darwen Grammar School, which had proper goal nets, a real bonus. Looking back it seems remarkable that we seemed to know instinctively where there was a game to be had. There were no mobile phones to find out where to go, we just knew.

Only heavy rain got in the way of playing out. As an avid reader this was not a disaster. My mother instilled a lifelong love of books. I was given a train set for Christmas at the age of five although of course at that age I believed that Santa had brought it down the chimney. It was a wonderful present and remains in the family at my brother's home. He is only waiting for one of his children to move out so that he can set it up again. Despite the fact that it is a family heirloom like my father's gold watch, my favourite childhood present was the encyclopaedia I received at Christmas 1961, this time not from Santa Claus. It was veritable treasure trove of knowledge and like the Pear's encyclopaedia from the 1930s that I found in a drawer, it was read over and over again. In the same drawer I found a copy of "The Fifty Most Amazing Crimes of The Last Hundred Years", published in 1936. I managed to read a few chapters including the one on Jack the Ripper before my mother confiscated it as being unsuitable. Some four decades later I found a copy in a second hand bookshop in Petersfield, retailing for the princely sum of 70p. It has sat on my bookshelf ever since.

I was not terribly interested in Saturday morning children's cinema, which was in any case becoming much less fashionable by the early 1960s. Our local cinema was The Empire, known as the barn or the fleapit. It had double seats on the back row for courting couples. I can remember going to the cinema in the evening and watching both the first James Bond film "Dr No" and World War Two epic "The Longest Day" with friends at the Empire when I was ten years old. At the age of fourteen I would watch my first "X" rated film, "The Family Way" at the same cinema. The age restriction for adult films was then sixteen – not eighteen – an age I could pass for without difficulty, unlike a number of my friends. Back in 1967, adult rated movies were still pretty tame stuff compared to what would be on offer in a few short years as boundaries that had held for years were smashed down. As I recall The Family Way broke new ground in tackling the subject of male impotence, but the newspapers were more interested in the fact that the bare backside of Hayley Mills, then a leading British actress was on show. In modern Britain this film would get a "12" certificate.

We were not cosseted by our parents. The expectation was that we would come home for meals and the pre-instructed bedtime. So long as no adults complained about us to our parents, we were pretty much left alone. Darkness was not a necessary reason to be confined to the house, and certainly not in the lead up to bonfire night. We had a bonfire to guard and raids to organise. On one occasion, which would have been in 1963, a group of small boys could have been observed carrying a very heavy telegraph pole across Bolton Road on their collective shoulders. I cannot recall whose bonfire was relieved of this item, but they certainly made no attempt to retrieve it. Despite the fact that our upbringing was much stricter than it is for the modern child, the reality is that we had much more freedom and were healthier for it in both body and mind.

Chapter Three

Primary School: Terror by Penguin

Most children will tell you they don't like school. Some will loathe it with a passion that continues into adult life. Even those children who really like school, largely because it validates them as successful young people, will not admit it to their peers or their parents, not least because it is un-cool. The vast majority of children, including those who really like school, will at some point resent its intrusion into their personal freedom, largely because of homework but also because teachers may intrude in other ways, like imposing dress codes that are at odds with the way adolescents would prefer to dress. It is natural for children to find discipline irksome, but it is necessary if young people are going to cope with the world of work. Bill Gates, founder of Microsoft, is reputed to have said to a class: "If you think your Mom is tough, wait until you get a boss." If the employers quoted at intervals in the Daily Mail are correct then parents are not tough enough and, if Education Secretary (2010–14) Michael Gove is correct, then a generation of children have been let down by a child centred uncompetitive system that has lacked both rigour and discipline. I can recall being told by a very traditional Headmaster on my first teaching practice in Oakengates, Telford, back in January 1975, to forget about (Jean) Piaget, one of the gurus of child centred, sometimes known as progressive education, whose ideas were beginning to catch on in Europe and America during the 1960s.

Whether or not the Sisters of the Passion had ever heard of Piaget I do not know. There was little to suggest in retrospect that either they or their lay colleagues were in any way influenced by academic theory. Indeed, their teaching methods and the religious curriculum appeared to owe more to a combination of unbending Victorian rectitude and the Jesuit mantra of: "Give me a child when he is seven and I will give you the man." I loathed primary school with an all-consuming passion. On occasion I begged my mother to move me to St Peters, not realising in my naivety that it would have been out of the frying pan into the fire. There was no escape from the nuns. I have often described my early years of school as "terror by penguin", and I know that many of my generation who had the misfortune to encounter the sisters of one religious teaching order or another feel exactly the same way. The only difference between primary school and a Magdalene Laundry was that we got to go home at night.

Let me be clear, I am not one of these people whose loathing of school has made them reject the whole concept of school discipline. Children should be silent when the teacher is speaking, should study diligently and, where necessary, be punished for breaches of discipline. I have no objection in principle to corporal punishment provided that it is reasonable and moderate and imposed only for serious disciplinary offences, such as bullying, assault and persistent disruption of classes. I can only describe St Edwards RC Primary School, Darwen, which was the closest Catholic school to our home and where I was a pupil from 1957 to 1964, as bleak and oppressive. The whole ethos of the school in that era was to intimidate and humiliate. Not only were we vessels to be filled, we were sinners who had to be made to suffer in the name of God. I struggle to remember a single instance of Christian charity being displayed. You never knew from one minute to the next when you would arouse the seemingly random wrath of those in charge of our education. It was an environment in which you never felt safe.

Children have a deep desire both to trust and please adults. Neither of these was possible at St Edwards. In his song "Working Class Hero" John Lennon sings a line: "They hate you if you're clever and despise a fool." Although Lennon was not a Catholic he captured perfectly what it was like in that one sentence. Indeed, being clever was in its own way more dangerous. You could not be allowed to get above yourself. Being top of the class in my final year was a source of danger rather than pride. The nuns liked nothing better than to hack down a tall poppy. It is one of the grim ironies of our education in that era that being successful at school exposed you to greater risk from the staff than it did from fellow pupils. The kind of primary education we endured would be incomprehensible to the modern child. The novel Jane Eyre has been adapted for television on a number of occasions. All the versions I have seen feature the brutal caning of Jane's friend, Helen Burns, in the first episode. Those readers who have seen it will know that the punishment was intended not merely to hurt but also to humiliate. Helen Burns is also seen to wear a cap with the word "slattern" printed on it. We watched it as a family in 1963 when I was ten years old. Although the caps marked slattern or dunce were no longer used, the early nineteenth century schoolroom seemed eerily familiar.

As I have said, I have no objection in principle to the use of physical punishment provided that it is moderate and reasonable and awarded only for the most serious breaches of discipline. However, those who inflicted it have to take as much share of the blame for the breakdown in school discipline as those social reformers who saw the cane and the tawse as instruments of an uncivilised society that deep down did not like its children. It is unarguably the case that corporal punishment was misused often, being the first resort of school discipline rather than the last. I doubt that mass punishment was ever truly lawful. Sadly, a minority of teachers can accurately be described as child abusers for whom corporal punishment was undoubtedly a source of sexual gratification. In that respect as a form of abuse it is perilously close to the paedophilic (or should it be paedophobic) spectrum, if not actually on it. Although only a small minority of teachers who used corporal punishment can be described in this way, I don't regard it as a coincidence that orders of nuns have virtually disappeared from the classroom since corporal punishment was abolished in the state system in 1987.

It may seem difficult to believe, but corporal punishment was once also a feature of British humour. A series entitled "Whack-O!" starring Jimmy Edwards as Professor Edwards the blustering, cane wielding, drunken Headmaster of a minor public school ran from 1956 to 1960 and again from 1971 to 1972. All told some sixty (!) episodes were made, though only four are known to have survived. To the best of my knowledge they have never been screened since, nor can I recall the spin-off film "Bottoms Up" (1960) being screened for very many years. My recollections of Bottoms Up are the frequent use of the phrase "Bend over, Wendover", Wendover being an errant pupil who was also the son of a Bishop, and Edwards' efforts to devise a means of caning five boys simultaneously using an extra- long cane to administer "six of the best", which would ultimately be the title of Edwards' autobiography! No wonder the French refer to flagellation as "the English vice".

I first had sight of the cane at St Edwards before I was five years old, the feel of it would come later. Four times a day we lined up outside in order to be marched into class. One of the male teachers, a Mr Bradley who I presume is long dead, would stand supervising the lines of children, cane in hand. Miscreants were ordered out of the lines and ordered to face the wall. The cane would be administered when everyone else had gone in, so as not to delay assembly or lessons depending on the time of day. When I commenced school in 1957, St Edwards was really still an elementary school. Those who did not pass the 11 plus mostly remained at St Edwards until they left school at the age of fifteen, as there were no Secondary Modern places for Catholic pupils in Darwen until 1960, when St Thomas Aquinas Secondary Modern School opened its doors, some sixteen years after the passing of the 1944 Education Act which legislated for secondary education for all, according to age, ability and aptitude.

The terrifying sight of Mr Bradley was one of the clues of the fate that would befall us when we progressed from what by St Edwards standards was the relatively safe environment of what was known as the "baby" class. We had a separate assembly, we were allowed free play with crayons and Plasticine most afternoons and our teacher, Mrs Sumner, was a relatively benign individual who did not use corporal punishment. However, assembly was usually presided over by the Deputy Headmistress, Miss Eccles, of whose formidable reputation we quickly became aware, and religious proselytising began on our very first day when we were herded into a large classroom, lined up between the desks and had our first taste of morning prayers. The school assumed that as Catholic children we already knew how to clasp our hands together, close our eyes and pray fervently to God with the words already made familiar to us by our parents. Well, they got that one wrong. However, it was quickly apparent that the older infants lined up between the neighbouring rows of desks knew what to do and, in fairly short order, we learned the Lord's Prayer and other prayers by heart. We also had religious instruction on a daily basis, although at this stage it was confined to stories about Jesus, Mary and Joseph, and also learned to sing hymns. Additionally, we were trooped off to Mass at the Sacred Heart church every Thursday morning. This was another set of actions and prayers that had to be learned; when to sit, when to stand, when to kneel, when to respond.

For some reason the Catholic Church was as obsessed with guardian angels as it was with original sin. Apparently, we all had our own individual guardian angels who were supposed to look after us constantly. That illusion was rudely shattered when we moved up to the senior infant class taught by Miss Eccles, a ferocious martinet, known throughout the school by the unoriginal and uncomplimentary nickname of "Eccles Cakes". I found myself in trouble with the redoubtable Miss Eccles on my first day in her class. We were instructed to print the date in the corner of our exercise books keeping all the letters and numbers above the line. Unfortunately, there is a "g" in August so using my common sense I rested the top half of the "g" on the line with the bottom half of the "g" underneath, which is as you would expect to find it to this very day. This aroused the ire of Miss Eccles, who thumped me several times in the back whilst berating me for my disobedience. Miss Eccles also introduced her class of forty plus infants to the strap. She employed it on a daily basis and no member of the class could get through a term unpunished. Miss Eccles also introduced us to her own unique method of toilet training. In the reception class we were taken for toilet breaks as a class each morning and afternoon in addition to the opportunity afforded at playtime. In Miss Eccles' class you had to ask and for your impertinence were given the strap before being permitted to leave the classroom!

For me, Miss Eccles was at her most terrifying when we had to learn sections of the Catholic catechism by heart. The parish priest's annual inspection was much feared by the teaching staff and this translated itself into a very tense classroom atmosphere with the strap used liberally to facilitate learning. Being a slow learner (and there were a number of them) or being so paralysed by fear that the memory of what had been learned disappeared at the crucial moment were vices presumed curable by the strap and the bollocking that accompanied it. At this time of year Miss Eccles assumed the guise of Mr Murdstone, David Copperfield's cruel stepfather who thrashed him for being unable to remember his lesson when, in reality, he was an intelligent but sensitive child whose eagerness to please was overwhelmed by fear. For the uninitiated, the catechism is a summary of Catholic principles. In the junior versions the catechism was in question and answer format starting with basic questions such as "Who is God?" and dealing with complicated concepts such as the

Holy Trinity, all of which we were expected to learn by heart. Religious instruction was given on a daily basis after assembly. At least as infants we still finished school at 15.45 and were allowed to play on a Friday afternoon.

It was a blessed relief when the year ended and the long summer holiday finally arrived. Back in the 1950s, school terms were a little longer than they are now. Our summer holiday was only five weeks long and we returned to school on the first Monday after 15 August, which is the feast of the Assumption. Its significance for Catholics is that it is what is known as Holy Day of Obligation, when all Catholics are required to go to Mass in the same way as they are required to attend on a Sunday. As Catholics were also required to refrain from servile works on the Sabbath and on the Holy Days of Obligation, which were also days off school, a boon not granted to my protestant friends. The autumn term was actually divided into three parts; the first of these was only three weeks long as school then broke up for what was known as the September holiday, a break which was part of the terms and conditions of local factory workers. Half-term came at the beginning of November and coincided with All Saints Day, which fell on the 1st of November. If we were really lucky it would fall on a Friday, thus we would get that day off as well as the following Monday and Tuesday, and even better Bonfire night would also be a school holiday. The spring and summer half-terms were also only of two days duration. We got a fortnight or so at Christmas, returning to school the day after twelfth night or the Monday after if that fell on a Friday or a Saturday. Again this was because of a Holy Day of Obligation, the Epiphany, which fell on 6 January. The Easter holiday began on Good Friday, which for someone unaccountable reason is not a Holy Day of Obligation despite its massive significance in the Christian faith. For the summer break the guidelines were secular. School finished at the commencement of the industrial summer holidays.

My protestant friends did a little less well in terms of

holidays, because they did not have the holy days and only got the two days in September that the millworkers got. However, I envied them in the summertime. The local Church of England school was less than a quarter of a mile from my home and inside the Blackburn town boundary where we lived, and had different holidays. The summer industrial break commenced a week later and the schools closed for six weeks, rather than five, meaning that school was not resumed until the beginning of September, a full fortnight of summertime after we had returned to school. It was agony. The extra summer week was taken off them at Easter, but I doubt that the children who went to the local school would have swapped with us.

Any pleasure or relief that we may have felt on being promoted to the junior school evaporated rapidly. Mrs Slater was another ferocious middle-aged martinet and the school day was ten minutes longer. We also joined the classes above us for the weekly hymn practice. Hymn practice still took place once a week in the main hall although, oddly enough, it was usually taken by one of the lay teachers. This required yet more rote learning and the atmosphere was at its most tense if Mrs Slater was presiding. To add further to our discomfort, Mrs Slater kept an extra beady eye on our religious welfare. Not even the nuns enforced religious conformity with the same zeal. Mrs Slater kept a Mass register in which every Monday morning she recorded our attendance (or not) at Mass on Sunday. I learned a very harsh lesson early on; whether you had been to Mass or not, say you had been. Telling the truth and shaming the devil was not an option. Put bluntly, the Catholic Church taught us to lie from an early age as the law of unintended consequences struck. One Sunday early in that academic year we had gone as a family to Blackpool for what was probably the last day out of summer. Like a fool I admitted in front of the whole class that I had missed Mass in favour of a trip to the seaside. I can only describe the bollocking from Mrs Slater as the most blistering I ever received in my school career. To do this day I cannot fathom how an educated woman can truly believe that a six-year-old child can have any say in whether or not their parents schedule a family outing across a religious duty. Yet, according to her it was me that was morally delinquent. Never again would I put myself in that position.

An even worse fate befell a classmate, Janet Oddie. It was her misfortune not only to admit to missing Mass, but to do so after we had been formally admitted to the church, i.e. having made our first confessions and holy communions as a consequence of reaching the age of reason, which for the Catholic Church was just seven. Poor Janet as a fully-fledged Catholic had committed a mortal sin and was therefore at risk of eternal damnation if she died before seeking forgiveness for this grave transgression. She was promptly whisked out of class and taken to the parish priest to confess her terrible sin. Not having seen her since we were eleven years old, I do not know for certain if like me she abandoned the church, but I can make a pretty shrewd guess. Once we had made our first confessions and communions, Mrs Slater also kept a register of those facets of our religious observance. In this year we were also introduced to the perils of the May procession, which cost us a precious Sunday afternoon of freedom on the first Sunday in May. Although the whole shebang including compulsory benediction lasted only two hours, it seemed like an eternity. For the nuns it was their annual opportunity to fill the church for benediction and they didn't waste it. There was also a procession after the first Holy Communion.

The annual May procession and the crowning of the May Queen was a classic example of Christianity absorbing pagan ritual from those which it had either converted or slaughtered. The May Queen symbolises the banishment of winter and the coming of the abundance of summer. At St Edwards the May Queen was normally selected from those who celebrated their eighth birthdays during the academic year. The honour therefore fell to a girl in Junior Two, taught in my year by Mrs Pearson. Anne Duckworth was May Queen that year. She was a member of one of Darwen's foremost Catholic families. Her father, Tommy Duckworth, was Head of PE at St Mary's College of which more in Chapter Six, and an important figure in local sport, chiefly swimming and football. As regards the latter, he supervised the inter school penalty prize competition held at Ewood Park, the home of Blackburn Rovers, during the half-time interval of matches for many years from the early 1970s onwards. It was perhaps fortunate for Anne Duckworth that she had got the role of May Queen before she aroused the wrath of our formidable Headmistress, Sister Paul of the Cross. On this occasion she was publicly berated at assembly for failing to acknowledge the Mother Superior in the street. I had never heard of the Mother Superior nor did I know what one was, but was able to work that she must be the Head Penguin in the convent round the corner from our school. Like everyone else in the school, I was just relieved that it was someone else's turn to be publicly humiliated. If it could happen to a scion of the Duckworth family, then truly no one was safe.

Mrs Pearson's class provided no relief from the strictures of religion. Not only did we have the May procession, we were also expected to pray for the conversion of Russia. As eight-year olds we knew nothing of the godlessness of Communism, we just prayed for the salvation of their souls. At about this time I began to worry that my father would go to hell when he died, as we were taught that only in exceptional circumstances could non-Catholics enter the kingdom of heaven. By definition, non-Catholics commit mortal sin every weekend as they do not attend Mass. However, I did not dare ask Mrs Pearson if my father was already a condemned man. The fact that my father said he was going to hell anyway did not make me feel any better and I had already learned that to say too much about our religious instruction at home was not a wise move. Nevertheless, the apparent cruelty and inflexibility of the Catholic interpretation of God's will was beginning to make an impact on me. Ultimately of course there is only one way to find out and death is a one-way ticket. One thing I am confident of is that if God exists and is both just and retributive, then many former members of the clergy and their lay outriders who expected otherwise will instead find themselves suffering eternal damnation.

The priest's inspection was not the only annual trauma to be survived. There was also the dreaded St Joseph's penny. At the beginning of Lent, we were issued what were called "penny prick" cards, each containing twelve squares. With each penny you contributed or collected you could "prick" a square. As you may have guessed our teachers kept exhaustive records and some of them had the nasty habit of posting public charts. It was all about shaming you into giving more. My sister and I were caught between two stools, as in our home there was no question of asking our parents for money and no prospect of keeping a low profile at school. Somehow I managed to dodge the inevitable inquisition until my last year at primary school and as ever at St Edwards it came as a nasty and unexpected surprise. One afternoon during Lent I found myself summoned to Mrs Pearson's classroom. At the time my sister Andrea had the misfortune to be in her class and had already suffered an inquisition about the absence of St Joseph's Penny contributions. I was subjected to a similar inquisition about the pocket money we received (not very much as only my father was working and overtime was almost non-existent) and publicly berated in front of a class full of eight-year olds about my supposed selfishness and general moral delinquency. It was a humiliating experience and one I never forgave or forgot. Nor did St Edwards get another penny out of me.

After leaving the school I bumped into Mrs Pearson on the odd occasion and she was affable and inquired after my academic progress at Grammar School, displaying a nicer side to her nature, which she had otherwise kept hidden. Like my two previous class teachers she had never shown the remotest empathy with her charges and it came as a surprise to me both that she reinvented herself as a reception class teacher and that my two youngest siblings spoke positively about her. If I was to be generous, it may be that as a young teacher she had felt under pressure from the nuns, and the pressure only dissipated when she taught the youngest children in the school who would not be old enough for aggressive religious proselytising and being bullied for their pocket money so that targets for raising money from St Joseph's penny could be reached. I readily accept that the intended recipients of St Joseph's penny, in what were then still the African colonies, were far worse off than we were, but instead of bullying children from working-class families the Catholic Church could have usefully considered disbursing some of its great wealth. As Christ says in the bible, "It is harder for a rich man to enter the kingdom of heaven than it is for camel to pass through the eye of a needle." During Lent the nuns did not hesitate to remind us of this, with no sense of irony.

I did, however, manage to avoid becoming an altar boy. I can't remember in which year altar boys were selected but I can remember being terrified of being picked. As it happened I needn't have worried. With the benefit of hindsight having a non-Catholic parent almost certainly ruled me out of contention. Added to that it was rare for me to attend the children's Mass, which took place every Sunday at 9am. We either attended the 10.15 Mass as the first bus of the day on a Sunday did not arrive until 10am or, alternatively, we attended Mass at another church. The nuns did not approve of you attending Masses other than at 9am, and were very unhappy if you attended the evening Mass as that, they said, was for those unfortunate enough to have to work on a Sunday. My own take on the matter is that attendance at other Masses or indeed other churches prevented them from closely monitoring your religious observance. Nevertheless, they restricted themselves to an occasional moan about non-attendance at the specially provided Mass unlike the experience of a good friend of mine from Grammar School, Bryan Snape, and his schoolmates. Bryan told me that at his primary school the Headmaster, who was a layman, took the view that any child not at the children's Mass in that particular parish had missed Mass, the punishment for which was the cane. It was the only time I ever felt that I had got off lightly as far as the nuns were concerned.

Probably the class in which I felt safest was Junior Three, taught by Mrs North. Although she was no less formidable than her three predecessors, I felt relatively comfortable in her class and did not regard each school morning with dread. Discipline was strict but consistent and if you got on with your work you were left alone. Life may have been easier for me, but it was no less hard for those who struggled academically. Although there was no dunce's cap, the less able were still made to feel that their failings were their own fault. I can remember one girl being told that she "wasn't a patch on her sister". It was hard enough being judged against your peers. In Mrs North's class there was a system for awarding stars for good work and I think there was a small prize for the child with the most stars in each half-term. It was fine for kids like me, but it can't have been much fun for those who could easily go through a half-term without a single star on the chart.

I spent two years in what was now the top class, Junior Four, being too young by a little over three months to take the 11 plus in 1963. As I lived in Blackburn, I was destined to sit that authority's 11 plus papers, which came in two parts requiring an initial non-verbal reasoning paper to be passed before you could sit part two. Those children who lived in Darwen sat the Lancashire county examination. The county permitted the examination to be taken a year early, but Blackburn did not and would not make an exception for me despite the pleadings of the Headmistress. I have to say I was disappointed at the time, not least because it would have allowed me to escape from St. Edward's a year early. The only way round it would have been for my parents to pay school fees at St Mary's College for the first year until I passed the 11 plus. That was never remotely an option. However, had we lived just a quarter of a mile further east over the boundary with Darwen, then I could have sat the 11 plus a year early and taken a free place which would also have opened up the possibility of me taking GCE O levels at fourteen and A levels at sixteen as St. Mary's College at the time selected an express stream after the second year. Gordon Brown may have gone to University at sixteen, but I always say that for me deferring Higher Education until I was twenty-one was the best thing that could have happened to me. I don't believe I was mature enough to have coped socially, emotionally and academically at eighteen never mind sixteen years of age. In any event it didn't happen and I remained at the mercy – more usually the lack of it – of the Sisters of the Passion.

The top class was taught by an older nun, Sister Rosalie, who early in my second year was replaced by another nun, Sister Winifred, who was much younger and who I believed abandoned the veil not long after I had moved on. Religion continued to play a huge part in our lives. The next main event was being confirmed in the church in our final year in the school. Just as with the priest's inspection, academic work was abandoned to bring us up to speed with what was required for Confirmation, which had to be learned by heart, or else. Sister Rosalie administered the cane rather than the strap and she administered it almost on a daily basis. It was the punishment for every misdemeanour. She also specialised in caning the entire class at intervals as it guaranteed that she got the culprit if no one would own up to talking or eating or whatever the transgression may be. We became inured to it. The cane stung, but Sister Rosalie did not have the strongest of arms. Sister Winifred preferred to use the strap. She was more discerning in its use than her predecessor but, like the Headmistress, you never knew when she might single you out for punishment. I preferred the more predictable regime of Sister Rosalie despite its harshness.

Corporal punishment was not just used for poor work and other transgressions within the classroom. It was also given for going out of school without permission and sometimes for lateness. Each morning those late for school had to stand at one side of the assembly hall so as to be distinct from those who had been in sufficient time to line up outside. Most mornings nothing came of it, but periodically there was a purge and Mrs Eccles would give the strap to all latecomers. A similar policy to tardiness in lining up in the playground when the bell was rung was dealt with in the same way. Using the school field on wet days was also punishable by the strap. Indeed it is difficult to remember a disciplinary infraction that was not. Even when the strap was not deployed they had other ways of making you suffer. Periodically, the Headmistress would reduce the length of morning and afternoon breaks as a punishment for it taking too long for the lines of pupils to get from the school yard to the assembly hall. The fact that it was exceptionally difficult for even the most efficient teacher to get 240 pupils from A to B in an orderly manner in less than three minutes cut no ice. As for truancy, very few dared. There was a story that circulated that a particular boy a year older than me had been beaten on the bare backside in the Head's office for truancy. No one knew whether it was true or not and no one dared take the risk of finding out. Former public schoolboys in their memoirs have confirmed that abuses of this nature took place in the private sector and, given the nuns penchant for humiliation, I cannot rule out this story being true. It has to be remembered that there was no point in complaining and Catholic parents no more dared to challenge the authority of the church than their unfortunate children.

Academically, the school was an 11 plus factory. It totally dominated my last two years. Sister Paul prided herself on getting pupils into the two Grammar Schools, St Mary's College, Blackburn, for boys, and the Notre Dame Grammar School for girls, also in Blackburn. Other than important religious landmarks such as the parish priest's inspection or the preparation for Confirmation, the curriculum was narrowed totally to what was required to pass this life changing examination that determined our destiny. After Religious Instruction had finished at 09.45, it was Arithmetic for the rest of the morning. We were expected to know our tables and were whacked if we did not. The afternoons were spent doing a mixture of English and non-verbal reasoning exercises. We had been introduced to homework after moving up from the infants, but there was rather more of it in the top class. We had books called Progress papers and a second volume called Further Progress papers. The format was the same. Each chapter of Arithmetic contained fifty mechanical problems and fifty mental arithmetic questions. The English and non-verbal reasoning books, the latter then simply called Intelligence, also had fifty questions per section. Thus, we laboured over comprehension, synonyms, antonyms, punctuation exercises in English and trying to work out what number, shape or symbol followed in sequence from those that had gone before. Homework was frequently fifty questions of one kind or another. At weekend we were given an essay to write, in those days referred to as English composition. It had to be a minimum two sides in length and we were supposed to write in rough first. I resented the time spent on doing things twice but, in order to avoid the cane, it was necessary to get it right on the first draft, a skill that would stand me in good stead many years later when faced with A level and Degree examinations. This was the daily diet for most of the last two years. In arithmetic our understanding of mathematical concepts was subordinate to that looming date in March. Being able to carry out the necessary drills was much more important than understanding them. We did not read any novels, did not learn any poetry and the class library was permanently closed. Looking back, it seems incredible that we were taught English without any regard for the literature that might improve our skills and knowledge. In my first year in the top class History and Geography were only taught after the 11 plus had been sat in March. Everything was geared to our date with destiny. There were even additional classes on Saturday mornings under Sister Rosalie and I was not excused them despite the fact that I was not sitting the 11 plus until the following year, something I bitterly resented at the time as weekends were short enough. We were given past papers to do under exam conditions at regular intervals. The Headmistress even succeeded in disguising the county 11 plus as a practice run in 1964 in a bid to squeeze out any disadvantage that might accrue from exam nerves. The Blackburn papers were taken a week or two earlier and given that only three of us sat them there was no possibility of us not knowing that it was the real thing. Only after the examination was over was there a slow resumption of something approaching a balanced curriculum. Geography, History, (dreadfully taught) and something called Nature Study reappeared on the curriculum along with Art and Craft. There was no Science other than Nature Study and only a very brief foray into modern languages. In our final few weeks Miss Eccles of all people took us for some basic oral French. Apparently, she had been having lessons herself for whatever reason. Oddly enough, in those final few weeks she seemed almost human.

Also reappearing on the curriculum were Games and PE. I had been more fortunate than some in that in my final year I was a member of the school football team. Only the team and immediate reserves were permitted to do PE in top class. I would guess that this dispensation was only available because the school team was coached by Mick McGrath, Blackburn Rovers footballer, Republic of Ireland international and important member of the Catholic community. His presence was an honour for the school as well as a source of delight and awe to a dozen small boys. Sadly, we were not able to emulate the previous year's team, captained by John Waddington who actually went on to play professionally for Blackburn Rovers in the 1970s, and lift the Darwen primary schools knock-out trophy. The other good thing about our sessions being taken by Mr McGrath was they were not subject to cancellation by capricious women teachers, who hated taking sport and would find any trivial excuse such as a drop of rain or someone talking out of turn to cancel an eagerly awaited outdoor games session. Unbelievably, in the final half-term, our teacher regularly allowed the boys to go out on the field for a full afternoon – well after Religious Instruction – to play cricket. We could not believe our luck. Some years later, as a student teacher carrying out teaching practice in a junior school, I remembered how we had been treated and ensured that PE always took place as per timetable. If a teacher cannot find a more effective sanction than cancelling much needed exercise for small children, they are in the wrong profession.

Although I have criticised St Edwards for the narrowness of its curriculum in the last two years, there was no question of any pupil being allowed to leave that school without a thorough grounding in what are still referred to as the "three R's", even though as I have said the fourth R from time to time took precedence. We learned our tables by rote chanting them out. Reading was taught using the phonic method, proven in its effectiveness, and its abandonment by trendy educationalists has done serious damage to generations of children. The Education Secretary at the time of writing, Michael Gove, vocalised his commitment to restoring phonics to its rightful place at the forefront of the teaching of reading. We were expected to learn to spell, punctuate and write grammatically. Fractions and decimals were then part of the primary school Maths curriculum. The expectation that we should write came early. In the second infants class we were issued with what were called news books and every Monday we were expected to write about our weekend or holiday if it was the start of a new term. This was the foundation for essay writing skills, which we knew as English composition. Only in the last two years did reading give way to the all-consuming beast known as the 11 plus.

The whole school ethos was competitive. I have in my possession primary school reports that go all the way back to July 1959 when I was just six years of age. The move out of the reception class brought with it twice yearly examinations and class positions based on performance in those examinations. Every year, in December and July, the whole of the school apart from the reception class was marched to the main hall for the formal reading of class positions from one down to as low as forty-two in each class. The bible stricture that the first shall be last and the last shall be first most definitely did not apply on these set piece occasions. The closer to the front you were the more you were likely to be one of the chosen few who made it to Grammar School. For those at the back it was the biannual humiliation, nature's way of letting you know that your future was a lifetime of toil. It was part of the suffering to be endured. I doubt if many of the children who stood at the back behind their more academic peers ever believed that they would get their reward in heaven.

Of course, we just accepted it because that was the way it was, and if we're honest about it being ranked against our peers across a vast spectrum of skills, attributes and talents is what happens throughout our lives. Being at the foot of the pecking order in one field does not prevent us being at the head of it in another. Interference with the natural order can actually reduce all round happiness. One obvious example is the insistence of some politically correct teachers in diluting competition on the sports field by fielding weakened teams in cup competitions so that everyone gets to play, regardless of ability. The outcome is inevitable. Instead of some winning a prize no one does because the team has been weakened. As for the poor kids who aren't very good at football, which is most of us, they are actually less happy as a consequence of playing because they are lumbered by their peers with part of the blame for the defeat. They would have been much happier cheering from the side-lines and sharing vicariously the pleasure of victory from that vantage point. Primary school academic life was harsh, but I believe we were better prepared for real life as a result.

I only know that my last day in primary school was Friday 10 July, 1964, because I took the trouble to check it on the calendar for that year. My only real recollection of the day was an exhilarating feeling of freedom, far greater than that which was normally experienced at the start of the summer holiday. There was no looking back and there would be no going back, apart from the one occasion some seven years later when I went to pick up my youngest sister, then just five years old. Mercifully, I did not bump into the Headmistress or indeed anyone else. As for the future, as an eleven-year-old boy, I thought only of cricket and the family holiday. Grammar School was a full eight weeks away, a lifetime for a small boy. However, it did mark the end for some friendships. There are two members of the school football team that I have never seen or heard of since in almost fifty years and I can remember all eleven names. We just moved on, because that was how it was.

Chapter Four

Listen to the Band

In our living room (working-class people did not call it the lounge), when I was a child, something called the "wireless" stood between the television and a utility sideboard. My father would refer to portable transistor radios as the wireless until his dying day. Not as tall as the television, it was every bit as important, particularly as the hours of television broadcasting were restricted and almost nothing was broadcast during conventional working hours. For my father's generation the wireless was as novel to them as children as the television would be to ours. If there was nothing on the television, my father would always put on the radio. On a Sunday morning, if he was at home, he always listened to The Archers and then to a request programme called two – sometimes more than two – way family favourites, aimed at the families of men serving abroad in the days when Great Britain still had a presence East of Suez as well as in Germany. It was many years before I learned that BFPO stood for British Forces Post Office. It was a massively important programme to those who had relatives serving in the armed forces far from home, and of course to the servicemen themselves, and until 1963, when the last national serviceman was discharged, this included conscripts.

The important thing was to get a mention. Actually getting the record of your choice played was another matter as your request would be bundled together with half a dozen others. If you did get the tune of your choice played there was every chance that it would be played by a BBC orchestra, rather than the version by the recording artist his or herself. This was because of restrictive practices by the Musicians Union, which negotiated restrictions with the BBC on what was known as "needle time". It seems hard to believe that a programme like Saturday Club, which began in 1958 and ran until 1969 and was aimed specifically at teenagers, was not allowed to play more than eight gramophone records in two hours. Indeed, only five hours per day of gramophone records were permitted at all on BBC radio stations. For young people who wanted to hear the artists they related to, this was especially frustrating. Not until 1967, when BBC radio stations were rebranded, was the agreement re-negotiated and not until 1980 did the BBC, under government pressure to cut costs, take on the Musicians Union and disband at least some of the orchestras that people did not listen to anymore. The last surviving orchestra – the BBC Radio Orchestra – was finally wound up in 1991. Three years earlier, in a long overdue ruling, the Monopolies and Mergers Commission determined that needle time was an unlawful restraint of trade.

On a Saturday morning, we always listened to Children's Favourites, introduced by Derek McCulloch known as Uncle Mac, which had first been broadcast in 1954. In 1967 the programme was renamed Junior Choice and broadcast simultaneously on Radio One and Radio Two, as the old Light Programme frequency on the Long Wave was rebranded. Its first host was another well-known children's entertainer, Leslie Crowther, and he was replaced the following year by Ed "Stewpot" Stewart, who hosted the programme for twelve years. Two years later Junior Choice disappeared from the listings, presumably no longer relevant. However, it returned at Christmas 2007 with Stewart back in the chair and has since enjoyed a new lease of life as an annual nostalgic treat. A look at the playlists was a reminder of the music played when I was a child. Readers of my generation and younger will remember Nellie the Elephant (not the punk version by the Toy Dolls), The Runaway Train, My Brother, Three Wheels on My Wagon, and Hello Muddah, Hello Faddah from the inimitable Allan Sherman. Perhaps the most played children's song of all was "I thought I Saw a Pussy

Cat", pronounced "I tawt I taw a puddy tat", recorded in the 1940s by Mel Blanc, the man of 1,000 voices, which included, amongst others, cartoon favourites from my childhood, Bugs Bunny and Barney Rubble. In less than three minutes the song documents the frustrations of Sylvester the cat as he tries unsuccessfully to sneak up on Tweety Pie the bird, and eat him for dinner. As ever in moral tales from those far off days, good always triumphed over evil. Rolf Harris was another established favourite in the children's slot. However, I think it is safe to assume that following his convictions for sexual offences in 2014, we have heard the last of Jake the Peg and the gruesome Two Little Boys. The last record of the programme was always a classical piece, played by a BBC orchestra in the compulsory high culture slot. As with two way family favourites, there were only a handful of current chart singles played and you got what you were given as far as requests were concerned. It never occurred to me to waste my time sending a request on a postcard as instructed.

I would guess that my early musical exposure was very similar to that of millions of other baby boomers. My father's real love was swing, but he was always keen on novelty songs. Classic examples from my childhood are My Boomerang Won't Come Back (Charlie Drake); Itsy Bitsy Teeny Weeny Yellow Polkadot Bikini (Brian Hyland); What a Mouth (Tommy Steel); Tie Me Kangaroo Down Sport (Rolf Harris); Speedy Gonzales (Pat Boone); the Yingtong Song (the Goons), and Goodness Gracious Me (Peter Sellers and Sophia Loren). These are just some of the ones I can remember. I have very little memory of rock and roll. My introduction to the record charts came via Pick of the Pops and Radio Luxembourg. Pick of the Pops was broadcast between 4pm and 5pm on a Sunday afternoon on the Light Programme, since 1967 known as Radio Two. The basic format of playing the new entries to the top twenty and then the top ten dated back to 1957, but Pick of the Pops did not become a programme in its own right until January 1962 when it was introduced by Alan Freeman. Apart from occasional stints by David Jacobs and Don Moss, Freeman continued to present the show until its initial demise in 1972. If my memory serves me well, the replacement programme was Solid Gold Sixty, which also featured the top twenty in full in the last part of the programme. On 1 October 1967, the day after Radio One opened for transmission, the newly transferred Pick of the Pops was extended to two hours starting at 5pm and for the first time played the top twenty in full, and there it remained until the BBC tired of it. The show has since been revived on both Capitol Gold and BBC Radio Two. Since 1997, it has been broadcast continuously on Radio Two as a purely retro chart programme, initially with Alan Freeman back in his old chair until he retired in 2000.

If my father was at home, Pick of the Pops would go on as soon as the Sunday afternoon film on ITV had finished. This was my first exposure to the top ten. Sometimes I would listen to it in the neighbouring farmhouse. My earliest memory of the show is that the Top Ten contained records by Elvis Presley, Cliff Richard, and The Shadows, then the three biggest selling recording artists in the UK. In this era, Presley was indisputably the top man, who had dominated the charts in the USA and the UK since his breakthrough in 1956. Good Luck Charm, which topped the British charts for five weeks in May and June of 1962, was Presley's eleventh British number one, and one of four number ones scored by him in the UK in 1962 alone. Cliff Richard, initially marketed as the British Elvis, was his closest rival. In 1962 he scored one number one, (taking his total by the end of the year to four) and three number two's, two of which were blocked from the top spot by Presley. The third of these, The Next Time, went to number one at the beginning of 1963, as you might expect replacing a Presley single. The record companies had no fear of head-to-head competition. The Shadows were Cliff Richard's backing group and were usually credited on his records, but also recorded instrumentals in their own right. In 1962, Wonderful Land, their third number one single, topped the singles chart for eight weeks, the longest run of the year. All told, these three artists combined headed the British charts for twenty-nine weeks, fifteen of them headed by Presley. The other significant artist in 1962 was Australian born singer, Frank Ifield, whose two number one singles totalled twelve weeks at the top. According to the BBC chart, which at the time was an average of four other published charts, only six other acts made the top spot, and four of these, Danny Williams, Bee Bumble and the Stingers, Mike Sarne and Joe Brown enjoyed just one week each with their only number one singles, such was the dominance of that year's big four.

Was this exciting? You have to be joking! The excitement of rock and roll (too early for me) was long gone, and entertainment bosses in both the USA and the UK made sure that the business swallowed rock and roll whole and regurgitated it as acceptable family entertainment. Presley's last true rock and roll single for many years was his 1961 double "A" sided number one, His Latest Flame/Little Sister. On coming out of the army in 1960, Presley was steered firmly to the mainstream and his first single after demobilisation, "It's Now or Never", a big power ballad, remains to this day his biggest selling single around the world. Presley had made the crossover. His songs could now be played on easy listening stations in the USA. Cliff Richard's career as a rock and roller ended after barely a year, before he made the crossover with the ballad, Travelling Light. Put bluntly, the artists who initially had appealed only to teenagers, now also appealed to the mums and dads. This explains why my parents, or more accurately my father, listened to Pick of the Pops, then the only BBC programme consisting entirely of gramophone records. Put simply, it played their music. Presley and Richard had joined the older generation of Frank Sinatra, Dean Martin and Nat "King" Cole from the swing era that my father loved, in the middle of the road. Add Frank Ifield and the obligatory novelty records to the mix and you have the state of UK music in 1962. With few exceptions, it was dire; dull, formulaic and utterly lacking in creativity or originality.

Just like in every other sphere of life, the establishment ruled. So why did I listen to Pick of the Pops? Partly because my father listened to it, partly to hear novelty singles that appealed to a child, such as Mike Sarne and Wendy Richard's, Come Outside, which spent eleven weeks in the top ten in the summer of 1962, but also because I was fascinated with charts. Some of my peers collected stamps, earlier generations had collected cigarette cards, but my interest was in the weekly change of positions in the record charts in the same way as I was fascinated by the league tables in football. Every man has his anorak tendency, charts and tables were mine. The weekly visit to my maternal grandmother's home allowed me to peruse the top 30 chart in the New Musical Express, at least until she cancelled it a year or so after the death of Uncle George.

As far as the singles charts were concerned, the early part of 1963 was almost a rerun of 1962. According to the NME, for the first three weeks of the year Elvis, Cliff, and the Shadows recording separately held the top three positions in one order or another. Dance On gave The Shadows their fourth number one before being replaced by two former Shadows, Jet Harris and Tony Meehan in the top spot. At the beginning of February 1963, for the only time in chart history, the top three records were all instrumentals. According to the industry's own chart, the next three number one singles were by Frank Ifield, Cliff Richard, and the Shadows again with an instrumental made without Cliff Richard. However, change was just around the corner. In January 1963 I heard the kind of sound the likes of which I had never heard before. It was two minutes of magic by a new act called The Beatles from Liverpool. The song was titled Please Please Me, and it entered the industry chart on 24th January 1963, just one day before The Beatles played at Darwen Co-op Hall. Sadly, I was not there but ten-year olds just did not attend pop concerts in those days. No doubt those who were lucky enough to be there treasure the memory. There was now music that appealed to me. The Beatles were the complete breath of fresh air that the complacent music business sorely needed. Music snobs tend to gloss over the first couple of years of Beatle dominance as one where they were either doing American covers in much the same way as an earlier generation of British rock and rollers, or as one of twee songs, with simple innocent lyrics about the agonies of teenage love. Whether the lyrics of Please Please Me are quite so innocent is a matter of interpretation. Whichever way you look at it, nothing would ever quite be the same. Please Please Me was actually their second single. Their first single, Love Me Do, had peaked at number 17 on the Industry chart, but outside of Liverpool it did not register as a significant cultural event. How wrong can you be? Re-released in 1982, Love Me Do would eventually outsell Please Please Me.

There is an urban myth that Please Please Me was not a number one single. Well, I can tell you it topped the NME chart at the end of February 1963, and more importantly that it topped the BBC chart, which was an amalgam of the four main published charts that related to sales. Unfortunately, thanks to the Guinness Book of Records, the one chart not topped by The Beatles second single the industry's own chart published in the Record Mirror, has been given the accolade as being the official chart, from what I can gather on the basis that it was the only chart in that era publishing a top 50. The reality is that none of the charts were accurate compared with the exact computation now available with IT, but the industry chart was probably the least accurate of all, taking its returns from a mere thirty shops. The NME used one hundred shops. Even in 1969 when the BBC moved over to a computerised chart ever since then recognised as the official chart, only 250 shops were initially sampled. Given that Please Please Me topped the other three charts and the BBC amalgam chart, it is ridiculous to pretend that it was not a number one single. It is unfortunate that the BBC charts pre 1969 have never been published, although they too had anomalies. As a points system was used with the other charts to determine the BBC position it was a regular occurrence that positions were shared. Inevitably, it finally affected the number one spot and did so in a way that brought the chart into disrepute with three records tied for the number one spot when the chart was read out on Pick of the Pops on Sunday 1 September, 1968. Joint positions were also common in the NME. A tie for the top spot was not uncommon in a system that awarded the position not on the basis of actual numerical sales, but on the number of shops reporting a single to be the top seller that week.

So, in the depths of the bitter winter of 1963, the worst in living memory, teenagers and those a bit younger got their own music. An industry that had decreed that "groups are out" suddenly found that the very opposite was true. 1963 was the year the Beatles conquered Britain and the following year they would conquer America, with a British invasion following swiftly behind. It is no exaggeration to say that there has not been a more exciting time in popular music in the half-century that has passed since. The dominance of Elvis Presley, Cliff Richard and The Shadows and the new crooner on the block, Frank Ifield, ended abruptly. In 1963 Elvis Presley topped the singles chart for precisely one week compared to fifteen in 1962. Cliff Richard did better with six weeks, the same as the previous year, but three of those weeks came right at the beginning of the year with a single released in 1962. The Shadows clocked up two weeks in the top slot in their own right, compared to eight the previous year and Frank Ifield managed five, down from twelve in 1962. These are figures from the Industry chart. The NME chart shows a slightly different distribution, but what really matters is the change that was heralded. Elvis Presley and Cliff Richard had no number one singles in 1964. Neither The Shadows nor Frank Ifield ever made the top spot again. No longer could Presley or Richard's record companies release any old rubbish and expect a number two single at minimum. In 1963, the Beatles topped the NME charts for a grand total of eighteen weeks. Fellow Merseyside acts, now the centre of the musical universe, Gerry and the Pacemakers, The Searchers and Billy J. Kramer and the Dakotas added a further eighteen weeks at the top between them. The trend continued into 1964. The Beatles clocked up fourteen weeks at the top of the NME chart and Merseyside acts The Searchers, Billy J. Kramer and the Dakotas and Cilla Black clocked up a further twelve weeks between them. Statistically, it may not have been quite as impressive as the previous year, but it was still exceptionally noteworthy in what had become an ultra-competitive environment amongst the beat groups of the era. They were not known as bands in 1964. Even my home town of Blackburn had its own chart topping act – The Four Pennies – who made it to number one in 1964 with Juliet. The Four Pennies were Blackburn's one contribution to the swinging sixties, which our parents and schoolmasters were determined would pass us by. On 2 January, 1965, they played live in the centre circle at Ewood Park as the pre-match entertainment. An above average attendance of 18,292 then watched Rovers win 5-0 against Aston Villa, who clearly didn't fancy the frozen pitch. John Byrom scored a hat trick, which uniquely in his Rovers career was not against West Ham.

Television programmes that showcased the music popular with young people were not new but the Beatles breakthrough and the subsequent "beat boom" gave them new impetus. As far back as 1957 the BBC had screened the "6.05 special", named after the time at which it was shown. However, although the programme was a genuine pioneer in that it featured rock and roll acts, it was also a magazine programme. Its frustrated producer, Jack Good, defected to ITV and produced "Oh Boy" in 1958, the first programme dedicated exclusively to the music sung by artists bought by young people. It survived only until the following year by which time rock and roll had gone mainstream. In 1959 the BBC first screened Juke Box Jury, a programme in which a panel was asked to vote a new release a "hit" or a "miss", based on a snippet of the song that lasted less than a minute. Juke Box Jury continued until 1967 and was revived in 1979 and 1989-90. Despite its staid format, the programme was hugely important as one of the few outlets available to artists to get their records played.

Thank Your Lucky Stars first aired on ITV in 1961 and ran until 1966. The Beatles appeared on eight occasions. TYLS was a prime target for the Musician's Union as all artists mimed until 1965 when they were forced to perform live, backing music provided courtesy of members of the Musician's Union. Saturday Club – which was the second most important radio programme after Pick of the Pops – got round the problems with the Musician's Union by getting acts to come and pre-record live slots for the show. Thanks to the law of unintended consequences there are now two superb live albums entitled "The Beatles Live at the BBC", released in 1994 and 2013 respectively, which remind you of just what a good live act they were before they quit touring and became a studio band in 1966. If anything, because Saturday Club had the freedom to interview acts and showcase more than one song by them, it had more to offer its young listeners than Pick of the Pops, which was essentially chart show with a few new releases selected by middle-aged BBC executives unduly influenced by powerful record companies. Ready Steady Go, often known simply as RSG, a new programme that first aired on ITV in August 1963 was much more akin to Saturday Club than it was to Pick of the Pops. Indeed, it aimed to set trends rather than reflect them. The TV equivalent of Pick of the Pops arrived on BBC with Top of the Pops on 1 January, 1964. It would become the most influential music programme on television by a country mile, particularly after 1967 when RSG was dropped by ITV and pirate radio stations were silenced.

Until pirate radio arrived in 1964, the only alternative to the minimal output of the BBC was Radio Luxembourg, which broadcast on 208 metres on the medium waveband. Radio Luxembourg was the forerunner of both the pirate stations and modern commercial radio in that it obtained revenue from advertising, still to this day forbidden on the BBC. More importantly, it was beyond the reach of the Musician's Union. Programmes were actually broadcast from Luxembourg, although some were pre-recorded in London. From 1960 onwards, it began to target the teenage market and by 1963, apart from advertising, its output was entirely gramophone records. Radio Luxembourg broadcast only in the evening and night – but not through the night – and the signal was very variable, being prone to fading in and out. In our home, my father put on Radio Luxembourg on a Sunday evening only during the religious slots on TV before Sunday Night at the London Palladium was screened. This was the bonus opportunity to listen to pop music. At Christmas 1963 I received a small transistor radio as a present. Its arrival coincided with the period before my brother moved into my room and allowed me the opportunity to do the same as countless other kids and listen surreptitiously to Radio Luxembourg underneath the blankets.

However, in 1964 Radio Luxembourg became very last year as pirate radio, the term used to describe unlicensed and unregulated radio stations, which also broadcast during the daylight hours, found its way into our lives. Pirate radio actually broadcast from ships moored offshore, just outside the three-mile limit of territorial water. Thus, although unlicensed and unregulated, they were not illegal and the signal was far better than Radio Luxembourg. Pirate radio cocked a snook at the BBC, the Musicians Union, and the establishment in general. In this last respect, they embodied the spirit of the age. The offshore stations chose unused radio frequencies, although national governments claimed that unregulated use of broadcasting frequencies interfered with legitimate transmissions and put shipping at risk. However, to the best of my knowledge, no maritime disaster ever occurred as a result of pirate radio on the airwaves. In my view, the only legitimate criticism of pirate radio is that the owners paid no royalties to the writers and artists, but I would have to argue that the much greater exposure of their products contributed to the spectacular rise in the sale of singles experienced in the mid-1960s, thereby creating additional income that otherwise would not have been earned. Our own pirate station was Radio Caroline North, anchored off the coast of the Isle of Man. By 1967, there were ten pirate radio vessels dotted around the British Isles.

Musically, the pirate stations were not particularly adventurous broadcasting a largely top 40 format and proving just as susceptible as the BBC to the provision of financial and sexual favours to promote records. Nevertheless, they were a breath of fresh air. You no longer had to wait until Sunday afternoon to hear your favourite chart single for perhaps the only time that week. Instead, you could expect to hear it several times a day during school holidays. It brought home just how little the BBC provided for young people, and that what it did provide was strictly on its own patrician terms. It was normal when we played football or cricket for a transistor radio to be playing just behind the touchline or behind the wicket. As the wicket was often a crate, dustbin or even a tree, the radio was perfectly safe behind it. Older teenagers gathered outside shops or at meeting points in the town almost invariably had a radio by their side. The message was clear; young people did not need the BBC and would not be patronised.

Pirate radio, as my generation knew it, lasted until 1967 although Radio Caroline continued to broadcast until March 1968 when its ships were seized by a salvage company working for a Dutch firm that was owed a considerable sum of money by the station's proprietors. The Marine Broadcasting Offences Act piloted through the House of Commons by one Tony Benn, then a quintessentially establishment figure rather than the better remembered and by some revered radical figure of the 1970s and 1980s, made it unlawful for any British citizen to supply goods, services and advertising to unlicensed and unregulated radio stations. At a stroke, it cut off their revenue and outlawed British disc jockeys such as Johnnie Walker who continued to work for Radio Caroline. All the other stations accepted the inevitable and shut down some as late as midnight just before the new law came into force on 15 August, 1967. For a while we continued to listen to Radio Caroline, supplied from Holland which did not sign up to the European agreement on unregulated broadcasting until 1974.

However, on 30 September, 1967, the BBC introduced Radio One to the airwaves in a massive restructure of its output that finally acknowledged that young people had legitimate expectations of the national broadcaster. In the interim period, the BBC had been busily recruiting a string of disc jockeys made redundant by Act of Parliament. At 7am on 30 September, listeners on what had until the day before been the frequency for the Third Programme heard the dulcet tones of Tony Blackburn as he introduced the first ever record played on Radio One, Flowers in the Rain by The Move. Any Third Programme listeners not aware of the change would have been shocked to discover that the highbrow classical music station they knew and loved had been rebranded as Radio Three and moved to another frequency. The Light Programme was rebranded as Radio Two and remained on its long wave frequency. What little pop output it had previously had moved to Radio One leaving Radio Two most decidedly as the mums and dads' channel. The former Home Service was rebranded as a Radio Four, retaining its role, as it does today as a serious news and current affairs channel that wrestles with intellectual controversies.

Radio One lacked the spontaneity of pirate radio and never matched it for freshness and verve. However, it made national celebrities out of the disc jockeys who had no choice but to defect to the establishment, but it also to some extent clipped their wings. On board ship no one told them what records to play (unless they'd been paid) or what order in which to play them, just so long as the jingles and the advertising arrived on cue. At Radio One, DJs in peak listening slots had to follow the instructions of a producer, work loosely from a script and stick to the BBC playlist. In fairness, in off peak slots Radio One did make shows introduced by DJs such as John Peel that skied off-piste and introduced listeners to acts with something original and different to offer potential record buyers. In this way, the BBC did its bit for album orientated rock and later for punk. Nevertheless, controversy was frowned upon and DJs were expected to be almost as circumspect as a BBC newsreader. Inevitably there were clashes. The most high profile sacking was of Kenny Everett in 1970 for jokingly suggesting that the Transport Minister's wife had bribed the instructor when she finally passed her test at the umpteenth attempt. Everett was already in BBC bosses sights for his scathing comments about the restrictive practices of the Musician's Union in the Melody Maker magazine, made in defiance of a ban on him giving interviews. In 1976, Johnnie Walker – then presenter of the lunchtime slot which on a Tuesday featured the all-important new singles chart – found himself eased out the station for seeing fit to choose some of his own favourite music to play and for being highly critical of the Bay City Rollers, then massively popular with pre- and early teenage girls, describing them as "musical garbage".

Looking back, it seems that the BBC liked its disc jockeys to be bland, lightweight, family friendly entertainers who fitted a corporate image, particularly when seen on TV. The revelations about the late Jimmy Savile in particular paint a rather different picture of what was really happening behind the smiles and bonhomie that we saw on our screens. There is a superb song from the late Harry Chapin released in 1974, about the up and down career of an American DJ, now working for a fictional top 40 radio station called W.O.L.D. (the title of the song), which contains the classic world weary line "feeling all of forty-five, going on fifteen". Just like anyone else, DJs had bills to pay and going down market was an unavoidable part of that if it was the only radio work available. However, some DJs, in particular Noel Edmonds and Tony Blackburn, appeared to adapt effortlessly or maybe they were simply a perfect fit for establishment radio and found their niche. This kind of DJ, lost in a time warp circa 1970, was mercilessly parodied by Harry Enfield and Paul Whitehouse who in 1990 introduced the characters of Smashie and Nicey to our screens. The show is credited with so much influence that it is reputed that the cull of veteran disc jockeys by the BBC in 1995 and the rebranding of Radio One as the youth station it had once been, can be traced back directly to the brilliant satire of Enfield and Whitehouse.

The rebranding of Radio One also allowed Radio Two to break away from its own time warp. In 1986, a decision to reposition Radio Two, which had evolved as contemporary middle of the road radio, as a station appealing to the over 50s effectively going back to the days of the old Light Programme, cost it listeners to album orientated rock commercial stations, which had been licensed as early as 1973. Radio Two also suffered heavily from losing sport to Radio Five in 1990. James Moir, who took over as Head Of Radio Two in 1996, targeted a mature rather than specifically older audience, and specialist programmes by recognised genre experts became a significant part of programming. Thus, for example, if you were fascinated by doo-wop then you could listen to a series of programmes presented in the evening by Suzi Quatro. You could now make the journey to Radio Two and feel that you had found your natural radio home as you approached middle age. Familiar disc jockeys like the late Alan Freeman, Tony Blackburn, Brian Matthew, Johnnie Walker, and the recently deceased Terry Wogan all made the journey with us at various points. The fact that Chris Evans, who was not even born when offshore pirate radio began, is now also on Radio Two is not only a reminder of my age, but also that another generation is now a consumer of Radio Two's output. Radio Two is now far and away Britain's most listened to radio station and listening figures for programmes such as Chris Evans' breakfast show regularly compare favourably with all but the most popular TV programmes.

The moguls who ran record companies in 1963 could never have conceived of a future in which there would be retro programmes, indeed wholly retro radio stations that cater for people who wish to enjoy the music of their youth. To them pop music was disposable ephemera. A record had a shelf life the length of its chart run (if it charted at all) and then it was deleted from the catalogue and the record shops returned any unsold copies, presumably to be melted down. Nothing was more frustrating than coming into some money on your birthday and going down to the record shop to buy a disc you had wanted for weeks, only to be told that it had been deleted. There was no point asking if a copy could be ordered. It was gone forever, or so it seemed at the time. It symbolised the contempt in which the record industry held not just its young buyers but those who sang the numbers usually written by professional songwriters. A solution to my problem would come with the opening of shops that sold second hand seven inch 45 rpm records, which had replaced the rather more breakable twelve inch 78rpm records from about 1958 onwards. I can't remember the exact year Blackburn Record Exchange opened, though I think it was 1968. I discovered the shop on St James St quite by accident, taking a fairly roundabout route from school into town one afternoon and over the next five or six years built a collection of second hand mono singles that came almost exclusively from that one shop. As far as I know, Blackburn Record Exchange is still in business.

The real revolt against the record companies came not from niche shops, but from the acts themselves. The most successful and the most talented, in other words those capable of surviving beyond eighteen months, wanted to be recognised as artists, not as something manufactured by record companies to be tossed aside when the public got bored. There was no good reason why acts as talented as The Beatles, The Rolling Stones, The Kinks, The Hollies, The Who and the late David Bowie should not stake a claim to artistic freedom. There was no good reason why songwriters as talented as John Lennon and Paul McCartney, George Harrison, Mick Jagger and Keith Richard, and my personal favourite, the incomparable Ray Davies, should not be recognised as composers in the same league as Bach, Brahms and Beethoven. My apologies if I have left out your personal favourite. There is nothing intrinsically superior about classical music simply because our so-called betters regarded it as high culture. I have no doubt that the music of Lennon and McCartney will be played in three hundred years' time and therefore prove to be as timeless as the great classical pieces. There is, of course, a great deal of throw away pop, indeed some out and out rubbish. Even the greatest artists are culpable. I doubt anyone can see any artistic merit in Paul McCartney's Mary Had a Little Lamb, a ditty only marginally less irritating than the Birdie Song. Equally, I am sure that the great classical composers had days when they were less than inspired. Fortunately for them their own worst efforts were not immortalised on vinyl for posterity.

Commercial success brought about artistic freedom and opened the way for acts that specifically rejected the two and half minute single. Artists wanted to explore their creativity by recording albums, or as they were still known in 1963, LPs, short for long player. The modern LP had been invented as recently as 1948. They were twelve inches in diameter and played at a speed of thirty three and a third revolutions per minute. The typical length was thirty-five to forty minutes when both sides were added together. In 1963 they represented an underdeveloped market. At the time an LP at number one in the album chart could expect to sell on average around about one sixth of the copies sold by the comparable single and so on down the chart positions. Record Retailer, which published the industry chart, compiled a top twenty from March 1960, expanded to a top in 1966, and thence to a top 50 in 1968. Apart from the leading few positions, their veracity must have been very dubious given the small sample of shops and sales at the lower end barely worth counting. In 1963 an LP record cost around five times as much as a single. If memory serves, a single was 6s 3d, 31.5p in decimal currency, and an LP retailed at around 30s, £1.50 in new money. I'm less certain of LP costs if only because it was 1966 before I could afford to buy one. Pre- Beatles, like the singles chart, the album chart was the domain of Elvis Presley, Cliff Richard and The Shadows but with one important difference.

The dominant genre at the top of the album charts was soundtracks from major west end shows and popular films. South Pacific, released in 1958 actually topped the album chart for a total of 115 weeks, seventy of them consecutively including the whole of 1959, was the daddy of them all and was the only million selling album released in the 1950s, going on to top the two million mark. The Black and White Minstrel Show (!) topped the album charts in 1961 and 1962 and the soundtrack from West Side Story topped the album charts in 1962 and 1963. Elvis Presley and Cliff Richard were on screen rather than stage and topped the charts with film soundtracks. Presley topped the album chart in 1961 with G.I.Blues and in 1962 with Blue Hawaii. The films were dire and the songs average at best. Whatever Elvis did, Cliff did as well though not to the extent of signing a ten-year contract with MGM. Richard topped the chart with The Young Ones in

1962 and Summer Holiday in 1963. The latter held off another Presley film soundtrack, Girls, Girls, Girls, at number two. Presley did actually record a studio album in 1962, titled Pot Luck, which also made number one. The Shadows had a number one album with Out of the Shadows. The monopoly was broken only by The Best of Ball, Barber, and Bilk, cashing in on the popularity of trad jazz in 1962. If you thought the singles charts of that era were dull, try the album charts and you would have soon abandoned all hope.

At the beginning of May 1963, everything changed. Please Please Me entered the industry album chart at number one and stayed there for thirty weeks. Musically, it was a mix of Lennon and McCartney songs and an eclectic bunch of American covers. Its significance lies in the potential it showed for an expansion of the album market. It was succeeded at the top by the Beatles second album, With the Beatles, which not only topped the chart for twenty-one weeks, but actually sold well enough at its peak to reach number eleven in the NME singles chart. Indeed, between May 1963 and April 1965, only their greatest rivals, The Rolling Stones interrupted them at the top with their first two albums. Incredibly the Beatles released four chart topping albums in eighteen months. Now you are lucky if a top artist releases four albums in ten years. The duopoly was finally broken by the legendary American singer songwriter, Bob Dylan, who reached the summit twice that year. The Beatles would have two further number ones that year, Help, and Rubber Soul. The only threat to the dominance of three of the greatest recording artists in history came from another west end soundtrack, The Sound of Music, which enjoyed stints at the top in 1965, 1966 and 1967, exclusively between Beatles and Rolling Stones albums until 1967, when the Monkees were massively popular and scored two number one albums. Between them they prevented America's top group the Beach Boys, with their most celebrated album, Pet Sounds, and their first compilation album, Best of the Beach Boys, from reaching the top spot.

1967 was the year Sgt. Pepper's Lonely Hearts Club Band was released by The Beatles, and until surpassed by Queen's Greatest Hits was the biggest selling album of all time. It continues to sell to this very day and has now passed the five million sales mark in the UK. This album is perhaps musically the most important album ever released, as it laid down an artistic benchmark for others to follow. It is the artistic reference point for the 1960s, even though their previous album, Revolver, is arguably superior. An oddity occurred in December 1967 when Irish crooner Val Doonican briefly topped the album chart and 1968 featured eleven chart topping albums, at the time the most ever in a single year. Suffice it to say, they were all big name artists. 1969 marked the year that progressive rock first reached the summit and the divergence between the concept album culture of the LP chart, and the perceived throwaway pop of the singles chart was now becoming clear. Two of the acts that topped the album chart in 1969, the Moody Blues and Blind Faith, did not feature in the singles chart at all. Two other progressive rock acts, Cream and Jethro Tull, also had number one albums. Led Zeppelin, who broke through in 1969, would release twelve studio albums without ever releasing a single in the UK so precious was the integrity of an album. Record companies liked there to be at least one single to help promote sales. Initially, The Beatles did not take singles from their albums but once they relented it became the norm apart from purists like Zeppelin.

I have to confess I am not a fan of progressive rock (often shortened to prog rock). As a genre I found it boring, introspective and worst of all, pretentious. That is not to say that there were not some great songs. Readers will no doubt have their own favourites, but I think few would quibble with the timeless quality of Led Zeppelin's Stairway to Heaven, the magnificent guitar work of Jimi Hendrix on his interpretation of Dylan's All Along the Watchtower, and the all-consuming power of Won't Get

Fooled Again, by The Who. It must also be reiterated that progressive rock wrenched music firmly out of the creativity stifling straightjackets of the three-minute single and the fourteen track album. Before Hey Jude in 1968 only three number one singles out of 257 chart toppers had exceeded four minutes in length. These were Harry Belafonte's Mary's Boy Child (1957), The Animals' House of the Rising Sun (1964) and Procul Harum's Whiter Shade of Pale (1967). Indeed, relatively few had even exceeded three minutes. As ever, The Beatles broke all the rules. Hey Jude was an incredible seven minutes long and provided the last of six UK million selling singles for the world's top act. There would not be a single longer in duration go to number one until 1992. There was now a template to follow.

My real beef with progressive rock was not the inevitable dross, which after all is common to all musical genres, but the notion that somehow it was a cool artistic revolt against commercial values. The growth in album sales stimulated by The Beatles was a "win win" situation for the artists and the record companies alike. Successful artists got to be both as self-indulgent as they wished and make money, and the record companies could look forward to albums selling as many if not more copies than a single reaching a comparable chart position and, therefore, generating at least five times the amount of cash. Indeed, album sales have gone on to far outstrip those of singles. By 2005 a total of sixty-six albums had gone on to achieve two million or more sales in the UK compared to only seven singles. The record companies could squeeze the market even more by releasing one or more singles from the album with the exception of dedicated purists like Led Zeppelin. Of course, the artists had to appeal to a fan base in order to sell albums.

The record companies quite rightly were not prepared to repeatedly advance money to acts whose music did not sell. In other words the product had to be commercial regardless of whether or not it was dressed up as modern high culture. The music business is capitalism in the raw and like it or not the artists cannot pretend that they have not embraced that which a number of them publicly affect to despise. It is always good when successful performers put something back into the community, but we should not confuse philanthropy with socialism. The blunt truth is that once there is no market for your product, then the only future is the retro circuit, a type of resurrection almost unique to the music business, which does have the benefit of earning a modest living as part of a package tour, just as it was in the '60s until the rules were rewritten and artists gave concerts in stadiums showcasing their latest album. Before the retro circuit there was cabaret in the nightclubs. Unfortunately for progressive rock acts they are as ill-suited to the retro circuit as they were to cabaret.

Being perceived as cool is important to teenagers, as it grants status within the group and it was no different in the '60s and '70s. The Rolling Stones were never less than cool because they symbolised decadence and were in their time perceived as so much a threat to the social order that the establishment conspired unsuccessfully to destroy them. The Beatles were initially the four lovable mop tops singing simple love songs, but their writing prowess and reinvention of the group as a studio band ensured their position at the top of the pecking order was rarely threatened. It was always cool to like the Beatles, but by the late '60s it was not cool to dig out copies of Please Please Me. Similarly, the Beach Boys were cool provided you were listening to Good Vibrations rather Surfing USA. The ultimate American cool figure was Bob Dylan, who survived being accused of selling out when he swapped his acoustic for an electric guitar. Progressive rock was cool because it fooled people into believing it was art. Fellow denim rockers Status Quo were a cool band for the opposite reason. Folk music was also considered cool as a minority intellectual pursuit.

Sometimes what was cool and not was very random. Sha Na Na, an American retro act that performed rock and roll and doo-wop classics were cool, whereas Showaddywaddy, who dressed up as teddy boys and did exactly the same job in the UK, were not. I doubt they cared. Most definitely not cool were the Monkees, Herman's Hermits and, sadly, on occasion (if you don't believe me play Jennifer Eccles), the Hollies, who vied with The Kinks for the accolade of Britain's number three group behind the Beatles and the Rolling Stones. The departure of Graham Nash told its own story. In the USA Britain's number three group were unarguably the Dave Clark Five, who appeared a record eighteen times on America's most influential TV programme, the Ed Sullivan Show. Clark's heavy drumming style, perfectly showcased on the group's biggest song, Glad All Over, resonated with rock luminaries such as Stevie Wonder, Elton John and Bruce Springsteen as well as influencing progressive rock. The Dave Clark Five became cool retrospectively and were deservedly inducted into the hall of fame in 2008.

To like black music was cool, but to like Tamla Motown attracted criticism from purists that the label's output was "whiteyfied" soul. I'm not a Motown fan particularly, but much of the output of the Temptations in particular, Marvin Gaye and Stevie Wonder cannot be fairly characterised as throwaway pop. It's a personal opinion, but I also think that the late Levi Stubbs of the Four Tops was one of the greatest lead singers ever to get behind a microphone. Northern soul, which specialised in black American artists that were obscure but to my ear commercial sounding, was much cooler. Its devotees danced in celebrated clubs like the Twisted Wheel in Manchester, the Golden Torch in Tunstall, Stoke-On-Trent, and the Wigan Casino. Northern Soul would find its way into the singles charts in the '70s as records favoured by its devotees were re-released and caught the pocket of the mainstream audience. The Tams "Hey Girl Don't Bother Me", was the most successful, making number one in September 1971. Purists preferred the output of the Stax label from Memphis Tennessee. Black music from the former slave states had the authenticity that the sound of the motor city, Detroit, was perceived to lack. Ultra purists stuck to the blues. However, at the end of the '60s, another genre of black music became popular, that was reggae from the Caribbean. Its principle devotees were the skinhead gangs who were almost entirely working class and considered cool only by themselves. Although skinhead gangs were crudely racist when it came to Pakistanis, young black men known to their white counterparts as "spades" were welcome. Reggae survived the short lived skinhead cult and came into the mainstream in the next decade thanks to Bob Marley, who was most definitely a cool figure with his anti-imperialist politics and support for the legalisation of cannabis. Thanks almost entirely to Bob Marley, reggae achieved full credibility as a genre.

Almost the ultimate in cool was the music and the politics emanating from San Francisco in the summer of 1967 when nothing was more hip than hippies. However, incredible though it may seem given that 1967 was dubbed the summer of love, the singles chart of that year was the grimmest since 1962. It was dominated by the music your parents bought. Crooners were most definitely in. Engelbert Humperdinck was the dominant artist enjoying a total of twelve weeks at number one on the BBC chart, with the top three selling singles of the year all sung by him. He even managed to prevent a Beatles single from reaching the number one spot, interrupting a run of twelve consecutive number one singles on the BBC chart. I can remember being totally affronted. How was this allowed to happen? Amazingly it did and there was no reprieve from the NME chart on this occasion. The double A-sided single Penny Lane coupled with the magnificent Strawberry Fields Forever stalled at number two. Moreover, it stuck at number three for three weeks before reaching that position as the Petula Clark ballad, This is My Song, written by of all people Charlie Chaplin, also outsold the Beatles. Could it actually get worse, we wondered. Well in one sense it already had as the year began with Tom Jones at number one with the country dirge, Green Green Grass of Home. Gruesomely, there was a rival version of "This is My Song" by Harry Secombe, which peaked at number two. Only marginally less gruesome was another number two single about a Swiss wild flower, Edelweiss by Vince Hill.

Things did not improve. Engelbert Humperdinck was succeeded at number one by Frank and Nancy Sinatra with Something Stupid, successfully revived by Robbie Williams and Nicole Kidman in 2001. After that it was the turn of the Eurovision song contest as we teenagers suffered Sandie Shaw's Puppet on a String in the top spot. I suppose, looking back, that I should have been more disappointed at the time that the Tremeloes' Four Seasons cover, Silence is Golden, which was the next chart topper, somehow prevented the classic Waterloo Sunset from reaching the summit. After the Tremeloes we endured the ultimate in arty farty crap in the guise of Whiter Shade of Pale, which to this day critics seek to lionise. If I'm honest, I remember trying to like it at the time but was secretly glad as it dropped off the chart. Following that was probably the Beatles worst ever single, All You Need is Love. Authentic San Francisco it was not. That came next from Scott McKenzie and I can truthfully say that San Francisco (Be Sure to Wear Some Flowers in Your Hair) was the only number one single from that year that I really liked.

There were three more dirges to endure in the top slot before the year was out; more Engelbert, The Bee Gees with Massachusetts, and Long John Baldry's rendition of Let the Heartaches Begin. Only at the beginning of December was normal service resumed with the Beatles at number one. At Christmas, they repeated the feat they achieved four years earlier of holding both the number one and number two slots. 1967 was the year of easy listening as far as the singles charts were concerned. Our parents ruled in the music market place, just as they did in the home. Its small wonder that acts ceased to define their credibility in terms of hit singles. I just wished at the time that the music aimed at our parents was excluded from the charts. At the age of fourteen I didn't understand that was neither practical nor ethical.

The antidote to both progressive rock and easy listening came in the early seventies with the advent of glam rock. It was most definitely not cool (other than David Bowie who was the ultimate in cool despite the glitter and the make-up) but I loved it and so did the old school friends that I socialised with at weekend. Indeed, not all the acts that carried the glam rock label actually wore glitter, make-up, and outrageous clothes. Suzi Quatro simply wore leather. We did not care a shit that glam rock was not cool. Glam rock was not a musical genre like rock and roll or doo-wop. What bound the acts together was a collective desire to entertain and make rock music fun again. The dressing up was part of that although androgyny was not compulsory. Dancing was most definitely permitted. The audience was most definitely part of the performance. By contrast, attending a progressive rock concert was like attending an exhibition at an art gallery. You were there to sit in silence affecting awe at the true art unfolding before your eyes, or more accurately, ears.

I'm always amused by the artistic snobbery that pervades the music business. Some years ago the BBC produced a programme to celebrate the top ten glam rock acts. It was introduced by Tony Blackburn and David Hamilton, DJs who are always linked with mainstream pop. Curiously neither David Bowie nor Queen featured on the roster of artists. Someone in the BBC's culture department must have decreed that a programme about glam rock could not be sullied by including such rock luminaries. In a 1972 interview when Bowie was in his Ziggy Stardust phase, he stated that he was quite happy to be categorised as glam rock. The main difference between Bowie and many other glam rock performers is the success he enjoyed in reinventing himself over the years, making both commercial and critically acclaimed records, long outlasting his contemporaries. To airbrush Bowie from glam history is artistic censorship. Queen came slightly late to the scene in 1974 but they bore all the hallmarks of glam with an androgynous lead singer in Freddie Mercury, garish clothing and terrific stage presence to go with the driving rock anthems they played. The critics were not initially impressed dubbing them a glam rock act. I say there is no disgrace in that but in 1974 it could not possibly be predicted how high Queen would soar in the pantheon of rock. So thirty years later rock history had to be rewritten. Queen were serious artists and therefore could not possibly be categorised with the likes of Marc Bolan, Slade and Sweet.

I enjoyed glam rock. It was fun, there were some great songs, and the top names were underrated. Sweet began as a pop act recording numbers by Nicky Chinn and Mike Chapman, the Stock, Aitken and Waterman of their era. They matured into a terrific rock band with distinctive high falsetto vocals. The early twenty-first century rock band, The Darkness, could have been a reincarnation. Sweet hold the distinction of being the only British glam rock act to crack America, scoring four top ten singles. Slade are usually remembered for that Christmas song, as indeed are fellow glam act, Wizzard, fronted by Roy Wood. Slade were the most successful glam act of all in the UK with six number one singles and two number one albums. As a live act they were in a class of their own. Their musical legacy influenced The Ramones, Quiet Riot, and the biggest UK band of the 1990s, Oasis. Whereas Slade and Sweet were contemporary rock acts, Wizzard were distinctly retro updating doo-wop for a 1970's audience. Roy Wood, who had found fame with The Move in the 1960s, was a virtuoso who could play almost any instrument, including the bagpipes. These were seriously talented people who deserved better than to be sneered at by rock critics. Finally, despite being exposed as a paedophile, Gary Glitter should not be airbrushed out of glam history. His songs were covered by people as diverse as American rock chick Joan Jett, and Sheffield based electro-pop act, The Human League, and he is cited as an influence on both punk in the mid-seventies and Britpop in the mid-nineties. Rock and Roll Parts 1 and 2 will never again be heard on radio, but censorship on the grounds that the singer was a pervert will never change the fact that it is a great record.

I can't remember exactly when I stopped listening to Radio One, although I would guess that it roughly coincided with my teaching career. There are few things more toe curling than teachers trying to be hip discussing the latest musical trends with their charges. In the early '80s the New Romantic movement dominated the singles charts and I happily confess – although not to the children I taught – that to this day I still love Fade to Grey by Visage. Although the movement grew out of punk, the clothes and the make-up owed more to glam rock. Like glam and unlike punk and disco, new romanticism was a genre of style and attitude rather than music. Punk did little for me and disco did even less. I did like Electro-pop and my collection of videos (now transferred to DVD) does include a Human League compilation. However by the mid-eighties I had given up on contemporary music. Hip-hop, rap and garage were not for me any more than the products of the Stock, Aitken and Waterman hit factory. From then on, I was strictly Radio Two or independent retro stations. I retreated quite happily into my '60s time warp where you can relive your youth without the angst of adolescence, and as such have been a regular listener to Sounds of the '60s on a Saturday morning since it began twenty-five years ago. It helped me discover that there was musical life between rock and roll and The Beatles. New York's Brill Building in the late '50s and early '60s housed some great songwriters like Goffin and King, Sedaka and Greenfield, Mann and Weil, and Jeff Barry and Ellie Greenwich, whose day job it was to write songs that would make the Billboard top forty. I discovered or rediscovered their songs sung by the original American artists, having often only been familiar with the British cover version. As in England, the artists were secondary and many have only the status of a rock and roll footnote, but at the other end of the spectrum Dion Di Mucci and Frankie Valli would both be inducted into the hall of fame.

Musically, I may have become a grumpy old man, unlike DJ the late John Peel who effortlessly embraced new genres. Fortunately we baby boomers have our own music that protects us from ever becoming our parents. And then I discovered recently that Bob Dylan was releasing an album of Sinatra covers...

Chapter Five

Grammar School

I entered the hallowed portals of St Mary's RC College, Blackburn, for boys on the first Monday of September 1964. Our new school was built on the site where Blackburn Olympic, FA Cup winners in 1883 had played in their short history. There were five of us from St Edwards: Brian Scott, Paul Bury, Colin Beresford, Tony Hurn and I, and we huddled together in the quadrangle, almost like penguins for the protection of familiarity, as we awaited instructions. We had some idea of what to expect as our parents had attended a prospective parent's evening shortly before the end of the summer term. As I recall, there was a bundle of paperwork packed with school rules and uniform requirements. Wearing a tie and a school cap on a daily basis was mandatory. Blazers could only be removed in the classroom with the permission of a master. They were not referred to as teachers. There was no escape from short trousers for at least the first year. Prefects were to be addressed by surname, not by first name or nickname, a rule that proved impossible to keep in the second year when our form prefect's name was William (Bill) Haley! The Headmaster, Father Green, also told our parents that we should not expect the masters to be patient or softly spoken. There was also a warning from boys already there who lived locally that new boys could be on the wrong end of initiation ceremonies, such as having your head shoved down a toilet bowl, which was then flushed.

Our first day was actually very short. We were sorted out into forms and told to come back the following day by 9am. It came as a relief to discover that all five of us were in the same form, 1C, which didn't impress my father, who believed I had been placed in the bottom class when in fact we were un-streamed in the first two years. Life must have been rather harder for Chris Watson, another good friend of mine, who was the other boy in our class to pass the 11 plus, as his parents sent him to Stonyhurst College, the Jesuit foundation near Clitheroe, where he would have had to negotiate the first day along with the rigours of boarding on his own.

The following day, it was in at the deep end straight after assembly. As first years we did not immediately join the rest of the school in assembly in the main hall. Instead, we assembled in one of the science laboratories and assembly was taken by the Deputy Head, Father Graystone. He seemed quite a reasonable individual but we would discover that his bite was much worse than his understated bark. We had barely found our classroom when the Headmaster came in and, briefly, we froze in terror. The moment passed. He had only come in to introduce Foster, our form prefect. We actually did not meet our form master until the Wednesday and knew our timetable only because some bright spark spotted it on the wall. The lack of a form period allowed us to claim our own seats and I sat next to the familiar and reassuring figure of Brian Scott, who had been a friend of mine since he was placed next to me in primary school on arriving from Scotland two years earlier. There was no question of being bullied in his company. I was careful to show my gratitude and ensure that he never failed any tests and found himself on the wrong end of a beating. Somehow we survived a full year without being split up, as our form master had a nasty habit of making boys move desks.

The first lesson was French with Mr Bolger of whom more anon. Forty minutes later that was followed by Maths with Mr Collingridge, who was unoriginally nicknamed Pythagoras. I blotted my copybook on day one when he spoke sharply to me for writing in pencil as we had done at primary school. Fortunately, I had a fountain pen in my pocket. Last period of the morning, before break, was English with Mr Rose, who to this day I regard as the most influential teacher of my school life. The initial impression was of a very nice man, but we would swiftly discover that we were being taught by one of the school's most renowned disciplinarians. He was nicknamed "Fred Drag" on account of his reputed forty a day smoking habit. In our first year he gave up smoking at the age of fifty and by all accounts replaced the habit by taking snuff. Neither habit could have done him much harm as he only died as recently as 2007 at the grand old age of ninety-three. We had early lunch followed by General Science in the Physics lab with Father McDonald, affectionately known as "Beppo". He was killed in the Paris air crash in 1974.

After a forty-minute break, we returned to the classroom for a triple period of Art and Craft. We were split into two halves; one half going to the Art room and the other half, which included me, remaining in our own form room with Miss Burns, who doubled as the school's head cook, for something called leatherwork. We passed a leisurely and relaxed first afternoon, a pleasant change after going straight into the properties of solids, liquids and gases in the Science lab. On arriving home I changed and spent some time kicking a ball around with Chris Watson, who did not start at Stonyhurst until the following week. It would be five years before we met again.

Day two, however, was a good deal less relaxed. It began with English and Mr Rose was on the warpath. We had been instructed to back our exercise books in order to protect them and many of us had simply forgotten. He then proceeded to tell us about his own first week in Grammar School, when his whole form were punished with three strokes of the ferule (a strap made of whalebone encased in leather) for failing to learn Archimedes' principle by heart. After making around half the class sweat he settled for giving fifty lines. At the end of the lesson we were given two spellings to learn that night and continued to do so for the rest of that first half-term. Every morning – we had English every morning – a boy would be selected to write them on the board. You can guess the punishment for not getting them right. Mr Rose carried his own personal strap, concealed by his gown, which obviated the need to send a boy to the staff room to collect the official instrument of punishment. Towards the end of half-term we had a spelling test composed of thirty words, which included words like onomatopoeia, alliteration, and occurrence, the last of which can cause trouble for even the best of spellers. The penalty for misspelling was one stroke per error, although mercifully for the poor spellers he capped the maximum at six.

After that first half-term he never used the strap again in my class nor indeed further up the school, when I was taught by him for a further two years. Mr Rose was a martinet, but he was a gifted and inspirational teacher, the best in the school. He also played the violin and was a noted local cricketer in his younger days, playing for Cherry Tree in the Ribblesdale League. Fred Rose had impossibly high standards, often ordering that work with just a single comma missing was repeated. We had to practice addressing envelopes and heading letters and he was a stickler for correct grammar. For him, correct grammar and punctuation provided the essential framework for his charges to express themselves in our beautiful language. Mr Rose was not averse to having the best essays read out publicly. Unlike the nuns, he gave out praise for high quality work. To this day, when I put together a piece of written work, I ask myself: "Would this have satisfied Fred Rose?" I'm sure he would be delighted to know that I have never used a spellchecker in my life.

Later that same morning we met our form master, Mr Smith, for the first time. Joe Smith was a young man in his first teaching post and he took us for Latin. He was on old boy of St Bede's College, Manchester, well over six feet tall and possessed of a powerful left arm. At weekends, in the summer, he opened the bowling for Ribblesdale Wanderers in the Ribblesdale League, whose club captain at the time was Keith Weaver, another master at the school. On a good day he could be an entertaining man, but on many other days he was in foul humour and it paid not to attract his attention. For my sins, after two years of Latin with Joe Smith, I opted to study Greek and found myself subjected to his not very tender mercies for another two years. After that he left the school on promotion to Head of Classics at Nantwich Grammar School. If memory serves we had another Maths class that morning and then the middle two lessons saw us out on the sports field. In winter, Games equalled football and I will say more about Games and PE later in this chapter. In our first two years our lunch break followed the morning break, which was taken from 11.15 to 11.30am. Typically, we ate at around 11.40 and were back in class by 12.10pm, except on Wednesdays when we did Games on a full stomach. The main break was 13.20 to 14.00.

In the afternoon on that second day, as well as meeting two new masters, we had another French class with Mr Bolger, who I think it is fair to say is fondly remembered by most old boys. He was a genuine eccentric, deeply religious, and something of a polymath. As well as teaching French, he also taught Latin and was a published botanist, a fact we discovered when a classmate found one of his books in the local library and produced it in a lesson much to this modest man's embarrassment. Mr Bolger was a genuinely nice, if rather shy individual and that, coupled with his eccentricities, led to an over reliance on the strap to keep discipline. In the second year, when we were rather braver as a class about pushing our luck, Mr Bolger sent for the strap on a daily basis. The second most familiar sentence that passed his lips was, "Mullen, go and fetch the strap," and this often happened twice in the same forty-minute lesson. John Mullen must have received more strokes of the strap than any other boy in our year. Eventually, Mr Bolger resorted to using a gym shoe from one of our kit bags, to save sending for the strap yet again. The most familiar sentence to pass his lips was, "Flynn, put his name down." Tim Flynn was form captain, whose duties ranged from collecting dinner money on our form master's behalf, through distributing books to being expected to keep the class in reasonable order between lessons. You got the job either because you were deemed to the most responsible boy in the form or, alternatively, someone likely to become more responsible as a result. It did not work in my case when I got the job a couple of years later. Unfortunately, Flynn's duties during French lessons extended to noting down the names of those who were to be given extra work. This could be very difficult as Mr Bolger would simply bark, "Flynn, put his name down," and Flynn was simply expected to know who it was, as Mr Bolger never called out the errant boy's name. Tim Flynn was bright enough to work out straight away that there was no point in asking whose name to put down as extra work was never given anyway.

Mr Bolger also had the habit of chanting out his instructions: "All corrections must be done before the homework is begun," would be chanted without fail on homework days. The same method was used to teach difficult French spellings. V-I-E-I double L-E was chanted out rhythmically by Mr Bolger as he attempted to get across the spelling of *vieille*, the French adjective for an old person of the feminine gender. The only trouble was that as a class we continued to chant long after Mr Bolger had finished and we would only be silent after Flynn had been ordered to take names, and Mullen sent to fetch the strap. Mr Bolger also had a remarkable range of facial gestures, which were most in evidence when the Deputy Headmaster came round to read out the weekly marks. Typically, for our class, this would happen on a Wednesday afternoon during French. He was not capable of a poker face. Mr Bolger would stand arms behind his back and during the time it took for thirty-five boys to stand and hear their marks he would nod disapprovingly, suck in his cheeks and screw up his eyes when poor performance was revealed. It is fair to say that, apart from when your own marks were read, all eyes were on Mr Bolger, as it was first class entertainment.

It was during the reading of the weekly marks that we discovered that our Deputy Headmaster, Father Graystone, was not the pussycat that he appeared to be at morning assembly. The system was straightforward. In descending order each academic subject was marked from six to two. Six represented excellent performance, five was good, four was average, three was poor, and two was very poor. The marks were entered on the back of what would become your bi-annual report card. Your examination results were on the front along with class positions. There was also a mark for conduct which was a default five, unless marks were deducted by your form prefect. If you had an excess of threes over fives, or, much more rarely, twos over sixes you were in detention on Friday afternoon after school. However, on this occasion, the Deputy Headmaster went beyond the random interrogation of poor marks and decided to make an example of David Maudsley, who was booked for detention yet again in that first half-term. He produced from his cassock the longest thickest strap I have ever seen and proceed to leather Maudsley's backside with a truly brutal six of the best. As we sat there watching in horror and gripped with terror, even Mr Bolger winced. At the end of the beating Father Graystone simply said, "Remember, Maudsley, your father is paying for your education." Whether Mr Maudsley would have approved of how the school discharged its duty to his wallet is not known to me. As I recall, four boys in my class were the sons of fee paying parents, three of whom had originally failed the 11 plus including Maudsley, and the other a Blackburn boy who had been to a private primary school and therefore not allowed to sit the examination a year early, whose parents elected to pay for him to attend Grammar School at the age of ten. I recall he duly passed the 11 plus, thus relieving his parents of the financial burden, but I cannot recall whether the other three fared any better at the age of twelve. They did all remain in the school for a full five years.

Looking back, there was a clear element of shock and

awe about discipline in that first half-term. It was all about laying down markers for the rest of our career in the school. It was about ensuring that we learned very swiftly what the standards were, who was boss, and where the lines were rigidly drawn. Sometime after half-term, we were finally admitted to the full school assembly, except that there was one last demonstration of power, this time by the Headmaster himself. We had barely shuffled into the front of the hall when the Head instructed his Deputy to get those dreadful boys out of his hall and not bring them back until they were fit to be seen with the rest of the school. I think we all wondered what on earth we had done to offend and only on reflection, after leaving school, did we realise that this was pre-rehearsed and stage managed for our benefit. It was rather like one of those army inspections that feature routinely in the recollections of national servicemen, that no matter the standard of your kit and the quality of your foot drill, you failed. It was pure bull. As it happened, we were invited to assembly again a couple of weeks later and it passed off without incident. The back of the hall had floor to roof screens which, when opened, revealed an altar where Mass was celebrated. High on the screens were engraved the names of the former and current Headmasters in bold capitals and, below them, the names of the head boy in each year going back to 1925 when the school was founded by the Society of Mary, hence the name of our school, a religious order founded in France. The Marists who taught in our school were also ordained as priests, in addition to taking the traditional monastic vows of poverty, chastity and obedience. On this basis, they were entitled to be addressed as Father rather than Brother. The Headmaster himself always took assembly from a stage at the front of the hall, flanked by the school's two longest serving masters. Prior to the arrival of the Head and his retinue, the entire school was controlled by one man from his position on the stage, the Discipline master.

During my seven years at St Mary's College, there

were two anointed discipline masters, Basil Holden and Fred Arkwright, the latter an old boy of the school. Mr Holden held office for my first three years and Mr Arkwright for the last four. Basil Holden taught Chemistry and Biology and was a gifted teacher with a ready wit. I was taught by him for only one year and, considering the position he held, the atmosphere was remarkably relaxed. However, he lived up to his fearful reputation when dealing with a miscreant in another class who was stupid enough to mess around with acid in the Chemistry lab. Eighteen strokes of the strap, six on each hand and a further six on the backside inflicted publicly at the front of the lab is believed to be a school record. Basically, the Discipline Master was responsible for every facet of discipline outside of the classroom. He whacked the smokers, those who disrespected the prefects and those caught out of school without permission. Mr Holden also had the task of conducting haircut inspections, at a time when long hair on men and boys was seen as almost the ultimate challenge to authority. An entire year would be selected at random to stay behind after assembly and Basil, one of those whose nickname was actually the same as his real name, would walk behind the lines of one hundred plus boys and tap the shoulder with the strap of those boys whose hair was considered too long. The ritual was those thus selected would go out to the front to be whacked after the inspection was complete. Only when a new Headmaster was appointed in 1967 did beatings for having hair too long finally cease. I should add that what was considered long in 1965 would be positively short by 1969. One only has to look at photographs of the Beatles and Rolling Stones in those years to see the difference.

Mr Arkwright took over the role at the same time as a new Headmaster arrived. He was feared even more than Basil Holden, partly because he almost invariably administered the strap to your backside and never less than four strokes, but also because we schoolboys believed that he actually enjoyed that part of the job, and unlike Basil

Holden, did not need to be genuinely angry in order to lay it on hard. Looking back over the best part of five decades, hindsight tells me that it was all part of the image, for him a necessary accompaniment to being effective. Fred Arkwright was still under thirty when he undertook the role. He understood that our perceptions enhanced his authority. Quite how the Discipline Master was selected I do not know, neither do I know whether he received an enhanced rate of pay. However, it would be interesting to learn how the interviews were conducted! Thus, although the Discipline Master was supported by two other masters, he was on duty before school, every break time, and every lunch time although he was excused supervising the dining hall. Fred Arkwright conducted most beatings outside the staffroom before afternoon school began. Crowds of boys would gather at the top of the stairs opposite to watch the sport. Fred Arkwright had the gift, when wielding the strap, of finding a sweet spot on boy's backsides guaranteed to make them visibly flinch. As well as the 1.55pm daily ritual, Fred Arkwright happily dispensed punishment on the spot. Smokers caught in the boys toilets could expect to have to bend over facing the urinal when punishment was administered. I should add that he was a fine classroom teacher, despite the fact that I failed my Geography "O" level.

Fred Arkwright could take you getting one over him, probably working on the basis that his day would come. My day to get one over him was in December 1968 on the last day of term when lessons were suspended to allow older pupils to watch the annual staff versus boys football match. Around six of us took it as our cue to sneak off to the nearest pub, the Sportsman, which considering that only a couple of us had turned sixteen never mind eighteen, and that we were in school uniform, was probably pushing it. The other boys pushed me to the front as my sideburns (then very fashionable) made me look the oldest of our group. I had just taken a couple of half pints into a side room when Mr Arkwright stormed into the pub and ordered my friends out. I shot under a long seat and huddled under it, behind the open door. Whether he looked in the room I do not know. All I do know is that he failed to catch me. I waited a few minutes, knocked back the drinks, called into the paper shop to get some mints and duly climbed back over some railings into school. By the time my friends had returned to the football match, suitably chastened, I was already there. Fred Arkwright appeared a few minutes later. I think he said something about six boys being reported as going towards the Sportsman but somehow only five had been caught. Oh dear, what a shame.

However, there was one occasion when he did not take being thwarted in good part, and it was his own silly fault. On this occasion there had been some snowballing that had probably got a little out of hand and a particular boy had taken exception to it. For whatever reason, Fred Arkwright took us to the Headmaster's office, a place I had never been before. The Head, Father Cassidy, gave us a short lecture and then took a strap out of the drawer. Fred Arkwright then said, "I recommend you strap these boys on the backside, Father." We could barely contain our laughter when Father Cassidy responded, "Oh, no, I wouldn't want to hurt a man's dignity." Fred Arkwright stood there with a face like thunder as we each received three strokes on the hand. In that moment our respect for the Head based on fear evaporated. We could not conceive of a Headmaster incapable of giving out a good beating.

As I have said, other masters were rather less reticent and kept their own straps or slippers. One referred to his personal strap as a "thunder flash", which is something of a contradiction in terms, especially coming from a physics master. Another, one of the Art staff, used the fearsome two-pronged Scottish version of the strap, the tawse. According to John Mullen, who must have been whacked by just about every teacher who used corporal punishment, this was the most painful punishment of all, even though it was administered to the hand and not the backside. There was another member of staff reputed to use a cricket bat on boys' backsides. One can only guess whether he was practicing his pull shot or his straight drive. Finally, there was another individual, Mr Diaz, who informed us all solemnly, at the commencement of our second year, that he did not use a strap or a cane. Sighs of relief were stifled instantly when he said that he threw a chair at an errant boy instead. In the fullness of time a stool was seen to fly across the Art room, fortunately missing its intended target. There were others who threw chalk and even board rubbers. Fred Arkwright himself had an alternative punishment to the strap for first years only. He would command the errant schoolboy to stand on the dreaded spot and slap him sharply across the face. One boy only, Steve Ansbro, the captain of our year football team, managed to duck. To his credit, Fred Arkwright accepted it and sent Ansbro back to his seat.

Competitive sport was hugely important in my school, as it was in all Grammar Schools. On a Monday morning the Headmaster read out his own version of the classified check starting with the First Eleven and finishing with the under twelve's. On one occasion in my first year the under thirteen's had lost 9-0 to another school having only been one down at half time. The Head ordered the team captain to report his office immediately after assembly. The irony of the situation is that the captain, John Waddington, was one of only three boys in the history of my school to go on a make a career in professional football. Waddington was a member of Blackburn Rovers Third Division Championship winning side in 1974–75, Rovers centenary year. The other two were Brian Miller, who spent his entire professional career at Burnley and won one England cap, and Mike Duxbury who played for Manchester United and England before a stint at Blackburn Rovers. The truth about the under thirteen side of 1964–65 is that it wasn't just substandard, it was crap. Most years at least one of our year teams would grace Ewood Park for the local schools knockout trophy finals. In 1966 the Head threatened to withdraw teams from local cup competitions if there was any repetition of spectators' behaviour that year. As I recall, it was pretty tame stuff, a bit of chanting, bits of paper being thrown up in the air, and some occasional booing. The season just ended had seen the first nascent outbreaks of hooliganism at Ewood Park, in a dreadful campaign that had seen the town team relegated to the Second Division. A few weeks earlier I got a bollocking at school because the Head of PE had seen me join a sit down demonstration on the terraces against the Rovers' Board. Sportsmanship and the proper acceptance of defeat were cardinal virtues. On one notorious occasion, two years later our year captain, Steve Ansbro, was withdrawn for arguing with the referee, a master from the other school involved. In those days substitutes were still only permitted to replace injured players, so we were down to ten men.

The sporting highlight of the year was not the seemingly annual appearance of one or more of our soccer teams at Ewood Park, it was the school sports day typically held on a Saturday in June. Although participation was voluntary (maximum three events which had to be a mixture of track and field), attendance most certainly was not, which caused some difficulty for the Rossendale Valley contingent whose special bus was not provided by the local authority on that day. I have to confess that I only participated in the first year when my limitations both as a sprinter and a high jumper were ruthlessly exposed. My heat contained a boy called Bernard Dickinson who unknown to me was lightning fast. The 100 and 220 yards events (the UK only acknowledged metric distances for Olympic purposes in those far off days) were simply non-events as competitions and Dickinson simply sprinted away with the junior Victor Ludorum trophy. As for the High Jump, I never did master the Fosbury Flop. Bernard Dickinson was also an excellent footballer, an inside forward in the parlance of the time who added the advantages of a low centre of gravity and bewildering body swerve to the blistering pace he displayed on the Athletics track. Sadly, his sporting prowess was curbed by a broken leg sustained the following year playing football for the school, which he never again represented.

A slightly lower key event was the school swimming gala held at the long defunct Belper Street baths in the autumn term. It was an evening event and attendance was not compulsory, but I would guess that our Head of PE, swimming enthusiast Tommy Duckworth, probably regarded it as at least on a par with sports day. I have to confess that my back stroke was no more noteworthy than my sprinting. The highlight of the evening was the water polo match between staff and boys teams.

Rugby was not introduced to our school until 1968. In Wales it was a caning offence in some schools to be caught kicking a football rather than a rugby ball. In many Grammar Schools in England, rugby was seen as a suitable sport for aspiring young gentleman, whereas soccer was associated with the great unwashed. So we were unusual in that rugby was not played at all until Mr Rigby, known as Joe Beak or Ollie Beak, introduced the sport. Joe Rigby was a terrifying figure with a bald head, glasses perched over a very long hooked nose, and hunched shoulders that made it appear as though his gown was on a coat-hanger, even when he was wearing it. For those not good enough to represent the school at soccer, it was an opportunity both to learn a new game and challenge the existing sporting pecking order. I have to say regretfully I did not take up rugby. Ollie Beak, who had acquired the alternative nickname courtesy of an ITV children's programme, which featured an owl puppet of that name, was simply too austere and formidable a figure. Others were not daunted and Rugby Union gradually got off the ground and improved the quality of its fixture list.

In summer, it was Cricket and Athletics when it was a pleasure to be outside, unlike winter, when no concessions were made. We were out on the field not just in torrential rain but also when the overused school pitches were icy and rutted. There was no such thing as Health and Safety and we just got on with it, running around furiously to keep warm. This was no help to the goalkeepers and one occasion the PE teacher did take pity on us was when one of the goalkeepers was clearly distressed and had to be thawed out in the pavilion. Otherwise, if we wanted sympathy, we would find it in the dictionary, somewhere between shit and syphilis. Not that any of our teachers would have used that expression but we did have one, the legendary Joe Stewart, who was not averse to calling boys frozen turds. Joe Stewart, or more accurately Father Stewart, was one of the school's legendary masters. He was the school's longest serving staff member who had earned the right to stand at the right hand of God (the Headmaster) at assembly. Father Stewart also ran the school tuck shop. He was tall and broad and in no way diminished by advancing years. His sheer physical presence dominated a room and he had a reputation as a ferocious martinet. Somehow I managed to get through Grammar School without ever being taught by him. He was truly terrifying.

As well as competitive sport, there were competitive examinations, twice a year every year. In the fifth and upper sixth forms – which for younger readers equate to years eleven and thirteen – the second set of examinations was the real thing, our GCE "O" and GCE "A" levels respectively. There were class positions in each academic subject and overall class positions, something we were already used to from primary school. However, we were spared them being called out publicly at a full school assembly. Following internal examinations, individual reports were compiled for our parents on the back of the card already used to record your weekly marks. These were to be signed by our parents and returned to the form master. One of the odd things about your schoolfellows is how your memory of them is frozen in time if you did not see each other again as adults. So it is with Jimmy Drew, who attempted to persuade the form master, Mr Smith, that his parents had refused to sign his report as opposed to the truth, which was simply that he was too scared to take it home. It goes without saying that Mr Smith was having none of it. At the end of two years we were streamed based on examination results and Jimmy Drew and I went in separate directions. Although he remained in the school until he was sixteen, I simply have no memory of him after we were sorted into rank order. Grammar schools were tough places for those who struggled with academic work.

Examinations were very strictly supervised and it did not pay to try and cheat as two boys found out when caught by one of the Biology staff, Mr Cooper, during an examination being held in the Biology lab. To try and prevent cribbing, the school often used a system whereby boys were seated alternately with boys from a different form or even year sitting a different examination. What the two boys were doing exactly, and how they came to be caught, I do not know. What I do recall are the consequences. Readers of my generation will not be waiting in suspense. Out of the desk drawer came a long and fearsome looking strap, which was duly administered six times to each posterior. Their papers were of course cancelled and a big fat zero entered on their report cards in the particular subject. Quite how O'Callaghan and Ansbro explained it to the parents is not known to me. As for Mr Cooper, who taught me "O" level Biology, he proved to be a rather less fearsome individual when you got to know him. Indeed, as I recall, he was the only master who routinely used our Christian names in class. He was also the unsuccessful Liberal candidate in the Darwen constituency in four consecutive General Elections between 1970 and 1979.

Perhaps the most surprising aspect of Grammar School was how little religious policing of our lives there was compared to primary school. We had religious assemblies, just like primary school, we attended Mass once a week, just like primary school, and we had RK (religious knowledge as it was known) just like primary school. On the Monday of the second week I was convinced that someone, perhaps the Deputy Headmaster, would interrogate our attendance at Mass the day before, the frequency of our confessions, and whether or not we took communion. It didn't happen then and it never did, not even at Easter when all Catholics were supposed to attend Confession and receive Holy Communion even if they did not do so at any other time of the year. Neither was there the annual St Joseph's Penny collection. Great dark shadows had been lifted. Altar boys were selected from volunteers who had carried out the task at primary school. Typically, the priests used either Peter Wilkinson, who himself went on to become a priest and was Roman Catholic chaplain of HMP Manchester during the Strangeways riot of 1990, or Paul Bury who was a friend of mine from primary school. Unlike Peter Wilkinson, Paul Bury was not everyone's idea of an altar boy. Paul was the third of six sons sired by Allan Bury, former naval petty officer, services boxing champion and devout Catholic. Like his father, he took crap from no one and his attitude to prefects frequently landed him in trouble with Fred Arkwright, in addition to being caught smoking and going to the pub. None of this in any way diminished his Catholicism but, as schoolboys, we could never get our heads round the alter ego of subservient altar boy.

On set piece occasions, when the whole school attended Mass, we trooped down to the Good Shepherd church, less than ten minutes' walk from the school. One of these, I recall, was for a Requiem Mass for Jimmy Smith, a boy in my year who died of after an asthma attack at the age of fifteen. Back in 1968 there was no counselling and emotions were expected to be suppressed. There is a line in a Catholic hymn, De Profundis (in English this translates as Out of the Depths): "Waste not in selfish weeping one precious day," which illustrates perfectly how we were expected to move on once the Requiem Mass was over. Those who were close to Jimmy Smith had to keep him alive in their hearts, as his memory was expunged from the school in the same way as his name from the register. At least there was a service for Jimmy Smith. Peter Wolfenden, who had the misfortune to be killed in a motorcycle accident at the age of sixteen, died during the summer holidays without any public acknowledgement of his contribution to the school. I had already seen the unsentimental attitude to death of the Marist order further down the school.

One of my classmates in our second year, Irving Walsh, had the misfortune to lose both his parents in a car crash, though as I recall his mother did not die straightaway. Walsh returned to school while his mother was in intensive care. One afternoon the new Deputy Headmaster walked into the classroom and without any preamble simply said in front of the entire class, "I'm sorry, Walsh, your mother is dead." Even to those of us emotionally hardened by our experiences at the hands of the nuns, this came as a shock. To the modern generation, which prostrated itself in counterfeit vicarious grief over the death of the former Princess of Wales, this would probably be seen as child abuse. The response to her death in 1997 showed how we had changed as a nation to a secular almost atheistic one, which saw life as a tragic end rather than a glorious beginning. For the churchmen that educated my generation, death marked the start of eternal life (for the virtuous) at the side of God and was therefore not a cause for weeping, indeed quite the reverse it was something to be celebrated. Earthly suffering was over. Unlike the modern Church of England, they did not make compromises with secular values, but unlike the nuns who blighted our primary school lives, the Marist fathers were not habitually cruel or unkind.

Nevertheless, Irving Walsh, who was a popular classmate, was now an orphan. He would be brought up by an aunt and grow up like his father to be a businessman and at the tender age of eighteen became manager of what I suppose we would now call a young men's fashion outlet. Walsh also liked a bet and introduced me to the perils of dog racing at the Blackburn track on Hill Street, not long after my sixteenth birthday. Filling the void in his life led him to consult a hypnotist in order to try and give up gambling. According to a mutual friend, he lost the fee for the second appointment at the dog track! At the time we roared with uncharitable laughter, but gambling can easily become a lonely business rather than a pleasant social habit. Looking back, I sometimes wish I had lost rather than won on that first occasion as it might have put me off betting for life, or maybe not given my maternal grandmother's love of horse racing. Towards the end of her life, it was my job to take her bets down to the bookies on a Saturday afternoon. My very last conversation with her was about what might win the 1972 Lincoln Handicap at Doncaster the following day.

Returning to the theme, I can't actually remember very much about Religious Knowledge classes. Nor indeed did everyone study GCE "O" level Scripture. In our first year we were taught by of all people Fred Arkwright, rather than one of the priests. I can't recall Religious classes at all in the sixth form, although it may be that I simply didn't bother to attend. What we did have that was different was the annual Retreat held for two days in February after half-term. Only the most senior years, the fifth and sixth forms attended. The rest of the school had an extra two days' holiday. Instead of normal lessons, we were split into groups led rather than taught by a series of masters and contemplated not only merely the meaning of a Christian life but also some of the great moral issues of the day. We were no longer vessels to be filled and to our surprise and delight saw a human side to those staff who we had previously regarded as unbending and unapproachable. Informality did not go as far as the use of our Christian names, but it did extend to a relaxation of the requirement to wear school uniform. Come the following Monday morning the Retreat had been put back into its box for another year and normal school discipline resumed.

If the Retreat was the private face of the school, then the annual speech night was its public one for which preparation actually began before the summer holiday. Held in late September or early October and always on a Thursday night, it was the highlight of the school year and the speeches made by the Headmaster and the guest speaker were given extensive coverage in our local evening paper, the Lancashire Evening Telegraph. The most prominent guest speakers in my time were Barbara Castle, the local MP from 1945 to 1979 who was the foremost female politician of hers and any other era in Britain until eclipsed by Mrs Thatcher a few years later, and Leonard Cheshire VC, founder of the Cheshire Homes. They handed out prizes to the first three in each form in the first five years plus other prizes awarded for exceptional achievement and also for effort and improvement.

The second half of speech night was the music recital, featuring the orchestra, the choir, and the recorder group. Somehow the school's one and only music master, the volatile Mr Holt, found time under extreme time pressure to prepare and rehearse the participants so well that if there were any wrong notes they were undetectable. It was Ken Holt's annual triumph – particularly so in 1966 – when he had been absent ill for most of the previous summer term after the stresses and strains finally caught up with him. After my time, the school would finally employ another music master, Peter Rose, an old boy and son of the aforementioned Fred Rose. Speech night was of course a compulsory school attendance but there was the not inconsiderable consolation of the Friday being a school holiday, ritually proposed by the guest speaker and graciously approved by the Headmaster. There were also no lessons on the Thursday afternoon as we were marched down to King George's Hall to rehearse where we would all be sitting that night. Our proud parents sat at the back and, assuming he was not working, my father would not only attend in his best (only) suit, but also arrive in a trilby hat to complement his overcoat so that he was fit to be seen by the town's middle classes in the lobby of King George's Hall. Our teachers wore the full academic regalia of the universities from which they had graduated. Fortunately, there were no animal rights activists around at the time to protest about the amount of fur being worn.

Once we were safely socialised into the norms of the school it settled into a predictable rhythm. Unlike primary school provided that you completed your work to a reasonable standard, behaved acceptably in class, and conformed at least outwardly with school rules, the average pupil could expect to be left alone. St Mary's College cared about the boys in its charge, did not look to hack down tall poppies and it did not regard children with one non-Catholic parent as in permanent danger of the fires of hell. It did not deal in the sort of hypocrisy that characterised the nuns who would happily justify the random humiliations they inflicted as being part of the divinely ordained suffering we were placed on earth to endure. The Marist Fathers could be harsh and, on occasion, excessive with their punishments, but they did not pretend that anyone but them was inflicting retribution or that anything other than earthly behaviour merited it. I cannot imagine any of the priests who taught me spouting the kind of drivel that the Headmistress of my primary school uttered to my mother when she was once daft enough to confide that she was broke. "The lord will provide," was the response. Quite how the nuns squared that with the annual St Joseph's Penny collection in support of those for whom the lord clearly never provided was not explained.

It was made clear to us from day one and reinforced regularly that we had entered an academic environment. The only content I can recall from any guest speaker's speech to the school at our annual speech night was on the subject of excellence and that it must be pursued relentlessly. Our secular education was geared to that purpose. Of course, not everyone can achieve excellence, but it was regarded as almost sinful not to achieve our potential. As a teenager, I went through a phase of rejecting these values but, in adult life, I cannot overestimate how much that has been part of my psyche. To this day, at the age of sixty-three and more than five years after retiring from the prison service, achieving my potential is still a driving force, the one that impels me to write.

In the summer of 1994, when staying with my parents for a few days prior to moving house yet again with the job I took a long walk and found myself in the village of Pleasington on the edge of Blackburn. My schooldays were the last thing on my mind when an elderly gentleman nodded to me from behind his garden gate. I realised immediately that it was Fred Rose. Of course he did not recognise me some twenty-three years after I had left school. I have to confess that I did not reintroduce myself. Part of me was not vain enough to think that he should remember one of the school's less distinguished alumni, but another part of me did not believe that I had done enough to gain his approval. So, the moment passed in a flash. Three years later, when I passed the Governor 1V Assessment Centre with flying colours and was appointed Head of Operations at Woodhill high security prison, might have been a better time but of course it did not happen. Indeed, I have never walked through Pleasington since. Looking back, I regret very much not engaging with an old schoolmaster who had so much influence on me, not least because there would never have been another opportunity. I'm sure, looking back, he would have been delighted to meet the grown man whose promise he had first nurtured thirty years earlier. However, this is not a sad story. Rather it is a reminder how a Grammar School education delivered by dedicated teachers committed to the highest standards could impact indelibly on working-class boys blessed with a degree of academic ability for the rest of their lives.

The English curriculum will be very familiar to fellow Grammar School old boys and girls. I'm not one of those people who can memorise poetry, but I did enjoy reading John Masefield's epic poems, *The Dauber* and *Reynard the Fox*. Probably my favourite poem was Samuel Taylor Coleridge's, *Rime* (correctly spelt) *of the Ancient Mariner*. Fred Rose also introduced us to the haunting *Elegy written in a Country Churchyard* by Thomas Gray in 1750, which I immediately called to mind at my mother's funeral in a peaceful Oxfordshire village in the summer of 2013. As one would expect, we studied Shakespeare and read a *Midsummer Night's Dream*, Julius Caesar, Henry IV Parts One and Two, and Henry V. For some obscure reason my form did not study a Shakespeare play for GCE "O" Level English Literature. Rather than study *Macbeth*, like some of my friends, we studied Robert Bolt's *A Man for All Seasons*. My guess is that had Fred Rose remained our teacher then the choice would have been *Macbeth*, but the Head of English had other ideas. Of course we were not consulted. No one pretended that schools were democracies in 1968. Something similar happened with the choice of novel for our "O" level English Literature.

Our new teacher, Mr Wood, handed out copies of Gavin Maxwell's *Ring of Bright Water*, a novel about the author's life with otters on a remote Scottish island, when I think most of us expected Dickens, Jane Austen or one of the Bronte sisters. I can't say I was energised by otters and felt this was Black Beauty for older youngsters. Nothing will convince me that *Ring of Bright Water* is great literature. Our "O" level poet was Keats, which also leaves me cold. Of the books we read in the school, I have to go back to my very first year for my favourite when we read Winston Churchill's *My Early Life*, which I found utterly compelling. Churchill died in January 1965 during my first year at Grammar School. The funeral was the dignified state occasion that our country does so brilliantly. I need hardly say that his passing was not greeted by the appalling display of emotional incontinence that greeted the death of the massively less substantial figure of Princess Diana thirty-two years later, which Fred Rose lived long enough to see.

My favourite subject was History and for five years I was taught by another formidable figure and war veteran, Mr Cowman, who was also my form master for the last three of those years. His nickname was Rawhide, no doubt derived from the TV series of that name about the lives of cattle drovers in the American West of the 1880s, which ran from 1959 to 1966, that first made the name of the young Clint Eastwood. Whether he was related to the proprietors of the celebrated Cowman's sausage shop in Clitheroe where he lived I do not know, but it is an unusual surname that I have not come across otherwise. Mr Cowman had a compelling delivery style and brought medieval history to life. I tried to model my style on him in my own short teaching career, though nowhere near as successfully. He also had a line in withering put downs that could reduce any boy daft enough to take him on to jelly. Although I never saw him use corporal punishment, it did not pay to cross him. As our form master he was stiflingly strict. Nevertheless, I wish he had taught me in the sixth form as I would not have dared take the liberties that I increasingly took.

No former pupil of St Mary's College between the mid-thirties and mid-seventies writing about his time in the school could possibly leave out the legendary Eddie Bell and expect his work to be taken seriously by fellow old boys. Mr Bell, Head of Classics, taught at the school from the mid-thirties until his retirement in 1974. He was a classmate of Fred Rose when they commenced their Grammar School education together at Preston Catholic College back in 1925, coincidentally the same year as St Mary's College was founded. At this time Preston Catholic College was an established school of some repute having been founded by the Jesuits in 1865. By the time I arrived at the school, Eddie Bell was the other master, along with Joe Stewart, who flanked the Headmaster at morning assembly. By contrast Fred Rose had joined the staff as recently as 1960. Mr Bell taught me for three years of Latin, and then one year of Greek after Joe Smith's departure. I can report that I passed my "O" level in both with something to spare. He was another fine teacher, strict but kindly, the St Mary's equivalent of Mr Chips. Mr Bell was an institution more than he was a disciplinarian and therefore it was a mark of moral turpitude to upset him. The fact that he was a lifelong Blackburn Rovers supporter also endeared him to me. I was even entrusted with the job of collecting his ticket for a fifth round FA cup tie in 1969, probably because I was the boy who lived nearest to the ground.

The best story about Eddie Bell is concerns his retirement presentation. Eddie Bell was an old-fashioned bachelor schoolmaster who did not even own a black and white television. His leaving present was a brand new colour TV. Mr Bell duly addressed the whole school and the entire staff, and after saying thank you, proceeded to deliver a stern lecture about the evils of television! Clearly he was convinced that not only ITV was a threat to the virtues of study and learning, but also that Lord Reith had failed in his historic mission for the BBC to be a source of education and information. History does not record how much television he watched in retirement (if any), which sadly was short as he died just six years later.

I entered the sixth form (years 12 and 13) in 1969. Until that year the minimum qualification for a place in the sixth form was five GCE "O" level passes, which effectively excluded around a third of the intake and the vast majority of boys who had been banished to the secondary modern at the age of eleven. The vast majority of secondary modern pupils left school at fifteen, without any formal qualifications but since their alumni had been graciously permitted to take GCEs from the early 1950s onwards the numbers staying on to sixteen had gradually increased. In 1967 the first examinations in the Certificate for Secondary Education were sat in the nation's secondary modern schools. The CSE was introduced in readiness for the proposed raising of the school leaving age to sixteen, which was due to take effect in 1970, although in the end it was put back to 1972. A grade one was deemed the equivalent of an "O" level pass. Thus in 1969 St Mary's College took its first step towards the comprehensive sixth form as a small number of boys from St Thomas Aquinas in Darwen, Holy Family in Accrington, and Blackburn's two Catholic secondary modern schools passed through gates that had seemingly been closed to them five years earlier. Equally amongst my own intake boys whose "O" level results would previously have seen them join the labour force returned in the sixth form to try and improve their qualifications. Now, not everyone studied three GCE "A" levels plus General Studies, rather there were combinations of "O" and "A" levels.

Superficially, nothing changed. We still wore school uniform, albeit with a different blazer and tie, were still addressed by surname, and prefects were appointed from our ranks. There was still a distinct hierarchy in the sixth form with the Oxbridge candidates at the top, those aiming at lesser universities just below, and after that those looking for polytechnic or teacher training places the latter of which in those days did not necessarily require candidates to actually pass two "A" Levels. At the bottom of the heap were those intending simply to leave school and go out to work. For this last category, careers guidance was none-existent. We were still very much connected to the rest of the school, despite enjoying the three distinct privileges of being allowed out of school at lunch time, no longer being subject to corporal punishment, and believe it not modern reader, the right to smoke in our own separate common room. My own sixth form academic achievements were modest. I added precisely one "A" level in British Constitution and "O" level General Studies to the six "O" levels I had garnered in 1969. I even managed to flunk "A" level History and didn't even bother to turn up for Economics having scored only six per cent in the mock examination. I got a grade "C" in History in my own time three years later. For reasons of immaturity, the desire for instant gratification, and simply not being ready for the challenge of higher education, I left school as a disappointment to my teachers. I was one that got away, but my time would come. Looking back, we probably had too much freedom, but I can hardly use it as an excuse when many others coped perfectly well.

St Mary's College was a rather more working-class institution than the average Grammar School, and significantly more working class than the venerable establishment on the other side of Corporation Park, Queen Elizabeth's Grammar School for boys, founded in 1509, known to all as QEGS. Clues as to this state of affairs can be found in the surnames of many of my schoolfellows. Traditional Irish surnames such as Riley, Flynn, Mullen, Kelly, Kennedy, Rafferty, O'Brien, McLaughlin, and of course Murphy were dotted around the form registers. Even though Irish migration had begun more than a hundred years earlier social mobility amongst Irish Catholics had been limited, certainly in comparison to Jews and later to Sikhs. With the novelty of full employment and the advent of free Grammar School and University education, this could finally be addressed. Additionally, we had a significant number of boys who were sons of Polish and Ukrainian ex-servicemen whose fathers had remained in England after the end of World War Two. Poland is a Catholic country and as is typical of first generation immigrants found themselves disproportionately working in manual jobs. Gorak and Gedzielewski, two of my most able classmates, were the sons of mill hands. Janusz Gedzielewski, a graduate of Warwick University has held the post of bursar of our old school for many years. Jan Gorak is also a graduate of Warwick University, though by a rather more circuitous route. After repeated clashes with our form master about his attitude, Gorak left school four months before the "O" level examinations. The brickyard was not good for his asthma and he duly took his "O" and "A" levels at the local tech before going up to Warwick just a year after Gedzielewski. Jan Gorak was a very popular classmate and provided more than one amusing moment. Having been made to kneel at the front of the class, he complained that the punishment was bad for his genital organs! Joe Smith promptly sent him back to his seat and didn't use the punishment again. Jan and I finally lost touch in the mid-eighties and his global wanderings finally took him to Denver, Colorado, where he is now Professor of English Literature and a distinguished author. I found an interview with him online and noted with interest that there was no mention whatsoever of his old school. It may be an omission of no significance, but our shared perception at the time was that he was driven out over fairly minor instances of adolescent rebellion. Thankfully, Gorak's talent was not wasted as a consequence of the school's uncompromising approach to the worst ravages of adolescence.

One of the contemporary criticisms of Grammar Schools was that free places were too frequently wasted on working-class children, the dropout rate was unacceptable and the staying on rate after the age sixteen was poor. It is fair to say that for some parents' Grammar School education for their children was simply a means to an end, a white collar job at the age of sixteen, thus delaying contributing to the family exchequer by only one year. This was particularly the case for girls. The staying on rate was to some extent addressed by the provision of student grants for higher education but the pre-"O" level drop-out rate was very much a product of the grammar schools imposing a culture that was often at odds with that in working-class homes. Uneducated parents with sons and daughters at Grammar Schools had to cope with children who brought home Latin and Greek passages to translate, poems to be learned, and a broader, more considered view of the social issues that they were encouraged to debate in the classroom, such as race relations. Bluntly, working-class parents needed an absolute blind faith in the education their children were receiving if they were not to send subliminal or just plain overt messages that their children were getting above themselves. I got the messages very clearly. Grammar School could also be expensive. Fortunately, when my youngest sister went to Grammar School, my parents could afford musical instruments. I was not musical but would have loved to gone on one of the school trips to Italy that were organised every summer, but it was absolutely out of the question.

Working-class Grammar School children were therefore often forced to ride three horses at once; at home, at school, and in their own neighbourhood, and it could be a very challenging balancing act. Fitting in is what gives children security, and if I have a significant criticism of Grammar School education it is that few allowances were made for the cultural inheritance of working-class children. It was all or nothing, assimilation not integration, classical music good, Rolling Stones bad. Girls' Grammar Schools were particularly uncompromising. Young ladies did not eat chips in the street, ride pillion on motor cycles and speak in a broad Lancashire accent, even when at home. However, because St Mary's College educated far more working-class boys than comparable non-Catholic Direct Grant Grammar Schools and schools in more affluent areas, we were not affected to the same extent by cultural dissonance. We had some ownership of our school. The fact that Fred Rose wrote dialect poetry was an important connection with our culture. Nevertheless, it was hard not to notice that your secondary modern counterparts in the next street were earning while you remained a schoolboy. Your contemporaries could afford records and clothes. It could be very hard to grasp at the age of fifteen that your education was an investment that would eventually result in a golden future, which for my generation was largely delivered.

It was also argued that that free Grammar School

education was a subsidy to the middle classes who previously paid for their offspring's education. As an argument, it is shot through with holes. There is no good reason why any parent should have to pay for their child's schooling, unless they choose to. Secondly, as a consequence of war and reconstruction, the middle classes paid much higher taxes and as such it was not unreasonable for them to expect something back. I would rather that the middle classes paid higher taxes and got back free secondary education than them pay lower taxes and be able to employ domestic servants as they did before the War. There is nothing fair about penalising those who value education.

For most of the UK (Northern Ireland did not abolish selection until 2008) the era of the free Grammar School lasted, at most, thirty years. The Labour party and the educational establishment felt that the existence of Grammar Schools was socially divisive, elitist, and caused gross distortions in funding within secondary education. There was mounting concern about the finality of the 11 plus, which as an argument was very useful to those opposed to the very principle of selection on academic merit. Hugh Gaitskell, then Labour opposition leader, speaking in 1958 called for all children to have access to Grammar School education. His protégé, Tony Crosland, vowed "to close every fucking grammar school in the land". Crosland became Education Secretary in Harold Wilson's Labour government and issue circular 10/65, which required local authorities to submit plans for comprehensive secondary schools, which would educate children of all abilities in the same institution. Harold Wilson wished to preserve Grammar School education within the comprehensive school, but the educational establishment would see to it that all too frequently all ability schools lead to mixed ability teaching. For the comprehensive zealots, internal selection was just as much the enemy as external selection by competitive examination. By 1970, when the Tories returned to power and Mrs Thatcher became Education Secretary, the vast majority had either gone comprehensive or had submitted plans. Although Mrs Thatcher made going comprehensive optional, in most cases the planning process was too far gone to be undone. As a result, we had the supreme irony of Mrs Thatcher signing off more local authority comprehensive schemes than the previous Labour government.

My school was not affected by 10/65. Like 178 other schools, St Mary's College was partly funded by what was called the Direct Grant, which came directly from government, as opposed to being wholly funded by the local authority. Direct grant schools received the rest of their income from local authorities in return for free places and from fees for which they could charge for up to twenty-five per cent of their pupils. Some direct grant schools were independently wealthy with significant endowments from benefactors. Although we debated comprehensive schooling in the classroom, and in those days I was very much in favour, what was happening in the state sector had no impact on St Mary's College. This was because not until 1975, when Labour returned to power, did the government announce its plans to phase out the direct grant. Thus, the last intake of eleven year olds entered the remaining 174 direct grant Grammar Schools in 1975. From hence these schools had the choice of joining the state sector or joining the independent sector. Sadly, only forty-six of these schools including mine, all but two of which were Roman Catholic foundations, entered the state sector. The remainder were lost to working-class children. Like most Roman Catholic foundations, my old school was disproportionately reliant on local authorities funding free places and was in no position to opt for independence. There were simply not enough well off Roman Catholics to successfully finance a move to the independent sector. The Roman Catholic hierarchy took the practical view and made their accommodation with the state, but it is fair to say that they were also conscious that their responsibility to their flock could not be discharged if the church's presence in free secondary education was significantly reduced as a consequence of reluctance to change. My old school became a sixth form college, which it remains to this day. Across park, QEGS joined the independent sector. In the state sector, Grammar Schools somehow survived in Kent and a few other random places despite the best efforts of the Labour government and have been left largely undisturbed ever since, although only since 2010 have they been allowed to expand provision.

I still support the comprehensive principle. What I do not support is the driving out of Grammar School education from under the comprehensive umbrella. The education of those fortunate enough to be academically talented, and who need stretching both for their own good and that of the country, is every bit as important as raising the achievements of those less advantaged. The loss of all but 164 of what was once an estate of 1,200 local authority Grammar Schools plus the 179 in receipt of the direct grant has produced two grim ironies; a decline in social mobility and a revival in the independent sector. At the start of the free grammar school era ten per cent of pupils were educated in the independent sector. This fell steadily to five and a half per cent as second rate public schools withered and died. Since the implementation of an almost fully comprehensive system, this has gone back up to eight per cent. This is not a healthy development.

In the summer of 1971, seven years of Grammar School education came to an end. My "A" level results were undistinguished to say the least and the prospect of joining a small band of third year sixth students to re-take examinations did not appeal. I did not want to be a nineteen-year-old schoolboy, but I did not have the qualifications for higher education. The only alternative was the world of work, of which more in Chapter Nine.

Chapter Six

The Idiot's Lantern

I sat down to write this chapter many months after I had given it the title above. Only then did I seek to discover the origin of the phrase used to describe the television. I remember my father using the phrase and also Mr Bell, legendary head of Classics at my old school. Google was not a great deal of help throwing up pages and pages of references to a 2006 episode of BBC sci-fi series, Dr Who, which carried the phrase as its title. Apparently, the writer of the episode remembered his father using the expression to describe the TV. A little more digging found an attribution to Labour Prime Minister Clement Attlee in 1950 from a Guardian archive. The Conservative leader, Winston Churchill, equally distrustful of the new medium, went further and described the BBC as a "nest of Communists". Quite what he would have made of the extraordinary bias exhibited by the BBC in the twenty-first century, one can only speculate. However, it is an urban myth that Churchill shut down the infant BBC television at the start of World War Two in September 1939 as he did not become Prime Minister until May the following year. The phrase was also used by the columnist Cassandra in the Daily Mirror in 1958 when he wrote that "the idiot's lantern was getting too big for its ugly gleam", following a BBC interview with Prime Minister Harold McMillan by a young Robin Day, which was considered ground breaking at the time for its lack of deference and willingness to ask impertinent questions. Robin Day would go on to be the grand inquisitor of slippery politicians and lead the way for such as Jeremy Paxman to follow.

Mr Bell and many like him were highly suspicious of the television, pretty much believing that young people's brains would atrophy as a consequence of gazing intently for hours on end at the box in the corner. For some politicians, there were concerns that television would be subversive and beyond their control. In 1956, during the Suez crisis the Prime Minister, Sir Anthony Eden, attempted to censor BBC coverage and ban opposition leader Hugh Gaitskell from replying to a ministerial broadcast. The BBC stood its ground, but this would not be its last encounter with politicians who thought that the BBC should be a vehicle for government propaganda. It is a tragedy that the BBC is now a conduit for the metropolitan cross-party elite who rule the country and that apart from set- piece confrontations it simply reflects the new secular religions of multiculturalism, environmentalism and the European project. Other commentators and politicians were concerned that television would have insufficient high cultural content (unlike the radio) and that its first Director General, John Reith's commitment to education, probity and the highest standards would be watered down. The Labour Party sought to demonstrate its commitment to equal cultural access for working people by opposing the establishment of a second channel, ITV, which would be funded commercially from advertising. That rather patronising approach cut no ice in parliament and ignored the validity of working-class culture. ITV duly began broadcasting in 1955, although it took until 1962 for all regional franchises to be awarded and the whole country covered. If you owned or rented a pre-1955 set, then you needed either to upgrade your television or purchase a converter in order to receive ITV.

Nevertheless, despite my reservations about manifestations of the nanny state, it has to be said that ITV did not hesitate to go down the populist route. It is true to say, as a generalisation, that the lower in the social structure a family was the more likely they were to be principally viewers of ITV. Would families who did not value education have read more books or listened to more classical music without trash TV to fill their evenings? Of course, they wouldn't do so. Looking back, ITV was swiftly colonised by American popular culture. We were saturated with cheaply bought American comedies and westerns, the latter much loved by my father. I was no fan of westerns (with the singular exception of Alias Smith and Jones), but would admit that as a child I did find some American comedies (and all the cartoons) amusing. The Beverley Hillbillies (1962–71) was a particular favourite, but I did outgrow it as I hit my teens. My mother was a particular fan of Lucille Ball. These days, I find American sitcoms embarrassing and cannot understand for the life of me why TV critics eulogise about the saccharine middle-American drivel that passes for entertainment. The only American sitcom I have ever enjoyed (for a time) as an adult was Happy Days. Initially sharp and witty with well-drawn characters, ultimately it went on far too long mining for gold in 1950's white middle-America where no teenagers smoked or drank and no one thought about sex until they were married. It was as though the ground-breaking film American Graffiti had never been made. Happy Days also spawned the gruesome spin-off, Mork and Mindy, which ran from 1978 to 1982, in which the late Robin Williams starred as an extra-terrestrial from the planet Ork. Readers of my generation may better remember My Favourite Martian screened from 1963 to 1966, which was sophisticated by comparison. However, what America lacked in quality sitcoms it more than made up for in producing perhaps the greatest stand-up comedienne of all time, the never less than lacerating and always brilliant Joan Rivers.

The earliest baby boomers will just about be able to recall life without the television. I was born in 1952 and for me the idiot's lantern has always been there. The big boost to television ownership came with the televising of the Coronation of the Queen in 1953 fronted by Richard Dimbleby, where, despite the obstruction of courtiers, the coverage was judged a great success. Those without televisions inveigled themselves into the homes of neighbours to watch what for many was a once in a lifetime experience. The longevity of the current monarch has seen to that. Television began in November 1936. When it was closed down in September 1939 there were just 20,000 licensed sets. BBC television returned to the air in June 1946 and by 1950 the number of households with television had grown to 350,000. By the time of the Coronation, around twenty-one per cent of households had combined radio and TV licences. Hereon television access grew exponentially and by the end of the decade combined licenses for the first time exceeded the number of radio only licences (these were abolished in 1971) and ten million households now had television, reaching three quarters of the population. By the early 1970s, only the eccentric, the mean, and the principled like Mr Bell did not have television. Everyone else was considering the upgrade to colour. It has taken another forty years for television ownership to fall again, albeit just slightly, as viewers who don't see any good reason to pay the BBC licence fee in the age of multi-channelled digital technology opt for programmes streamed to their laptops or alternatively use "catch up" TV, again viewed on their laptops.

My first television memory is of Watch with Mother. Neither of my parents is around to confirm things one way or another, but my best guess is that we got television in 1957 just before I started school. Again if memory serves, Watch with Mother was screened at 1.30pm, Monday to Friday, although that time slot did vary over the years. By the time I started viewing the programme there was an established batting order; Picture Book on Mondays, Andy Pandy on Tuesdays, the Flowerpot Men on Wednesdays, Rag, Tag and Bobtail on Thursdays, and finally on Friday, The Woodentops. I can remember being distinctly hacked off that starting school restricted me to watching these programmes in the holidays only. There was the small consolation of Listen With Mother (first broadcast in 1948) on the school radio in the first year of infant school, but after that we were considered either too old or too much in need of religious instruction in the second year of infants to merit the radio being turned on at a quarter to two in the afternoon. Watch with Mother actually began in 1950, although the programme name was not formally adopted until 1953 when the programme went out three days a week, and remained on air until 1974, by which time the concept was considered dated by BBC modernisers. All my siblings, therefore, also had the programme as an integral part of early childhood. Andy Pandy was actually first to hit the screen on Tuesdays in 1950. The Flowerpot Men followed on Wednesdays in 1952, and Rag, Tag and Bobtail on Thursdays the following year. Full weekday coverage was completed when Picture Book and the Woodentops joined the roster in 1955. For ten years the format was left undisturbed until new programmes joined the roster. Readers born between 1960 and 1970 will be familiar with Tales of the Riverbank, Pogles Wood, Trumpton, The Herbs and Mary, Mungo and Midge appearing under the Watch with Mother Banner. Episodes continued to be repeated in children's programme slots long after Watch with Mother disappeared from the schedules and in the late 1980s surviving episodes were released as video compilations.

My own personal favourite was The Flowerpot Men, which always ended with the man who works in the garden returning from his dinner (not lunch) and Bill and Ben being urged to return swiftly to their flowerpots by an increasingly anxious little weed, who did not want them to get caught. Shortly before the end there was always a song which began with the line: "Was it Bill or was it Ben?" which invited young viewers to call out which particular flowerpot man had committed some minor misdemeanour. Regrettably, I cannot remember whether it was Bill or Ben that had the squeaky voice, which was the best method of determining who had been a naughty boy that day. Watch with Mother was all very innocent and as small children we thought nothing of Andy Pandy climbing into the basket with Looby Loo at the end of each episode. Even the puritanical Wolverhampton schoolteacher Mary Whitehouse, Head of the National Viewers and Listeners Association, the scourge of sex on TV in the '60s and '70s noted for pouncing on even the faintest suggestion of impropriety, could find nothing wrong with that. However, during my student days, I can recall a rag week sketch when two female students who renamed themselves Randy Pandy and Looby Screw, proceeded to shut themselves in a laundry basket on stage, squealing in simulated delight. We were all very amused, not least because the clean-up TV woman had missed a trick.

The main slot for children's programmes was roughly between 5pm and 6pm on weekdays before the evening news. In the early days of television the network shutdown between 6pm and 7pm so that parents could get toddlers off to bed without missing any of the evening's adult delights. An early occupant of that slot was Muffin the Mule, which ran from 1946 to 1955, so before my time. I do, however, remember Noggin the Nog, King of the Northmen who battled his wicked uncle, Nogbad the Bad, which debuted in 1959. The two programmes provided an old friend of mine with victory in a university toilet wall graffiti competition. The joke was very simple: Question: "Is Muffin the Mule a sexual offence?" Answer: "No, but Noggin the Nog is." Clearly this also eluded Mrs Whitehouse. At the other end of the spectrum was the junior version of Criss Cross Quiz. The concept was very simple; nine boxes each containing a category arranged in three rows directly under each other. The defending champion had the advantage of going first in a bid to make a row of "X's" up, down or diagonally. To dethrone the champion the challenger had to make a row of zeros from the disadvantaged position of going second. Some games resulted in replays as the contestants blocked each other off. As a child with a thirst for knowledge and obscure facts, this was one of my favourite programmes. Nevertheless, I have to confess that I had no interest in

Blue Peter, the longest running children's programme in the world, and preferred ITV's Five o'clock Club.

I did, however, watch Crackerjack, which ran on the BBC from 1955 until 1984 (451 episodes, 303 missing). In case you have forgotten, every time one of the cast used the word "crackerjack" the audience were expected to shout "crackerjack" in return. Until I checked, I had no idea that it had lasted beyond the 1960s. Eamonn Andrews presented the show in my childhood which moved from Thursday to Friday evenings when Leslie Crowther (1964–68) took over. There were only three other presenters in the shows history, Michael Aspel (1968–74), Ed Stewart (1974–80) and Stu Francis (1980–84). Andrews and Aspel are perhaps both better known as presenters of This is Your Life. Crowther was the first presenter of Junior Choice (the revamped Children's Family Favourites) on Radio One and Two (later just Two), being succeeded by Stewart with whose name it would become synonymous. There were slapstick comedy sketches, a short play and a music spot, very important as it was one of the few opportunities to see our favourite chart acts. I couldn't tell you if the Beatles did Crackerjack, but they did do two songs on a children's programme called "Pops and Lenny". Lenny the Lion was the glove puppet of ventriloquist Terence (Terry) Hall, and was a children's TV staple between 1956 and 1963. Perhaps the most memorable feature of crackerjack was its quiz in which wrong answers were penalised with the award of a cabbage, right answers with a prize. Sadly, if the poor child dropped the prizes piling up in his arms, he/she lost the lot and went home with just the consolation prize of a crackerjack pencil.

Just to emphasise my liking for obscure facts, Blue Peter, which began in 1958 and is the longest running children's programme in the world with the same name, is almost unique in a UK series of this vintage in that there exists a virtually complete archive of the 4,000 plus episodes transmitted thanks to the programme's original editor, Biddy Baxter. Sadly, the BBC had the bad habit until well into the 1970s of recording over the tapes of programmes and losing them forever. This cultural vandalism has cost the BBC many episodes of iconic programmes such as Z Cars, Doctor Who and Top of the Pops to name but a few. Less than half of Z Cars 803 episodes survive. Only twenty complete recordings of the first 500 episodes of Top of the Pops (1964–73) survive, the earliest of those being the Boxing Day special from 1967. Only one piece of footage of the Beatles performing on TOTP survives, which is a dreadful indictment, and this is something of a fluke as it survives only as a consequence of being included in a Doctor Who episode that is itself a chance survivor. Some ninety-seven of the first 253 episodes of Doctor Who are missing from the BBC archive. Not until 1978 did the BBC desist from wiping tapes and thus deleting programmes forever. From time to time episodes of vintage shows turn up because they were retained and subsequently returned by overseas television stations which bought them, were recorded by the few fortunate enough to possess early video technology, or secretly copied by BBC staff. The BBC even managed to lose the first two series of Steptoe and Son to be recorded in colour, although mercifully there are black and white copies available. I live in the vain hope that someday episodes of Mickey Dunne (1967) starring the late Dinsdale Landen, which took its inspiration from the film "Alfie" starring Michael Caine, a huge box office success the previous year, will turn up. ITV were not necessarily any better. Not a single episode of Discs A Gogo, a pop music programme shown intermittently between 1962 and 1965, remains in the archive, although there is surviving footage from a one-off episode made in 1968.

One other obscure fact that rates a mention is that Sir Mick Jagger's late father, Basil (usually known as Joe), was not just a provincial PE teacher, but an occasional TV star in his own right. Jagger senior was seen in a number of episodes of ITV's Seeing Sport, which ran from 1956 to

1965, presenting items on rock climbing (one which featured a young Mick), canoeing and basketball. Despite its slightly inapposite title, the programme was aimed at getting children (mainly boys it has to be said) to take up sport as participants rather than spectators. Sporting luminaries such as England soccer manager Walter Winterbottom, England goalkeeper Ron Springett, England cricket captain Mike Smith, and England wicketkeeper Godfrey Evans were the kind of people children could expect to see and get coaching tips from. As I have indicated, the programme did not just concentrate on the major team sports. Seeing Sport was an earnest and serious programme of the type not normally associated with independent television's children's hour output.

ITV did have a fondness for adventure programmes, often far from historically accurate but enjoyable nevertheless. Two of the channel's earliest successes were The Adventures of Lancelot (1956–57), which I cannot remember and, rather better known, The Adventures of Robin Hood with Richard Greene in the title role. One hundred and forty-three half-hour episodes were made between 1955 and 1959 and almost unbelievably all survive and were transferred to DVD half a century after they were first made. The use of an outside production company may provide the explanation. The catchy theme song was released as a single in 1956 and reached number 14 in the charts. Not surprisingly, ITV mined the genre again and brought The Adventures of William Tell to our screens, starring Conrad Phillips in the title role, putting words to the famous overture at the beginning and end of episodes. 1950's crooner David Whitfield sang the lyrics. The first episode featured our hero and his legendary crossbow shoot through the apple perched on his son's head. Subsequent episodes would see William Tell regularly cheat death at the hands of his enemy, the corpulent Gessler, in much the same way as Robin Hood's merry men defied the Sheriff of Nottingham. Both programmes were notable also for their supporting actors, some already famous and others on their way up. The success of Robin Hood also encouraged ITV to go to the well of Richard The Lionheart's reign again with Walter Scott's fictional hero the knight of Ivanhoe, starring future James Bond, Roger Moore, in the title role, which also debuted in 1958 and ran for thirty-nine episodes. I have no memory of its theme tune. Unlike Robin Hood and William Tell, it is not yet available on DVD. Not satisfied with the bit part players, ITV could not resist bringing Richard the Lionheart to our screens with a series of his own in 1962, which like William Tell and Ivanhoe ran for thirty-nine episodes, and also cannot yet be found on DVD. Yet again, English history of the period was reduced domestically to a straight battle between the good and chivalrous King Richard and evil and treacherous younger brother Prince John, who would eventually become King. The truth of course is a good deal more complex and both men were equally capable of acts of great cruelty.

In 1970 the BBC would produce its own ten-episode mini-series of Ivanhoe, told as a continuous narrative rather than entirely separate episodes. As I recall, it was screened in the Sunday teatime slot often reserved for serious drama that was deemed suitable for a family audience. It was the slot where we saw adaptations of Oliver Twist and Jane Eyre. I mention it only for one abiding memory of how good drama, even allowing for dramatic licence, can be ruined by cack handed attempts to make a show relevant to a modern audience. During tournaments you could hear the local peasantry chanting "England", and the Norman guard chanting "Nor-man-dy" in response. Quite how football chanting worked its way into a medieval costume drama I shall never know, but I do know it left me totally unable to take the production seriously.

Another feature of children's TV has been its enduring love affair with animals. At the time of counting on Blue Peter's 50th anniversary in 2008, the programme's pets totalled eight dogs, nine cats, two tortoises and five parrots, although the incontinent elephant Lulu, a guest on a show screened in 1969, may be better remembered than all of them, other than perhaps Shep the dog. Shep featured in a spoof song, "Get Down Shep", recorded by the Barron Knights in 1978, thus immortalising John Noakes and his border collie for posterity. It can be found on you tube. The BBC flagship animal programme during my childhood was Animal Magic, which began in 1962 and remained on air until 1983 when the po-faced tendency determined that the anthropomorphic technique of introducing children to the exotic animals of Bristol Zoo was no longer appropriate. The show's presenter was Johnny Morris (1916–1939), a brilliantly gifted mimic, who played the role of Keeper Morris about his daily duties continuously for twenty-one years. Morris's voiceovers may no longer be politically correct but no one who grew up with Animal Magic can doubt his love and respect for the inhabitants of the animal kingdom and expect to be taken seriously. Johnny Morris was also the voice of the animals in Tales of the Riverbank.

ITV had actually beaten BBC to the punch with a serious zoo based programme about wild animals. Zoo Time hosted initially by renowned zoologist and all round polymath Desmond Morris (no relation to Johnny) ran from 1956 to 1968 and can be fairly described as a serious programme. Morris continued to write the scripts after he ceased to present the show, which was usually filmed at Regent's Park Zoo, but occasionally at Whipsnade in Bedfordshire. When Animal Magic joined the schedules, it was a rare example of BBC screening the more downmarket rival. Both channels shipped in children's drama series from abroad with animals as the stars. Thus in no particular order we had Champion the Wonder Horse, Lassie, Flipper, and Skippy the Bush Kangaroo. I'm sure there were others but these are the ones I remember, but not with any feeling of nostalgia. One imported series with animals in a supporting rather than starring role, Circus Boy (1956–58), featured a future pop star, child actor Micky Dolenz in the title role. Dolenz would go on to achieve fame as a member of the Monkees.

Cartoons were another dish in the staple diet of children's TV. Indeed, on ITV, cartoons were sometimes screened straight after the early evening news and therefore just outside of the children's slot, preceding regional magazine and news programmes such as Granada's People and Places covering the north-west region. The Flintstones and the Jetsons, which were half-hour cartoon sitcoms (less advert breaks), were shown just after six. That particular slot was also a favourite for American family orientated comedies such as The Beverley Hillbillies, My Favourite Martian, Just Dennis, and Mr Ed, all of which were eminently suitable for children. Mr Ed was probably the best loved. Ed the horse would only speak to his owner, Wilbur Post, who found himself in possession of the horse when he bought his suburban home next door to the cynical Roger Addison and his termagant wife who made Addison's retirement a misery. The horse, of course, was much smarter than any of them. Ed added some flavour to the familiar bland diet of affluent white-middle America. There was also a catchy theme and yes, it can be found on you tube.

Although I am a frequent carping critic about popular American cultural output, I have to say that I love Top Cat to this day. It is simply the best cartoon series ever. Top Cat was created by the two most celebrated screen cartoonists of all time, Joseph Hanna and William Barbera and there are just thirty episodes first screened in 1961–62, but still repeated to this day. *Can you name all the cats in Top Cat's gang?* For UK screening the programme was billed as Boss Cat because Top Cat already existed as a brand of cat food. Free advertising was definitely not permitted, especially on the BBC. In each episode the super smart TC, as he was known, ran rings round the hapless local beat cop, Officer Dibble, who was always exhorting TC and the gang who lived in dustbins, to clean up the alley and give up their petty schemes and rackets.

The character of Top Cat can be fairly described as the animal cartoon version of Phil Silvers' brilliant creation, Master Sergeant Ernie Bilko of the US Army motor pool. The connection is reinforced with the part of Benny the Ball being voiced by Maurice Gosfield, who played the terminally dim Private Doberman in the Phil Silvers show. For those of you who cannot remember, the other members of the gang were Fancy, Brain, Choo-Choo and Spook.

The first cartoon I remember was Popeye, which first hit the small screen in 1956 and was swiftly bought from America by ITV. Popeye the Sailor had first featured on the big screen in 1933, courtesy of Paramount Pictures. Altogether 231 episodes were made over three decades and the first DVD collection was made available in 2007. The Americans have been so much more careful in preserving their TV archives. Those of my generation will remember the classic formula of the villainous Bluto trying to steal Popeye's girlfriend, Olive Oyl, often giving him a beating in the process until Popeye happened on a can of spinach which, downed in one, gave Popeye superhuman strength swiftly putting the bad guy to flight. At the conclusion Popeye would sing: "I'm strong to the finish cos' I eats my spinach, I'm Popeye the sailor man." As a consequence, spinach sales increased dramatically In America, but nothing would have persuaded me as a child to eat the stuff. In more recent years I have relented and will eat Sag Aloo (Bombay potato with spinach) as part of a good curry. I also remember the Huckleberry Hound show again screened on ITV composed always of three separate cartoons. Huckleberry Hound was a pretty boring character as I recall and Yogi Bear was much more memorable. Yogi's adversary was Jellystone Park Ranger Smith, who sought to prevent him from stealing picnic baskets. The third cartoon featured Pixie and Dixie, two mice who always outwitted their sworn enemy, Mr Jinks, the cat who chased them with a broom shouting, "I hate meeces to pieces." The show first aired in 1958, the last episodes being made in 1961. The most popular character Yogi Bear left Huckleberry Hound after episode thirty-nine in 1960 to be replaced by Hokey Wolf. Yogi Bear got his own show in 1961 and thirty-three episodes aired during 1961–62. Supporting cartoons were Snagglepuss the mountain lion and Yakky Doodle duck. Perhaps less well remembered is the Quick Draw McGraw show screened originally from 1959 to 1962. Michael Maltese shared creators' credits with Hanna and Barbera.

If there were any decent British cartoons on TV, I cannot remember them, with the single glorious exception of Captain Pugwash which was first shown in 1957. Pugwash had actually debuted in the boy's comic, "The Eagle" in 1950 and featured in the Radio Times from 1960 to 1968. Cartoonist John Ryan adapted his creation for television and eighty-six black and white episodes were made between 1957 and 1966 and a further thirty colour episodes in 1974–75. The Britt Allcroft Company later bought the rights and a further twenty-six episodes were aired in 1998 bringing the cowardly pirate, the crew of the Black Pig and their sworn enemy Cutthroat Jake back to the screen for a new generation. For the record, the characters do not include Seaman Staines, Master Bates or Roger the cabin boy, whose name was actually Tom. Nor is pugwash Australian slang for oral sex. Pugwash's creator, John Ryan, successfully sued two newspapers in 1991 when they printed those myths as fact. Apparently, the myths emanated from student rag magazines of the 1970's. Ryan died in 2009 at the age of eighty-eight.

Children's television took its cartoons mainly from America but when it came to puppets it was British all the way, or more accurately Gerry Anderson all the way. Anderson was the creator of Supermarionation and his shows were rarely absent from the screen from the mid-1950s to the end of the 1960s. There were ten creations in all and I set myself the task of remembering them all in the correct order. I only got seven, but here is the full list: The Adventures of Twizzle (1957–59), Torchy the Battery Boy

(1960–61), Four Feather Falls (1960), Supercar (1961–62), Fireball XL5 (1962–63), Stingray (1964–65, the first to be filmed in colour), Thunderbirds (1965–66), Captain Scarlet and the Mysterons, Joe 90 (1968–69), and Secret Service (1969). I have to be honest and say that I had forgotten Joe 90 and never heard of Secret Service or the Adventures of Twizzle. The dates are those of the original run and all were screened on ITV. My own personal favourite was Fireball XL5, featuring the intrepid space explorer Captain Steve Zodiac, glamorous female Space Doctor, Venus, Professor Matthew Matic, and Robert the Robot, who guided the ship when the crew slept. Robert had the same one line every week: "On our way home." Accompanying the crew was an animal known as a lazoon. Back at base were Steve Zodiac's superior, Commander Zero, and his sidekick, Lieutenant 90. The theme tune, Fireball, sung by children's entertainer Don Spencer, reached number 32 in the British charts in 1963. Of all Anderson's creations, Thunderbirds is the one that will have meaning for the modern generation, being revived as a feature film in 2004. Gerry Anderson himself died in 2012 at the age of eighty-three.

The subject of puppets cannot be left without a mention of Pinky and Perky and Sooty. Pinky and Perky, who were puppet pigs, can fairly be described as an acquired taste. Nevertheless, they featured regularly on BBC (1957–68) before transferring to ITV for three years before the series was canned. Pinky and Perky were revived in 2008 with fifty-two episodes being produced. I think the reason I never acquired the taste was the mangling of chart hits of the day. Mike Sammes did the voices, which I'm led to believe were speeded up to twice normal speed with the backing track slowed to half-speed. Thus, children were induced to believe that this is how pigs sang. There were other puppets in the show including from 1963 The Beakles, who needless to say sang strangulated Beatles numbers. Quite how the show's producers got away with this I will never know, but then the Beatles' manager,

Brian Epstein, was never very good at protecting his leading act's copyright.

The Sooty show was much better. The original concept of Sooty and Sweep, very much based on Punch and Judy except that you could see presenter Harry Corbett, was simply the two glove puppets manipulated under the table with Corbett doing a commentary and occasionally whispering in Sooty's ear rather than providing the voices. Sooty also carried a magic wand and had a catchphrase voiced by Corbett: "Izzy wizzy, let's get busy." Indeed, Sooty did not speak at all and Sweep simply squeaked. Sooty, a yellow teddy bear with black ears and a black nose first appeared on the BBC in 1952 when Harry Corbett was the winner of a televised talent show. The Sooty show commenced on BBC in 1955. At this stage there was only the one puppet until Sweep (a dog) joined in 1957. I cannot recall Sooty without Sweep. Further characters joined the cast in the 1960s. By this time it was entertaining my younger siblings but I can remember Soo (a panda), providing Sooty with a love interest, and the Lancashire accented snake, Ramsbottom. For the uninitiated there is actually a town called Ramsbottom, which found itself transferred from Lancashire to Greater Manchester under 1970's local government reform. BBC cancelled the show in 1967 but as Harry Corbett owned his own rights he was able to strike a deal with ITV. Harry Corbett handed Sooty over to his son Matthew in 1976, but only for television shows. Corbett senior continued to take the puppet to provincial theatres right up until his sudden death in 1989. Matthew Corbett himself handed over to Richard Cadell in 1998, who eventually bought the rights in 2007. Sooty continues on children's ITV to this day. Were it not for the technicalities of name changes to the programme, it would have an undisputed claim to the title of longest running children's series usually attributed to Blue Peter.

The most iconic children's programme of all is Doctor Who. Like all good science fiction, it appealed to both children and adults (although sadly not Mary Whitehouse), and is one of those programmes that you don't necessarily drop when you put away the things of a child. Indeed, since its triumphant return in 2005 after a sixteen-year absence, it has always aired outside of traditional children's viewing times. For whatever reason, BBC bosses often treated the programme badly with a lack of investment in decent sets and special effects which are a sine qua non for science fiction series. Doctor Who ran originally from 1963 to 1989 and seemed dreadfully dated towards the end. When Doctor Who finished it seemed that the BBC had finally put an old retainer out of its misery, but not before real damage to the show's reputation had occurred. With no disrespect intended towards the actors, the programme declined and then decayed from 1981 when Tom Baker, who had played the title role for seven years, left the show. The programme should have been pulled at that point. Instead, Doctor Who continued regenerating while the programme was degenerating.

The first episode was broadcast on 23 November, 1963, less than twenty-four hours after the murder of President Kennedy. The first Doctor Who was veteran actor William Hartnell, who played the character as a clever but very grumpy old man who did not suffer fools. Doctor Who (always referred to in the TV series as The Doctor and addressed as Doctor) was in fact an alien in human form. He was an exiled Time Lord from the fictional planet Gallifrey who could not only travel through space but also back and forward in time. The concept of time travel entered popular culture via literature rather than science, which is understandably very sceptical, when H.G. Wells (1866–1946) novella "The Time Machine", was published in 1895. I can certainly remember reading it at grammar school. Externally, the spaceship looked like a police box used by police officers to phone into the station when walking the beat or indeed by members of the public needing to report a crime. A flashing light on top told the beat officer he needed to contact his station. The advent of two-way radio in the 1970s put paid to police boxes as working technology. The spaceship, known as the T.A.R.D.I.S (time and relative dimensions in space), was much larger inside. Crucially, the mechanism which allowed the T.A.R.D.I.S. to blend in with its surroundings was irreparable as so it was always the iconic police box wherever it landed. Where the T.A.R.D.I.S landed was a matter of random chance as the mechanism which set the co-ordinates was also broken, although it would be repaired in later series. Very importantly for the earthbound adventures, Time Lords were not allowed to change history where it was known.

The first ever episode which mercifully is not lost was titled "An Unearthly Child". The child was the Doctor's fifteen-year-old granddaughter Susan, who for some reason never explained, was attending school in London. The detail escapes me but somehow two of her teachers, Ian Chesterton and Barbara Wright stumbled into the T.A.R.D.I.S when attempting a pastoral visit. The Doctor does not trust the two teachers to keep his secret, takes off, and the four of them find themselves in the Stone Age. My memory is that the programme was originally screened at 5.15pm and lasted twenty-five minutes, being followed by Juke Box Jury. If we were having tea at my grandmother's home I could just get there in time walking from Ewood Park if there was a home game. The first series had four episodes, but it was the second series which established Doctor Who indelibly in popular culture. BBC had resisted what it called "bug eyed monsters"," but with nothing else in the kitty other than The Daleks, the second series was screened. With that screening Doctor Who became the most talked about programme on the television and such has been public demand for the dreaded Daleks that eighteen Dalek adventures featured in the twenty-six seasons of Doctor Who shown between 1963 and 1989. Since the programme returned in 2005, each season has contained at least one Dalek adventure. In the early years Doctor Who featured both adventures in alien worlds and

Earth's history. I suspect that this latter fitted with the BBC's mission to educate handed down from Lord Reith. The split may have also reflected the fact that of the two teachers on board, one taught Science and the other History.

The two teachers were eventually able to return to Earth via a liberated Dalek time machine. Susan had departed at the end of an earlier Dalek adventure to get married. Peter Purves, later a stalwart of Blue Peter, was the new companion. The companions have always been central to the programme. They can never outshine the Doctor but they have an indispensable role assisting the Doctor in fighting evil wherever it is found and each one brings something different to the table. Things are different in the twenty-first century reincarnation, but between 1963 and 1989 there was not even a hint of sexual frisson whatsoever between the various Doctors and the numerous female companions, and most certainly no suggestion of homosexuality when the companions had been male. Mary Whitehouse instead complained about it being too violent and scary for children. My sister was not the only child who hid behind the settee at certain moments. However, I have to confess that there was certainly sexual frisson on my part as regards one particular female companion, Jo Grant, played by Katy Manning, daughter of J.L. (Jim) Manning, a national newspaper journalist of high repute. The character of Jo Grant, a brilliant scientist although obviously not as clever as the Doctor, first appeared when the Doctor was made earthbound by the Time Lords, in reality by the tight-fisted BBC, which wanted to save money on special effects. Miss Manning wore very short skirts for the role and no doubt ensured that those who like me had watched the series as a child stayed the course as young men. She featured in seventy-seven episodes between 1971 and 1973, more than any other female character. At the age of eighteen I re-found Doctor Who and happily watched the programme with my two youngest siblings. In 1977 Miss

Manning posed nude wrapped round a Dalek for a glamour magazine called "Girl Illustrated", a publication I can honestly say I don't remember. The front page photograph, readily available on the internet, leaves virtually nothing to the imagination so one can only speculate what the centrefold was like. Only Billie Piper of the Doctor's former companions has been as publicly daring when she took the lead role in Secret Confessions of a Call Girl, which ran from 2007 to 2011. Nevertheless, despite the flesh on display, Billie Piper's poses are coy by comparison.

As a child you soon discover that there is television beyond the familiar slots. Some of it I saw simply because my parents were watching it and some of it because I was genuinely interested. Like most parents, mine were keen to censor certain adult content, which was tame by comparison to what is available now. Catch up TV and computers have virtually ensured that your twelve-year old can view programmes like Mrs Brown's Boys, The Inbetweeners, and the surely most risque comedy ever screened on television, Celebrity Juice, without parental interference. For our generation, censorship was enforced by bedtime. TV's in children's bedrooms, let alone modern gadgets, were not even a distant dream when I was being sent to bed because an edition of Z Cars, which began in 1962 when I was nine years old, was considered to have too adult a theme to be viewed by little me. There was no more question of separate television than there was of separate meals. Z Cars was ground-breaking in 1962. Dixon of Dock Green it was not. There was outcry when one of the officers beat his wife. The myth that the private lives of our policemen are irreproachable was not allowed to be shattered. Behaviour on duty was not necessarily any better. The programme made a star out of Stratford Johns, who played Detective Chief Inspector Charlie Barlow. It also spawned a hit record for Johnny Keating with the theme from Z cars peaking at Number 8 on the singles chart. To this day it is played when Everton take the field at Goodison Park. The character Of Charlie Barlow continued after Z Cars in Softly Softly and Barlow at Large. On the way, he was promoted to Detective Chief Superintendent. His no nonsense approach to criminals and general rudeness, particularly to lower ranking officers, set a template for the future still used today. Even Lynda La Plante, the creator of strong fictional female detectives Jane Tennison and Anna Travis, is not immune. Travis's boss D.C.I (eventually D.C.S) James Langton is Barlow for the twenty-first century oozing aggression, sarcasm, and excess testosterone.

The halfway house between the nostalgic Dixon of Dock Green and the gritty Z Cars was ITV's No Hiding Place, which grew out of two series that starred Raymond Francis as Detective Chief Superintendent Lockhart of the Metropolitan Police, Murder Bag and Crime Sheet. The series was screened from 1959 to 1967. No Hiding Place clocked up 236 episodes, although only twenty-five survive. From Murder Bag and Crime Sheet there is just one surviving episode. As I have said earlier, the various ITV regional franchises could be just as careless with their archives. P.C. George Dixon, eventually promoted to Sergeant, remained on screen on the BBC until 1976 running for 432 episodes from its debut in 1955. Only thirty-two episodes survive in full. Jack Warner, the actor who played Dixon was born in 1895 so was still wearing his policeman's uniform at the age of eighty! However, in the final series he hung up his handcuffs and became a civilian collator. At the start of each episode, Dixon was seen to salute the viewers and utter the greeting: "Evening all," an expression which entered popular culture. At the end of each episode, Dixon would deliver a short homily usually around the theme that crime doesn't pay, salute again, and this time say, "Goodnight all." By 1976, when Dixon of Dock Green was finally canned, another cult cop show which took testosterone to new levels, The Sweeney, had been on screen for a year; different world, indeed. Dixon of Dock Green was rarely on in our house, particularly if it clashed with a western on ITV.

My father loved his westerns. My mother referred to the genre simply as "Cowboys and Indians" and it is accurate to say that children of my generation did play Cowboys and Indians armed with cap guns that made a loud bang, but of course did no damage whatsoever. Cowboy outfits were sold in shops. In our modern politically correct era any shop selling Indian headdresses would have a crowd of unwashed anarchists demonstrating outside. In truth, it was largely the big screen that concentrated on wars between settlers and the native population. The small screen preferred the struggle to establish law and order and build a nation, and conflict was mainly between the opposing interests of settlers; crop farmers and drovers, prospectors and landowners, with disputes often settled at the point of a gun as the United States expanded both south and west from the original New England settlements. Masculine virtues such as the ability to shoot fast and straight, hold your own in a fist fight, and play poker skilfully in a saloon were heavily emphasised. Slavery was glossed over or ignored. The most popular western on British television during my childhood was Wagon Train (1957–65, 286 episodes), of which my father was a great fan. He also loved Rawhide (1959–66, 217 episodes), Cheyenne (1955–62, 108 episodes), Maverick (1957–62, 124 episodes) and Laramie (1959–63, 124 episodes) Wagon Train and Rawhide were definitely on ITV. I think the other three were also but cannot say with absolute confidence. One of the supporting actors in Rawhide was a young Clint Eastwood. The theme tune for Rawhide, sung by Frankie Laine, enjoyed a seventeen-week run in the top 30 chart peaking at number 6 in January, 1960. Rawhide was also the unoriginal nickname handed down by previous generations of boys for our form master, Mr Cowman.

The longest running western of all was Gunsmoke, which ran for twenty years (1955–75, 635 episodes), in which Marshall Matt Dillon fights to uphold the law in lawless Dodge City. The series was praised for its realism. It did not sentimentalise the frontier experience where life could be nasty, brutish and short. Second in the longevity stakes was Bonanza, a fourteen-year saga of the trials and tribulations of the Cartwright family (1959–73, 430 episodes). The distinctive theme tune was not a hit single but Lorne Greene, who played the family patriarch Ben Cartwright, had an American number one single in November 1964 with "Ringo", a song about a legendary American gunfighter, fast guns being a recurring theme in the Western genre. In the UK it peaked at number 22 in January, 1965. The vocal version of Bonanza, not used over the TV credits, was on the B side. The song was recorded earlier by Johnny Cash. The third long running Western was The Virginian (1962–71, 249 episodes) set in Wyoming at the end of the nineteenth century. The Virginian was the tough, taciturn foreman at Shiloh ranch whose name was never revealed. The most developed character in the series was that of Trampus, the top ranch hand played by Doug McClure.

There were less memorable westerns. My own recollections from my childhood stretched to Bronco Layne (1958–62, 68 episodes), Sugarfoot (1957–61, 69 episodes), The Big Valley (1965–69, 112 episodes), Lawman (1958–62, 156 episodes), and High Chapperal, (1967–71, 98 episodes). Eric Laxton watched them all with rapt attention. We children were not left out. There was the Adventures of Rin Tin Tin, which I can barely remember (1954–59, 164 episodes), Champion the Wonder Horse (1955–56, 26 episodes), Casey Jones (1957–58, 32 episodes), Hawkeye, (1957, 39 episodes), and the daddy of them all The Lone Ranger (1949–57, 221 episodes), which had begun life on radio in 1933 and had run to 2,956 audio episodes. Most of these I would have only seen on repeat runs as we did not have a TV before 1957 and, in the case of The Lone Ranger, I was not even born before that was shown on TV. Although Hawkeye was revived briefly in 1994–95, it is almost inconceivable that programmes such as Hawkeye and The Lone Ranger would be made today as they would be perceived at the very least as disrespectful to Native Americans and more likely as downright racist by our politically correct cultural guardians. In my childhood Native Americans were known simply as Indians and used expressions like: "White man speaks with forked tongue." When you stop to think about early American history and put aside for a short time the politically correct notion that this phrase is racial stereotyping, you might just come to the conclusion that there is more than a grain of truth in the observation. For the uninitiated, Rin Tin Tin was a dog and Casey Jones an engine driver on what the Americans call the railroad.

The western production line began to slow in the 1970s as the genre began to run its popular course. Nevertheless, my father's all-time favourite was made in that decade. That was Kung Fu (1972–75, 63 episodes), which chronicled the adventures of Shaolin monk Kwai Chang Caine in the American west, having fled the vengeance of the Chinese Emperor. The highlight of each episode for devotees was Caine using his martial arts skills against the bad guys who sought to do him harm. The decade also spawned the only western I do like, Alias Smith and Jones (1971–73, 50 episodes) based loosely on the film Butch Cassidy and the Sundance Kid. Joshua Smith and Thaddeus Jones are the aliases of Hannibal Heyes and Kid Curry, two outlaws who have to evade capture until the promised amnesty comes through. It contains all the familiar western clichés, most notably the gambling and the gunfights, but for me it was a rare gem. I most certainly did not like the gruesome Little House on the Prairie (1974–83, 204 regular episodes) and could not stand The Waltons (1971–81), the cloying, saccharine sweet saga of an extended family living in the depression hit Virginia mountains in the 1930s. There are no guns, no gambling, and no Indians, so I'm not sure it should even be classified as a western. It is not included in a Wikipaedia list of almost 200 western series, most of which I had never heard of and were not screened in the UK that were shown on American TV channels at some time or other. Less than fifteen per cent of the list was made after 1980.

My father's other great love was professional wrestling screened on ITV on Saturday afternoons. If he was not at work, he was guaranteed to be watching it. Professional wrestling was actually televised on ITV from 1955 to 1988. Initially shown only in autumn and winter, it became an all-year round programme with the advent of ITV's Saturday afternoon programme, World of Sport in 1964 through to that programme's cancellation in 1985. It then limped along as a standalone programme for a further three years. The peak of the sport's popularity was in the 1960s, making stars out of Jackie Pallo, Mick McManus, Big Daddy (late uncle of Huddersfield Giants Rugby League forward Eorl Crabtree), Giant Haystacks and the masked Kendo Nagasaki. A certain Jimmy Savile also wrestled professionally and participated in televised bouts. Not even the revelations in Sunday newspaper that televised bouts were all fixed could detract from wrestling's popularity at its peak. I have to say it wasn't for me. Worse still, as it did not finish until 4.50, I had to wait for the football results. Mercifully, from ten years old onwards, it wasn't too frequent an issue as I was at Ewood Park watching my beloved Blackburn Rovers, which often extended to watching reserve team games as well. When my father was out of the way I could put on the BBC, which brought results via the tele-printer from 4.40 onwards. There was that wonderful brief moment of tension as the printer began to print your team's result, which would swiftly result in elation or deflation, which the straight reading of the results on ITV could not replicate.

As I have said in Chapter Nine, there was very little live football on TV when I was a boy. Consequently everything stopped for the FA Cup Final, which was screened by both ITV and BBC. No other matches were played on that day. The FA Cup Final, which was played traditionally on the first Saturday in May – except for 1963 when it was put back three weeks because of disruption caused to the football season by the exceptionally hard winter – stopped the nation. No small boys were seen outside until the final whistle blew and then, miraculously, they would emerge on makeshift football pitches up and down the land to try and replicate what they had seen that afternoon. At least from 1964 onwards there were recorded highlights of one game on BBC and from 1965 on ITV. Highlights packages grew slowly. In 1969 we got a second game, a regional televised fixture on Match of the Day. ITV would network short highlights of televised games in other regions to supplement the main game in your area, but wall-to-wall coverage of cameras at every game had to wait until the Premier League era.

I would have been about thirteen before being permitted to stay up and watch the fledgling Match of the Day, but fortunately there was an ITV equivalent on a Sunday afternoon, which fortuitously had usually finished by the time my father got home from the pub and commandeered the TV for some old war film (there were lots of these both British and American) or western. The first real extravaganza of live football came when England both hosted and won the World Cup for the only time in 1966. We were on a family holiday in a chalet in Cleethorpes that year and our fortnight away encompassed the whole tournament except for the opening group games, and most importantly, the final. There were no motorways between Blackburn and the coast of Lincolnshire, the M62 being very much in the construction stage. Mercifully, we arrived home with twenty minutes to spare before kick-off and join the other thirty million people watching the game on BBC or ITV, which remains to this day the record audience for a UK television programme. Midweek football also became a regular feature during the season as highlights from the three European tournaments, the League Cup, and midweek FA cup replays were shown on Wednesday nights. Full live coverage, however, remained rare and very special.

Other sports were less coy. Both BBC and ITV covered the Wimbledon fortnight but without encroachment into evening schedules. My dislike of tennis stems from its annual clash with the Lords test match in which cricket coverage always came off the worst. Horse Racing was the first mainstay of BBC's flagship Saturday afternoon programme, Grandstand. The Grand National took fourth place in the viewing ratings for 1968. The National had first been televised live in 1960. Presumably, the audience were contemplating the possibility of the previous year's pile up, which allowed 100-1 shot Foinavon to navigate the carnage way in front of him and go on to win. It is hard to credit that horse racing is no longer shown by our national broadcaster. Neglect, complacency and, in the twenty-first century, a disastrous policy of cherry picking led the sport to conclude not unreasonably that its future lay on other channels.

Test match cricket was first shown as early as 1938 and became a regular feature after World War Two. When I began watching test cricket in the 1960s, all day coverage was still inconceivable. Restrictions on permitted broadcasting hours were part of the problem. Although play began at 11.30am coverage often did not begin until 12.30pm, except on Saturday. Lunch was taken at 1.30pm (forty minutes), but coverage often did not resume until 3.00pm and not even then during the Wimbledon fortnight. Cricket lovers would have to endure the test card on weekdays (for some reason Wimbledon was excused the test card) and competition from other sports on Saturdays. Tea was taken at 4.10pm and coverage did not resume until a few minutes before close of play at 6.30. There was no question of disrupting early evening schedules. These problems were only solved by the gradual easing of the broadcasting hours' restrictions and the use of BBC2, the high-brow channel which began broadcasting in 1964, to supplement coverage. It took until 1971 for a night time highlights programme to be available to cricket lovers who had been at work all day. As far as cricket's county championship was concerned, the only coverage we saw came on ITV's northern franchises for the annual Roses clashes between Lancashire and Yorkshire over the spring and August Bank Holiday weekends. The advent of one day knock out cricket in 1963 saw the game get greater coverage and enjoy its own cup final on the first Saturday in September. In 1969, when the John Player Sunday League was launched, an entire game was shown in its entirety on BBC2. Test cricket was not played on a Sunday in England until 1981 and did not become the norm for another decade after that.

I should not complain too much about tennis or restrictions on broadcasting hours because we did spend an enormous amount of time outside in the summer holidays. However, TV coverage from Lords or The Oval was very welcome if it was raining in Lancashire and the one hour's pre-lunch coverage clashed nicely with our meal time. So, I was privileged to see the English top cricketers of the decade, Ted Dexter, Colin Cowdrey, Ken Barrington, Tom Graveney, Fred Trueman, and Brian Statham in glorious black and white. The West Indies were terrific to watch in an era where scoring rates were lower than they are today. Gary Sobers was without doubt the top cricketer of the 1960s, but my personal favourite was his colleague and successor as captain, Rohan Kanhai. I was also lucky enough to see part of a televised game between an Old England XI and the Lords Taverners, which I'm guessing occurred in 1964. This was the only occasion that I got to see former England legends Len Hutton, Cyril Washbrook and Denis Compton bat, as they had been retired for several years. I can recall more recently retired Australian captain Richie Benaud being equipped with a microphone as he bowled, and being invited by the commentary box to bowl a delivery that would induce Compton to play the sweep shot he had popularised. It was only a friendly but technologically this was very radical. My apologies if I have missed your favourite cricketer.

Other sports that received plenty of live coverage in the 1960s were athletics, boxing, motor racing, motor cycle scrambling, and both codes of rugby. Henry Cooper's world title fight with reigning champion Mohammed Ali attracted not only 46,000 people into the Arsenal football ground where it was staged, but also one of the biggest television audiences of the year for the live broadcast. Athletics was a Saturday afternoon staple in the summer and motor cycle scrambling in the winter. Motorcycle scrambling took place over muddy terrain in the depths of winter and the contests for the various classes were short enough to be screened in bite sized chunks that interlocked with other sporting events being covered. It was on screen from the mid-fifties to the mid-seventies and the legendary motor racing commentator Murray Walker commentated on the sport from the beginning. The five nations (not six in those days) Rugby tournament was televised by BBC over successive Saturdays in January and February and the live second half of a Rugby League fixture was a staple before the football results sequence. The Rugby League Challenge Cup Final was screened live on the BBC the Saturday after the FA Cup final. These days I am a season ticket holder at Huddersfield Giants, but I can't say that I had any affinity for the game in the 1960s. Blackburn was not a Rugby League town and it was not a sport we played. Looking back Eddie Waring's commentary did the sport no favours. He was the voice of Rugby League right from the first live broadcast in 1948 through to his long overdue retirement in 1981. It's a harsh judgement, but his exaggerated accent and comical voice simply reinforced the image of the north as an alien land of whippets, flat caps and racing pigeons. It's only an opinion, but any chance of Rugby League breaking through as a national sport, as opposed to a regional one that emerged from its cocoon once a year at Wembley, was set back further with every year that Waring remained behind the microphone.

As well as sport, I loved quizzes, pop music programmes and British comedies. The adult version of a

Criss-Cross Quiz was a particular favourite as was Television Top of the Form, where nothing pleased me more than outscoring my fellow Grammar School boys around the country. Double Your Money and Take Your Pick were more vehicles for their respective hosts, the priapic Hughie Green and Michael Miles, than they were serious programmes. Nevertheless, Double Your Money offered the opportunity to win up to £1,000 on what was called the treasure trail, more than two years' wages even for a skilled working man in the mid-fifties. The top prize was rarely won, but one of the winners was future England world cup winner Bobby (now Sir Bobby) Charlton in 1959. The maximum wage for a professional footballer at the time was twenty pounds per week, so this was a serious windfall for the young Charlton. Take Your Pick had Miles bidding for the numbered box selected by the contestant who could either take the money or open the box. One of the ten boxes contained a star prize and there were three booby prizes lurking as well as other prizes well worth having. Only one box contained a cash prize, the fifty-pound treasure chest so obviously Michael Miles' maximum offer was always less than that figure. There was also box 13, activated when a contestant picked the regular box which contained its key. The programme began with the "yes-no" interlude in which contestants had to survive a minute's worth of questions without using those words or indeed nodding your head. It's much more difficult than you think. Both shows, originally broadcast on Radio Luxembourg, screened from 1955 to 1968, and apart from their last year were always in the top twenty most viewed shows. Take Your Pick was revived between 1992 and 1998 with Des O'Connor presiding. Other quiz shows I can remember were Concentration (1959–60, revived 1988–90 and Take a Letter (1962–64) hosted by legendary game show host Bob Holness, best known as the host of Blockbusters (1983–94).

Pop music shows are dealt with in Chapter Five – Listen to the Band, so to avoid duplication I shall move on.

My earliest memories of comedy programmes are the American shows mentioned earlier in the chapter. Probably the first British comedy made specifically for the small screen I can remember featured Harry Worth. I genuinely have no memory of Tony Hancock and my parents did not watch The Army Game (1957–61, the theme tune of which reached number five in the pop charts in 1958) or its spinoff, Bootsie and Snudge (1960–63). Harry Worth is memorable not for the gentle bumbling comedy of the hapless Harry, but for the optical illusion shown over the opening credits in which Harry raises an arm and a leg simultaneously, and because of the angling of the mirror to the camera it appears that levitation has occurred with both arms and legs off the ground. Nevertheless, Harry Worth's brand of comedy was rarely off the screen between 1960 and 1974, and there was one final series starring Harry as late as 1980. He died in 1989.

Both co-stars of my all-time favourite, Steptoe and Son, are also long dead. The title roles were played by Wilfred Brambell and Harry H. Corbett who found it necessary to adopt the "H" so as not to be confused with the aforementioned Harry Corbett of Sooty fame. Steptoe and Son, the saga of a retired rag and bone man Albert Steptoe, and his thirty something son Harold, who still lives with his father and runs the family business via a horse and cart, spanned the period 1962–74 (57 episodes), although there was a five-year gap between 1965 and 1970 and no series was screened in 1971. There were also two separate feature films made in 1972 and 1973. The series made a star of Shakespearian actor Corbett, but it was also the role he could never escape, just like his character could never escape his domineering and manipulative father. Steptoe and Son was not gentle comedy set in the suburbs. Albert and Harold Steptoe were not only working class, they were poor, they were disreputable (Albert was illegitimate), and they lived in squalor. Class was certainly a theme, but Harold's social mobility was blocked not just by his father and his origins, but by his own delusions of grandeur.

Albert Steptoe regarded his son with contempt, and his son regarded his father with loathing. Happy families this was not, but it was hilariously funny. The phrase "you dirty old man" entered the lexicon of comedy catchphrases. Steptoe and Son has worn well. Sadly, its co-stars did not. Harry H. Corbett died in 1982 at a mere fifty-seven years of age, his once formidable classical acting credibility eroded. Wilfred Brambell died three years later of cancer at the age of seventy-two. Sadly, Brambell is another celebrity on the receiving end of allegations of historic sex offences, in his case against young boys, some three decades after his death.

The other memorable comedy of my youth is Till Death Us Do Part (1965–75, but with a four-year gap between 1968 and 1972 apart from one special, fifty-four episodes of which twenty-three are missing from the archives). There were also two feature films. Like Wilfred Brambell, Warren Mitchell (1927–2015) played a character around fifteen years older than himself. This character was Alf Garnett, cockney, dockworker, and all-round bigot. The name of Alf Garnett has entered and remained in the lexicon as an adjective to describe individuals who voice racist and homophobic sentiments despite not being seen on the screen since a sequel, In Sickness and in Health, ended in 1992. Like Albert Steptoe he is a working-class Tory with very little to be Conservative about, but there the similarities end. Garnett was created by Johnny Speight as an antidote to racism; a man whose language and vitriol were so outrageous, he would become a pathetic figure of fun. Alf Garnett was supposed to be a satirical character, but the problem was that this was too heavy for many viewers who preferred instead to identify with his misogyny, racism and homophobia. Black comedian Lenny Henry described his experience of the programme as one which gave his schoolfellows a new racist insult to taunt him with each week.

His television wife was Else, played by Dandy Nicholls (1907–86), his daughter Rita by Una Stubbs, and his son-in-law Mike, played by Tony Booth, father of Cherie Blaire, one of his eight daughters by five different partners. Booth's character was dubbed "randy scouse git" by Alf. His wife was that silly moo, which also entered the lexicon. BBC would not permit the more obvious insult of silly cow. The series was about more than just the worst sort of working-class prejudice, it was also about intergenerational conflict in which Alf railed against the values of the young, or as he saw it the lack of them. Within the family, Alf was an isolated figure scolded by his daughter, taunted by his son-in-law, and put in his place regularly by his long suffering spouse. Alf Garnett is a lonely figure with no redeeming features, lacking both the intelligence and the cunning of Albert Steptoe. The series attracted the wrath of Mary Whitehouse for its coarseness, but Johnny Speight trumped her brilliantly by writing a script in which Alf voiced his support and admiration for Mary Whitehouse in standing against what she saw as a tide of filth. Till Death, to give it its reduced title for the 1982 revival on ITV, was pulled after six episodes but Alf returned again in the sequel In Sickness and in Health, back on the BBC as a much reduced and less obnoxious figure as he aged, although as much as anything it was because BBC bosses would no longer accept racist and homophobic abuse as satire. I loved the programme and it was much discussed at school the next day as was Steptoe and Son, but in terms of its contribution to fighting racism I tend to the Lenny Henry view. Johnny Speight tried again in 1969 with Curry and Chips in which Spike Milligan blacked up as an Irish Pakistani called Kevin O'Grady who worked in a factory. It lasted just one series and even with the benefit of hindsight and context it is pretty obvious that Johnny Speight, a thoroughly sincere man whose motives I would never challenge, got that one wrong.

So what did the affluent worker watch on the television when there was a choice? Well he/she did indeed favour ITV, but it would be wrong to believe that American imports dominated the ratings. Amongst the many imported Westerns only Gun Law, Wagon Train and Rawhide appeared in the top twenty most viewed programmes. Wagon Train actually rated at number one in 1959. In 1955, the first year of ITV, the only BBC shows in the top twenty were Highland Fling (sorry I haven't a clue) and professional boxing. From 1956 to 1961 inclusive there were no BBC shows in the top twenty of the ratings. The list of most watched programmes includes quizzes such as Take Your Pick (number one in 1957), Dotto (number one in 1958), Double Your Money, Criss Cross Quiz, Spot the Tune and Concentration. There were comedies, the Arthur Askey Show, the Army Game, Life with the Lyons, The Larkins, and America's sole representative, the Lucy Show. The first hospital drama, Emergency Ward Ten, was immensely popular and the first soap opera as the genre is now tagged, Coronation Street, entered the ratings in 1961 and has never left them since. For its fiftieth anniversary in December 2010, ITV screened the very first episode again and I was much struck by the narrow mindedness, hypocritical piety and unquestioning social conservatism amongst virtually all the residents. It was a very accurate portrayal of northern working-class life.

ITV may have been accused of going downmarket but a trawl through the ratings reveals a genuine commitment to serious drama. Armchair Theatre, a drama anthology series of single plays was a continuous member of the TV top twenty from 1956 to 1964. It was screened much too late for me at the peak of its popularity, but the series actually ran until 1974, so I did get to see some of its offerings. Armchair Theatre was not afraid to explore contemporary themes, which could make for uncomfortable viewing for those not comfortable without having their entrenched beliefs and prejudices challenged. The early series were live bringing the edginess of the stage to the small screen. Armchair Theatre was not alone. ITV also gave us Theatre Royal, Fireside Theatre, TV Playhouse, Play of the Week and Drama 1962 and 1963. These are just ones I have identified from ratings lists.

The most represented genre in the ratings was variety. The biggest show of all was the annual Royal Variety Performance. It was the most watched television programme 1960–63 inclusive and again in 1965, four times on ITV and once on the BBC. Only Steptoe and Son at the height of its popularity broke the sequence in 1964, despite the Beatles being on the show. The Royal Variety Show topped the ratings again in 1967 and a Special Royal Performance was the most watched programme of 1968.

Variety was not just an annual event. Sunday Night at the London Palladium on ITV was a programme not to be missed in the vast majority of households. It topped the very first ratings in 1955 (ratings were conducted on the basis of the number of homes viewing rather than individuals at this stage), and its popularity only dimmed at the very end. Highlight of the first half of the programme was the game "Beat the Clock", which established the template for game show programmes such as The Generation Game and Bullseye. An array of jugglers, acrobats and ventriloquists preceded Beat the Clock and the last segment was the province of the star guest, which in the true spirit of variety could be anything from Liberace to the Rolling Stones. At the end of the show, all the artists reassembled on a revolving stage.

In the pre Top of the Pops era the value of exposure on the Palladium for singers was almost incalculable. I remember being allowed to stay up and watch Lonnie Donegan sing "My Old Man's a Dustman" in 1960 when I would have been just seven years old. The impact on sales was massive as Donegan became only the second artist after Elvis Presley to enter the NME singles chart at number one. After the Beatles appeared in October 1963, their single "She Loves You", which had fallen from the number one spot began to go back up the NME chart and eventually returned to number one. It would remain Britain's highest selling single for the next fourteen years.

The programme, known since 1966 as The London Palladium Show, ended in February 1969, although it has been revived for short runs on a number of occasions since. It's very first compare was Tommy Trinder and it made stars out of Bruce Forsyth, Norman Vaughan and Jimmy Tarbuck. Sunday Night at the London Palladium was a live show and that seemed to have excused ITV from recording it. Consequently, very little footage survives. You have to wonder if ITV and BBC ever employed anyone with an understanding that the growth of television was an event of enormous historical significance.

A look through the ratings reveals a whole host of variety shows. Try this for a list; Val Parnell's Star Time, Saturday Showtime, Saturday Spectacular, Stage One, Hippodrome and the Blackpool show. As a consequence of exposure in TV variety shows, artists broke out of music halls and radio and into TV shows named after them. There was still variety but the shows were carried by a big name. Bruce Forsyth, Max Bygraves, Harry Secombe and Dickie Henderson are obvious examples. In the mid-sixties they gave way to Tommy Cooper, Frankie Howerd, and probably the biggest names of all, Morecambe and Wise, who were a ratings fixture until Eric Morecambe's untimely death in 1984. Intriguingly their shows tended to rate better when the duo signed to the BBC rather than ITV.

The 1960s ended with the Miss World contest at number one in the ratings and the next decade began with the Benny Hill Show sitting at the top of the pile. Anyone suggesting that Miss World return to the screen would be instantly certified by BBC mandarins and sent for re-education, oxymoronically known as Diversity training, since diversity of opinion is the last thing it seeks to inculcate. The 1970 contest was actually disrupted by women's liberationists, a public foretaste of the intolerance of militant feminism. The contest has long since disappeared from mainstream schedules, but it still exists and is organised by Julia Morley, widow of Eric Morley who staged the first contest back in 1951. However, in 2014 the swimsuit round was dropped. Miss World is now so far below the radar that I doubt even militant feminists noticed. The Benny Hill show can never return as he died in 1992, but the seaside postcard brand of humour with Hill often playing the role of a dirty old man leering at scantily clad young women has been utterly trashed by politically correct thinkers (another oxymoron). Hill's defenders argue that the comic stereotypes are simply harmless fun that no one takes seriously. Perhaps they should have tried the Johnny Speight defence and claimed that Hill's Angels were satirical.

Chapter Seven

Rovers Till I Die

"Rovers till I die, I'm Rovers till I die. I know I am, I'm sure I am, I'm Rovers till I die."

All small boys – and these days some girls – who spend any of their time kicking a ball around develop an affinity with a football club, regard its players as heroes, and pretend to be them in their own games on the street or in the school yard. It's a natural part of children developing their imagination. My club was and is my home town club, Blackburn Rovers, and its players in the 1960s were my boyhood heroes. I hold to the view that you can change your job, change your wife, and even change your political affiliation, but you can never change the football club you love. It's a lifelong attachment and even if the supporter does flirt with more glamorous suitors, the encounter is always unconsummated. Those supporters who do leave their club for long periods, through disenchantment and disappointment, are liked lapsed Catholics, they don't take their faith elsewhere. It's a bit like the Hotel California, you can check out any time you like, but you can never leave.

So if you are a Blackburn Rovers fan who wasn't around in the 1960s but has a very strong view about how the club has been run in the last few years, then I invite you to join me on a trip back in time to an equally frustrating era when the Board treated supporters with contempt and systematically wrecked the club we love. No doubt some readers will be tempted to skip the next few pages if they have no particular interest in Blackburn Rovers and their neighbours, but I ask them to continue reading as I'm sure that some of what I have to say will resonate with the supporters of most clubs in the football league. I am sure that your club will, at some point in its history, have suffered egotistical owners, useless boards of directors, incompetent managers and truculent players. Your club may have suffered administration, its players locked out of the ground, and in extreme cases gone bust and dropped out of the football league. Most of all, you will know from experience that the likelihood is that your pre-season optimism that this will be your club's year will be extinguished within a few short weeks often before the autumn leaves have begun to fall. By the end of September your club is way off the pace in the chase for promotion, your club is out of the League Cup, and your best player has jumped ship in the transfer window. The manager is already making excuses, and all that is left is the hope of a decent FA Cup run culminating in a glamour tie that will earn your club some money, and the hope that instead of a relegation fight your club can reach mid-table safety and dream of next season...because for football supporters, there is always next season.

The blunt truth is that in football there are very few prizes to go round. When I was a boy in the 1960s, only the league champions played in the European Cup, forerunner of the Champions League, unless they were the holders. The competition was a straight knockout. There was a competition for cup winners in European countries and additionally something called the Inter-Cities Fairs Cup, forerunner of the UEFA Trophy for which as now qualification was by league placing. Thus, there was a maximum of five European places compared to the current seven. The Football League Cup was inaugurated in 1960–61 but not until 1966–67, when the final was first scheduled at Wembley, did the big clubs enter. Blackburn managed to blow an opportunity to win the trophy in 1961–62, somehow losing 4-3 on aggregate in a two-legged semi-final with fourth division Rochdale, who succumbed to second division Norwich in the final. The League Cup remains the poor relation to the FA Cup despite the latter's fall in prestige. There were only two promotion places available from the second and third tiers compared to the current three, and no play-offs to keep interest alive for clubs not in contention for a top two slot. There was no Football League trophy for clubs in the two lowest divisions which, like the play-offs, offer a trip to Wembley, until the mid-1980s. Finally, there were only two points for a win, which made recovering from a poor start and coming from behind to challenge that much harder.

However, although there were fewer prizes on offer, the most important prizes, the League Championship and the FA Cup were not the almost exclusive property of an elite group of clubs as they are now. The absence of SKY TV is one reason, but the other is that the maximum wage was not abolished until 1961 and it took some considerable time for wage rates between wealthier and middle ranking clubs to diverge significantly. It seems unbelievable, looking back, that boards of directors comprised of people as insignificant as gents' outfitters, master butchers, and small factory owners could lawfully restrict the earnings of some of the best known entertainers in the land. Additionally, despite the Eastham judgement in 1963 which ruled the retain and transfer system unlawful, it continued in a watered down form until the Bosman ruling of 1995 allowed footballers to leave their employer at the end of their contract without the new employer being liable to pay a transfer fee...just like an employee in any other job. Prior to the Eastham judgement, the feudal system ruled employment in professional soccer. Once a player had signed a professional contract with a club, he could be made to stay there for the rest of his career. A transfer could only take place if the employing club consented. If they did not then when a player's contract expired he had no income from football as he was not at liberty to join another club.

Occasionally players resisted, but having no income coming in, combined with the threat of being evicted from a club house, brought them into line soon enough. Quite why the 1945–51 Labour government did not rectify this I will never know. The cap on wages was lifted in 1961, but the clubs conspired to ignore the Eastham judgement. For whatever reason, the Professional Footballer's Association colluded with the clubs and accepted an arrangement whereby if a club was determined to keep a player whose contract had expired, they simply continued to pay him the same salary. As anyone who knows anything about employment law will tell you, if you accept the money then you have accepted that you are working for that employer and the terms and conditions that go with it. In practice, players could and did force transfers, and as the removal of the maximum wage did its work and opened up a gap between rich and poor, then town clubs that once held on to players of the calibre of Matthews and Finney, could no longer do so. Thus it could be argued that a feudal system made football outcomes more democratic as opposed to the modern situation whereby player freedoms have made the game far more elitist.

In the 1950s the FA Cup was won by clubs such as Blackpool, Bolton and Nottingham Forest. In the 1960s the FA Cup was won by West Bromwich Albion and West Ham United. Even in the next decade, when the balance of power was swinging decisively towards the richer clubs, three second division sides, Sunderland, Southampton and West Ham all won the FA Cup in the space of seven years. As late as 1988 the football world was stunned by the victory of Wimbledon over Liverpool in the FA Cup final of that year. The league title was harder to win, but the roll of honour in the 1950s included Portsmouth, and Wolverhampton Wanderers on no less than three occasions. Burnley won the title in 1960 and Ipswich in 1962. In the 1970s the legendary Brian Clough managed both Derby and Nottingham Forest to the league championship. Since 1978 the only small club to win the top domestic prize, since 1992–93 the FA Premiership, was Blackburn Rovers in 1994–95, in that brief period when the club's beneficiary, Jack Walker, had both the money and the vision to challenge the top sides. It couldn't last and twenty years on Jack Walker's £300 million fortune would be insignificant compared to the billions that bankroll Chelsea and Manchester City, and irrelevant when compared to the worldwide commercial income that pours into the coffers of Manchester United, such is the glamour attached to their name. The ascendancy of Blackburn Rovers was brief, but their name will always be on the trophy, and it will never be forgotten by the fans. As for the Football League Cup, it was won by two third division clubs in the 1960s, Queens Park Rangers and Swindon, but none since.

In 1990 a group of five self-styled elite clubs were encouraged by ITV to negotiate their own separate television deal. These clubs were Manchester United, Everton, Liverpool, Arsenal and Tottenham. The initiative was squashed flat by the FA and paved the way for twenty-two clubs to resign from the Football League and set up the FA Premier League in time for the 1992–93 season. Back in 1960 Lancashire had its own "big five" of town clubs, four of which had once been wealthy on the back of the cotton industry, and the fifth one, Blackpool, providing the annual holiday venue of choice for the workers of those towns. Blackburn Rovers, Burnley, Bolton Wanderers, Blackpool, and Preston North End, all of whom had illustrious histories, could and did compete with the big city clubs. Four of them, Blackburn, Burnley, Bolton and Preston were founder members of the league. Between them the five could boast five league titles and fourteen FA Cup victories among other feats. Only after World War Two did their big city neighbours in Manchester genuinely emerge as bigger clubs.

As a measure of how things have changed, Manchester United's attendances in the early '30s, at the height of the depression and a nadir in the club's fortunes, were actually very similar to those of their small town neighbours. In 1930–31 when United were relegated from the first division their average was a mere 11,685. Liverpool, who would emerge as the dominant force in the fifteen years or so before the formation of the premier league, spent eight years in the second division 1954–62, and had suffered the humiliation of losing an FA Cup tie to non-league Worcester City in 1959. In 1959–60, Burnley became league champions and Blackburn Rovers were losing finalists in the FA Cup. Both Bolton Wanderers and Blackpool had won the FA Cup in the 1950s, and Preston North End had suffered the agony of both losing in an FA Cup final and being pipped on goal average for the league title. Lancashire's town clubs were still a major force and 1960 marked the zenith of their standing in the game. In 1947–48 and from 1958–59 to 1960–61 all the big five Lancashire town clubs competed in the top division. In that post-war period until the end of the 1960–61 season Preston spent two seasons in the second division, but it was Blackburn who let the side down with ten seasons out of the top flight. Nevertheless, old timers will tell you about the exhilarating football they played in the second division, they will tell you about the goal prowess of Tommy Briggs, and they will tell you that despite being in the second tier Rovers' legends Bill Eckersley, Bryan Douglas and Ronnie Clayton were England regulars. In this spell in the second division Blackburn Rovers also reached two FA Cup semi-finals. Rovers FA Cup run in 1960 saw gates in excess of 50,000 for the tie against Liverpool and the quarter final replay against Burnley, the last occasion this happened. An attendance in excess of 40,000 was recorded for the league game against Preston in the same season. On only one occasion since, a fifth round FA cup tie against Manchester City in 1968–69, has an Ewood Park attendance exceeded 40,000.

After the Ibrox Park disaster on New Year's Day 1971, ground capacities were gradually reduced as stringent safety regulations were adopted. By the time Rovers met Manchester United in the FA Cup in 1984–85, the capacity had been reduced to less than 23,000 for exactly the same ground. Only when the stadium was fully converted to all seating in 1994–95 did the capacity rise again to 31,367.

Home average attendance figures for Lancashire's town clubs in 1959–60 make compelling reading:

Blackburn Rovers	27,299
Burnley	26,978
Bolton Wanderers	25,998
Preston North End	24,552
Blackpool	21,783

This was the last occasion that the five major Lancashire town clubs all had an average attendance exceeding 20,000. The combined average was 25,322, less than the combined average of over 29,000 at the peak of the boom in the late '40s, but impressive none the less. Translated in another way, around twenty-two per cent of the population were watching home games regularly, and in the case of Burnley, the smallest of the five towns, the figure was in excess of thirty per cent for the club's greatest ever season.

Unfortunately it did not last. In 1960–61, Preston North End was relegated and has never returned to the top flight. Their average attendance fell below 20,000, also never to return to that level. In 1963–64 it was the turn of Bolton Wanderers and in 1965–66 it was the turn of Blackburn Rovers to take the big drop. In 1966–67 Blackpool followed suit but were promoted back to the top division in 1969–70. Sadly, they survived only one season before being relegated back to the second division along with Burnley. The 1970–71 season was the last occasion that Blackpool's average attendance exceeded 20,000. In the space of just a decade, all of Lancashire's town clubs had been relegated from the top flight. In fact 1970–71 was even worse than that as Blackburn and Bolton were further relegated to the third division. Preston had already experienced one season at that level. The only good news for Lancashire's top flight town clubs was the swift return of Preston back to division two. The effect on attendances was catastrophic. Compare the 1971–72 attendances (below) with 1959–60:

Blackburn Rovers	8,256
Burnley	12,893
Bolton Wanderers	8,173
Preston North End	15,136
Blackpool	13,483

The combined average was 11,588. The five clubs together had lost almost fifty-five per cent of their support in just twelve years. Blackburn and Bolton had each lost more than two thirds. Whereas around twenty-two per cent of the population of the five towns were watching games in 1959–60, in 1971–72 this had fallen to ten per cent. Oldham Athletic, who at this point had spent just one season above the third tier since 1934–35, exceeded the attendances of both Blackburn and Bolton when they won promotion from the fourth division in 1970–71. Readers who support Oldham and Bury may feel slightly aggrieved that I have left them out of the narrative but both clubs had dropped out the top flight in the 1920s and had long ceased to be significant players. I should say in fairness that Bury have an illustrious history winning in the FA Cup in 1900 and 1903 and that Oldham Athletic would return to the top division for three years in 1991, and for the first of those years they were the only Lancashire town club in the top division, the first to play there since Bolton were relegated in 1979–80. So, Oldham can claim a brief reign as top dog. I should perhaps add at this stage that I have used traditional counties and ignored the 1974 local government reorganisation which placed Bolton, Bury, Oldham, and also Wigan in the abomination known as the metropolitan county of Greater Manchester. The nadir of fortunes came in 1985–86, when the depth of the recession and appalling performances on the pitch produced these average attendances:

Blackburn Rovers	5,826
Burnley	3,204
Bolton Wanderers	4,847
Blackpool	4,536
Preston North End	3,502

The combined average had fallen to 4,383. There was no threat whatsoever to the massively reduced capacities of these now very shabby looking grounds. The clubs had now lost over eighty per cent of the support they had back in the halcyon days of 1960. Now only one citizen in twenty-six, a little less than four per cent of the population, was attending matches compared to twenty-two per cent in 1960. In Preston that figure was actually just short of three per cent of the population. For Bolton and Preston, these were the lowest attendances in their entire history. Burnley had not seen attendances this low since the first decade of the twentieth century, and Blackburn's attendances had not fallen so low since 1891–92 when crowds were estimated to the nearest thousand rather than accurately recorded, the infant football league was still only in its fourth season and the fifty-six-hour week was the norm for working men.

Blackpool's record low average attendance since before the First World War had come in 1982–83 when it fell to 3,002 and their improved showing in 1985–86 coincided with them winning promotion from the fourth division the previous year and holding their own back at the higher level. This modest achievement was the brightest note achieved in 1985–86. Preston North End endured the worst season in their history on the field as well as off, finishing next to bottom in their first season in the basement division. Burnley finished fourteenth in division four, also their first season at that level. Bolton Wanderers finished a dismal eighteenth of twenty-four in division three. Only Blackburn Rovers, of the five, were playing in division two and it took a nerve jangling relegation escape in the last match of the season to keep them there. For Burnley and Bolton, the nadir in terms of performance came the following year. Bolton plunged to the fourth division for the first time, although they did get promotion back at the first attempt. Burnley escaped relegation to non-league football amid high drama on the last day of the season, and it would then take a further five years before they climbed out of the bottom section of the league.

So what happened to the Age of Affluence for Lancashire's town clubs at the soccer turnstiles? Why did it end much earlier than it did for northern working-class households? The late Alf Thornton, for many years Blackburn Rovers correspondent of the Lancashire Evening Telegraph, had no doubt about the villain of the piece in his weekly lament about Rovers' struggles; the abolition of the maximum wage, which to him sloped the playing field permanently against the likes of Blackburn Rovers. To Alf Thornton it was the root of all evil, rather like the abolition of national service was for those who believed that the country was going to the dogs. I cannot pretend that there wasn't more than a grain of truth in what Thornton had to say, but I do have my own take on the situation. Looking back Alf Thornton was almost the mouthpiece for the board. In fairness, if Thornton had articulated the grievances that supporters had against the board and the club's managers, Jack Marshall (1960–67) and Eddie Quigley (1967–70), then he probably would have been banned from the ground, which of course would have made his employment position untenable. After Alf Thornton's retirement, even when the Board was supposedly more enlightened and open, they were able to force the local paper to remove Thornton's successor, David Allen, from his position as Rovers correspondent. This is how things operated and Alf Thornton was confined to blaming the abolition of the maximum wage, the failure of the townspeople to support the club, and those who back in those far off days were not allowed to speak up for themselves, the players. All of this deflected attention from the woeful mismanagement of the club at boardroom level in the decade that followed the FA Cup final loss to Wolves in 1960.

As a small boy, I can recall former supporters saying they would never go again after the cup final defeat. Indeed, attendances dropped by thirty per cent in the 1960–61 campaign, the season in which the maximum wage was abolished. So yes, the club was forced to pay higher wages just when income was declining. However, it is legitimate to ask what clubs did with the money in the good times when wages were held down and the fans were streaming through the turnstiles. It certainly wasn't spent on improving facilities for supporters, although in fairness the 1960 cup campaign did pay for a cantilever cover at the Blackburn End. Nevertheless, the toilets remained disgusting. The FA Cup final was a sore point, not particularly for the defeat which was inevitable after Dave Whelan's broken leg reduced Rovers to ten men (no substitutes in those days), it was do with ticket distribution. Back in those days, finalists got only 12,000 tickets apiece, and good numbers of that restricted allocation did not find their find their way to genuine fans. Supporters were also upset by players selling on their own tickets, some of which inevitably found their way on to the black market. Unfortunately, selling on tickets in this way was a rare opportunity for players constrained by the maximum wage to make some money. The third sore point was Derek Dougan's transfer request on the eve of the cup final.

For some supporters the rot actually started in February 1960 when Roy Vernon was sold to Everton, after repeated clashes with Rovers' manager, Dally Duncan, who had replaced Johnny Carey when he took the Everton job in the autumn of 1958. There is nothing unusual about managers moving on stroppy players, but the truth is that Rovers got a poor deal when accepting a fee of £27,000 plus Eddie Thomas from Everton. Thomas was a useful footballer, but was not remotely in the class of Vernon, who won a league championship medal with Everton in 1962–63 and was even made captain by Everton's notoriously hard line manager, Harry Catterick, who replaced Carey in 1961. In five years at Everton Vernon scored 101 goals in 176 league games. By contrast Eddie Thomas's return for Blackburn was nine goals in thirty-seven league games played between February 1960 and April 1962. Whereas Thomas did not play in the FA Cup Final, it is inconceivable that Vernon would have been left out. The Blackburn board recognised Duncan's deficiencies as a man manager by sacking him after the cup final defeat, but by the then the damage was done. While it would be unfair to blame Dougan's transfer request entirely on Dally Duncan, there is a real issue as to whether he should have been selected to play at Wembley at all. In addition to the transfer request as Dougan himself later admitted, he was carrying an injury and not fit to play. Dougan's injury was not exactly a secret. Duncan had two valid reasons for leaving Dougan out, and acted on neither of them. Derek Dougan would eventually become a football icon and prove himself to be an able, intelligent and forward thinking chairman of the Professional Footballers Association, and more than a match for FA and Football League bosses. However, at this stage in his career Dougan was disruptive, immature and petulant. He remained at Ewood Park for another year until the new manager, Jack Marshall, believed he had found the man to replace him, Fred Pickering. Less frequently noted was the sale of Peter Dobing, also at the end of 1960–61 season, to Manchester City. Dobing was a model professional, but was another who challenged the authority of the small town, small-minded local businessmen who ran the club. The move to Manchester City was ill starred, but he had better fortune at Stoke, where he played out the rest of his career and won a League Cup winners medal in 1972.

Also on his way out of the club at the end of the 1960–61 campaign was future Scotland manager, Ally McLeod. Just turned thirty years old, McLeod was the club's senior professional now that goalkeeper Harry Leyland was no longer a regular in the side. In five years at the club McLeod had played in 192 of Rovers' 210 league matches, scoring a very creditable forty-seven goals as an orthodox left winger. He was Rovers' best player in the 3-0 FA Cup final defeat in 1960. There was no evidence that his powers were waning, yet the board refused to offer him any pay rise subsequent to the abolition of the maximum wage despite offering twenty-five per cent rises in basic pay to its other senior professionals. The long and short of this tawdry treatment was that McLeod returned to Scotland and Rovers' short sighted, mean spirited board left the manager, Jack Marshall, with a position that was not adequately filled until the signing of Mike Harrison in September 1962. The loss of McLeod was severely felt in the 1961-62 season. Even the club's star player, Bryan Douglas, was moved to ask for a transfer the following season. The request was denied and, mercifully, the Blackburn born England international settled down again and saw out his career at his home town club.

However, the greatest betrayal of all came in March 1964 when the board sold Fred Pickering to Everton, one of our main rivals for the league title. Other than during Kenny Dalglish's reign as manager 1991-95, the 1963-64 season remains the only occasion when Blackburn Rovers were genuine title contenders in my lifetime. The only comparable transfers since are the sales by Leeds and Newcastle of Eric Cantona and Andy Cole respectively in 1992 and 1995, both to Manchester United. *Who was Fred Pickering?* Well he was the Blackburn born captain of the 1958-59 FA Youth Cup winning side that beat a West Ham youth team that included future England world cup winning captain, Bobby Moore, and 1966 World Cup final hat-trick scorer, Geoff Hurst. Pickering played at left back but, when tried in the first team, he did not look an obvious successor to the injured Dave Whelan who himself had replaced Bill Eckersley. So, Jack Marshall experimented with Pickering at centre forward in 1960-61 where he scored seven goals in ten games. 1961-62 was rather less productive with only eleven goals in thirty-four league and cup games, but the following season, after being left out for the first five games, Pickering missed only one more competitive match, scoring twenty-eight goals in forty-three league and cup outings, cementing his place in the team. In 1963–64, before his transfer, he was ever present scoring twenty-six goals in thirty-eight league and cup games. In a three-year spell in the number nine shirt Pickering scored seventy-three goals in 125 competitive matches. It was an outstanding record that attracted the attention of England manager, Alf Ramsey, who picked him for the under-23 team, although he did not make his full debut until after joining Everton. Fred's crime was to want to be paid what he was worth, and then to let the press know about it.

What was Pickering being paid? Obviously we are reliant on his memory but there is no reason to believe that his account is untruthful or exaggerated. In an interview given to an Everton fanzine in 2012, Fred stated he was only being paid fourteen pounds per week when senior players, presumably Ron Clayton and Bryan Douglas were on twenty-five–thirty pounds per week, which sounds about right for them. After the abolition of the maximum wage in 1961, senior players (except Ally McLeod as mentioned earlier) saw their basic pay increase from twenty pounds to twenty-five, hardly riches compared with what Fulham paid Johnny Haynes, one hundred pounds per week, as soon as the wage ceiling was lifted. According to the player he asked for a small rise of five pounds per week, still well behind some of his teammates despite banging the goals in week in and week out. The response of the board was to place him on the transfer list at a British record fee. Wealthy Everton called the bluff, paid the fee reputed to be £85,000, and Pickering was on his way. The board happily sold the team's prospects down the river for the sake of a fiver a week. To them players were members of the working class who must know their place and doff their caps to local worthies whose importance to the community did not go beyond the sale meat pies or of overpriced school uniforms. These were the kind of businessmen who regarded themselves as socially superior to the likes of Fred Pickering. Fred's career was not without its disappointments at Everton, missing the 1966 FA Cup final, but he was every bit as prolific scoring seventy goals in 115 competitive appearances, including a hat trick on his debut against Nottingham Forest. He is as much an Everton legend as a Rovers legend.

The board through its mouthpiece, Alf Thornton, claimed that the club needed 20,000 plus attendances to compete in the top division. Well, in 1963–64, Rovers got those numbers through the turnstiles on a Saturday, averaging 21,543. Not until the premiership winning season of 1994–95 was that figure exceeded. The people of Blackburn supported the club in those numbers because we had a great side, a side capable of winning the league title, and if not the absolute best team Rovers have ever had, it was the most exciting I have seen in my lifetime. The first choice eleven trips off the tongue: Else, Bray, Newton, Clayton, England, McGrath, Ferguson, McEvoy, Pickering, Douglas, and Harrison. In those days there were no substitutes, no squad numbers, and the shirt numbers represented the position on the field, although increasingly teams were moving away from the old 2-3-5, or W formation as it was sometimes known, that had dominated the English game since the off-side law was changed in 1925 to formations that appeared to be more fluid and dynamic. This Rovers team scored lots of goals. In the 1962–63 season Rovers scored seventy-nine League goals in forty-two matches. In 1963–64, eighty-nine goals were scored, although only nine goals were scored in the last eight games after Pickering's departure. At Christmas, Rovers were top of the table deposing Liverpool by winning 2-1 at Anfield. On Boxing Day 1963, the day on which a record sixty-six goals were scored in ten top flight matches, Rovers won 8-2 at West Ham.

It was not the only spectacular performance that season. Blackburn defeated Tottenham Hotspur 7-2 at Ewood Park in September and in November won 4-2 away at the defending champions, Everton. Before the season unravelled, Rovers also won 5-0 at Bolton, with Pickering netting a brace. I can remember on that Boxing Day that our group of small boys, pretending to be our idols, had a transistor radio on behind the makeshift goal to enable us to keep up with game. The goals just kept going in. Sadly, the return game three days later was lost 3-1. Rovers were unchanged and West Ham made just one change, Eddie Bovington replacing future world cup winner, Martin Peters. Exactly the same line-up was on duty for West Ham when they won the FA Cup final at the end of the season. The defeat was part of an inconsistent spell where only one of the next seven league games was won and club bowed out meekly from the FA Cup at fourth division Oxford, one of the most stunning giant killing feats of the decade. Nevertheless, Rovers bounced back to trounce Bolton 5-0 and Leicester 5-2 when the board stepped in to crush our dreams. Less than a fortnight after the transfer, Pickering returned with his new club for a vital match of two genuine title contenders. Rovers lost 1-2 and the season petered out dismally with only one more victory at home to Ipswich, already doomed to relegation, on the last Saturday of the season.

The search for a replacement centre forward began immediately. For many fans that search only ended with the signing of Alan Shearer twenty-eight years later. As it happened, the answer lay under their nose in another Blackburn born boy, John Byrom. However, the club signed promising eighteen-year-old George Jones from Bury. Jones scored two goals in eight games at the end of the season and one in two games at the start of the 1964–65 season before giving way to Byrom, who did not miss another match and scored twenty-seven goals in forty-five league and cup fixtures. Byrom had broken through to the first team as a seventeen-year old in 1961–62, wearing the number 10 shirt and partnering Pickering up front. He scored eight goals in eighteen games including a "hat trick" away to West Ham on Boxing Day, the first of three career hat tricks Byrom scored for Blackburn against West Ham, and the first of six hat tricks scored by Rovers' strikers against West Ham in five seasons. In 1962–63, as in his debut season, he competed with Ian Lawther for the right to partner Pickering up front and returned eight goals in nineteen games. However, the following season the reinvention of Andy McEvoy as a goal scoring inside forward reduced Byrom to just three appearances and one goal. In 1964–65, with Byrom almost as prolific in the number 9 shirt as the departed Pickering, Rovers should have been competing for the title. At halfway they were just off the pace, but in the second half of the season won only five of the twenty-one fixtures, relegation form in anybody's language. Goals were not a problem as eighty-three in forty-two league games attests. The only other significant change in the side was at full back where the tough tackling Joyce replaced the equally tough tackling John "tank" Bray, with Newton moving over to right back to accommodate his new partner.

However, the game was changing in ways that seemed to be leaving Rovers behind; organisation and dirty play. Blackburn's rivals were looking to Italy for defensive solidity and to Brazil for fluidity. Although there was nothing new about hard men playing a hard game, the game became decidedly more dirty when Leeds United joined the first division in 1964–65. They had a great side, but their snarling physicality, blatant intimidation and crude tackling plunged the game to new depths. Other clubs fought fire with fire and unleashed their own hard men in an era when two footed tackles from behind were not considered dangerous by most referees. The FA had no coherent policy for cleaning up the game and it is only in the last fifteen years or so, with the growth of the premier league brand, that dirty play has been properly punished and dirty teams no longer reap a reward. Blackburn Rovers had two of the best defenders in the league in Keith Newton and centre half Mike England, both members of the FA youth cup winning team that Pickering had captained, yet despite the presence of such quality the club leaked seventy-nine league goals, the fourth worst in the division. Two of the three that were worse than Rovers were relegated. The club still played with traditional wing halves, Ronnie Clayton, club captain and former England skipper, and Mick McGrath, both highly regarded players. However, other clubs were innovating with formations and developing the role of the modern midfielder. Rovers' old-fashioned approach to organisation and tactics was having an adverse impact. The perception of spectators was that Rovers did not hunt as a pack but were a collection of individuals, always a problem against organised and robust opposition. The game was no longer simply about one-to-one contests between individuals in fixed opposing positions. The club's most skilled players, Bryan Douglas and Mike Ferguson were prime targets for the hard men, although it seemed to me that left winger Mike Harrison was particularly singled out for treatment. Harrison had joined from Chelsea in the autumn of 1962–63 and had also played in an FA Youth Cup final, but on the losing side when Chelsea lost to Wolverhampton Wanderers in 1958. He was blisteringly fast, had the most ferocious left foot shot, and missed only one penalty in his five years at Ewood Park. Home fans were not too sympathetic, as his tendency to hurdle challenges and avoid physical contact was perceived by some fans to show lack of moral fibre. The truth was that some full backs set out to injure him deliberately, and certainly the injuries just took the edge of his pace. At his best he was the fastest winger to play for the club in my lifetime. I think also there was a psychological issue. After all, if the board didn't value success, why should the players? It only takes the smallest loss of focus to affect results on the field. Needless to say, attendances dropped which allowed the board to claim, with their usual lack of self- awareness, that the public were not supporting the club.

At the start of the 1965–66 season the manager retained not only the support of the board but also the fans. Despite the poor end to the previous season, Jack Marshall was the man who had created the exciting team that had threatened to win the league in 1963–64. He was the man who had converted Fred Pickering from a lumbering full back to a lethal centre forward. He was the man who had reconverted reserve wing half Andy McEvoy to inside forward and found he had unleashed a penalty box predator, who for two seasons matched Jimmy Greaves almost goal for goal. Greaves remains to this day the top career goal scorer in top flight football in football league history. Marshall was the man who moved Bryan Douglas back inside from the wing to operate as playmaker. Marshall was the man who pinched Burnley born teenager Mike Ferguson from the wreckage of Accrington Stanley's demise for a mere £2,500, from under the noses of local rivals and moved him out on to the wing to take Douglas's old shirt. So, Jack Marshall had plenty of credit in the bank in the eyes of supporters who like their football to be played on traditional lines. The season was a disaster and the worst in the club's history in terms of points gained; a mere twenty from forty-two fixtures. Twelve of the last thirteen games were lost, as Rovers were relegated without a fight. Yet at the end of the season manager Jack Marshall remained in his job, and the board remained in their seats.

Two urban myths have developed about this gruesome season; that Rovers were badly disadvantaged by a polio outbreak in the town that delayed the start to the season, and that the absence of Douglas for twenty-six of the forty-two matches was the prime cause of relegation. Both these claims are rubbish. Precisely two games – one home and one away – were postponed because of public health concerns. As far as the Douglas argument is concerned, Rovers won precisely two of the sixteen games in which he played (and scored his only goals of the season) at Burnley and Nottingham Forest. Although the return of six wins from twenty-six games without him was still dismal, it was still almost twice the percentage with him. Douglas also appeared in one FA Cup tie and one League Cup tie, one drawn and one lost. Mike Ferguson, who routinely deputised for Douglas in the number 10 shirt, was the only ever-present player, which tells you just who was consistent in that awful season. Goals from McEvoy and Byrom dried up, apart from in the FA Cup. Marshall experimented with moving Mike England to centre forward, where he scored seven goals in thirteen games. For a nine-game spell England was partnered up front by a recalled George Jones, who scored nine goals. Unfortunately, it was Jones' only prolific spell and he scored only one goal in his other nine appearances. Sadly, while goals were going in at one end they were being leaked at the other. During that spell where England and Jones were paired up front three cracking home wins by margins of 4-2, 5-0, and 6-1 were more than offset by six defeats. There was no discernible strategy and as the season deteriorated the team changes became more frequent and panicky. As for the board of directors, it sat on its arse like a sphinx without a riddle. An attempt by twenty-seven-year local house-builder Derek Barnes to join the board was unceremoniously rebuffed. Mr Barnes' company, Northern Developments, specialised in building new semi-detached houses for newly affluent workers seeking to trade up from the traditional terrace.

Apart from the win at Burnley the only real joy that season came from an unexpected FA Cup run in which McEvoy and Byrom re-found their mojo. Rovers firstly knocked out Arsenal, and then West Ham. Byrom hit his third career hat trick against West Ham in the 3-3 draw at Upton Park, and his strike partner Andy McEvoy performed the same feat in the replay which Rovers won 4-1. In round five Norwich were defeated at Ewood Park also after a replay. The home replay against Norwich provided the biggest attendance of the season, 33,135. The directors' response to the cup run was put up prices twenty-five per cent for the home quarter final against Sheffield Wednesday. The response of many supporters was to boycott the game. The gate was nowhere near the hoped for full house of 52,000. The official attendance was exactly 33,000 and nearly half of those came from Sheffield whose supporters were given extra tickets after selling out their 13,000 allocation. The greed and stupidity of the Board actually ended up costing the club money when it was most needed. As for the result Rovers performed disappointingly in line with their league form rather than their cup form and lost 1-2, despite a quite brilliant equaliser from John Byrom, footage of which can be found on you tube. Once Rovers had bowed out of the FA Cup supporters became much more vociferous in calling the head of the manager and the resignation of the board. Chants of "sack Jack", "sack the board", and "fuck Forbes", a reference to Norman Forbes, a former chairman who remained on the board, a descendant of Johnny Forbes whose name was over the shop front of Blackburn's best known gents' outfitters and school uniform suppliers echoed around the ground. Johnny Forbes closed down in 1973.

The British disease is sometimes described one-dimensionally as that inflicted on the country by trade unions, which enforced over manning and rigid demarcation, went on strike went they didn't get their own way, and whose members when at work were lazy, unproductive and indulged in overlong tea breaks. The other side of the British disease often ignored is the complacency of Britain's bosses who thought their markets would be there for evermore, regarded their workers as an alien and inferior species, and were more than a match for the laziest worker with their long boozy lunches and afternoons on the golf course. Of course, not all bosses and workers were like this but the stereotype had more than enough traction in it to hamper the British economy. Companies run by this sort of boss were already in trouble in the 1970s and some had already gone to the wall before a sharp blast of Thatcherism in the early '80s finished off not just the complacent companies but many viable ones as well. In football, the decline began earlier and the historic Lancashire town clubs and their supporters were victims of complacency, class based snobbery, and a provincial outlook in a global game. They opted to manage decline by selling the family silver and blaming the customer for no longer patronising the business.

As long as there were players with a transfer value, there was no risk of going bust and as I have also said it was not just Blackburn Rovers. Starting with the sale of Jimmy McIlroy in 1963, Burnley's obnoxious and dictatorial chairman Bob Lord, who owned a chain of butcher's shops, sold star players at regular intervals and somehow got away with it until a very fine side that had emerged from the first relegation in 1971 was broken up and a second relegation in 1976 finished Burnley as a force. After Lord died in 1981, fans would discover just what a financial mess had been left behind. Once considered a visionary chairman who encouraged Burnley's famous youth policy and bankrolled the facilities in which it could prosper, Bob Lord lived on as a dinosaur that expired all too late for Burnley's good. Not that Lord's immediate successors were much better. They dispensed with promotion from within, hired John Bond as manager in 1983, and then allowed him to spend money that club hadn't got. Some years later when Bond was managing Shrewsbury and they were drawn away to Burnley in the FA Cup, Bond was advised not to attend the game such was the depth of feeling against him. I blame the clowns that employed John Bond.

Blackpool sold prize asset Alan Ball after the 1966 World Cup and were relegated the year after. The sales would continue. Blackpool's board were so far up their own class conscious backside that there was even a debate as to whether one of the club's greatest players, Jimmy Armfield, should be awarded a testimonial when he retired in 1971. In 1986, the club's board attempted to sell the ground to a supermarket chain with the intention of moving in with Blackpool Borough Rugby League Club, whose equally ramshackle ground doubled as a greyhound stadium and was refused a safety certificate the following year. Mercifully, the local council refused planning permission otherwise Blackpool may have anticipated by a decade the wanderings of another seaside club used and abused by its directors, Brighton and Hove Albion. Bolton Wanderers did sell part of their ground to a supermarket chain when a large section of the Railway embankment was sold to Normid in 1986. As a consequence, Burnden Park became the league's ugliest ground. Their long serving manager, Bill Ridding (1950–68), who later became physiotherapist at Lancashire County Cricket Club, incredibly doubled up as club secretary. Ridding was the manager who famously rejected the young Alan Ball telling him to go off and be a jockey. He also rejected Keith Newton. Ridding guided Bolton to their FA Cup win in 1958 but presided over relegation in 1964. Performances deteriorated year on year and his departure in 1968 was long overdue, even before quality players like Francis Lee and Wyn Davies were sold. The story was similar at Preston. In ten years in division two, before being relegated again in 1971, North End challenged for promotion only once, in 1963–64, the same year they lost to West Ham in the FA cup final, and a promising side was gradually broken up. The club's star player of that era, Howard Kendall, was sold to Everton. Eventually, Preston fans would have to endure an application for re-election in 1986, the last season before automatic promotion and relegation between the Conference and the Football League was introduced, the conversion of their hallowed turf to a plastic pitch, and the employment of managers such as John McGrath and John Beck, whose agricultural methods made Wimbledon's crazy gang appear almost sophisticated. As a Blackburn Rovers fan it is some comfort that boardroom stewardship improved at Blackburn early enough to avoid the ignominies heaped on our neighbours.

Returning to the narrative, eventually with thirty games gone and Rovers already needing snookers to stave off relegation, the club entered the transfer marker and purchased West Ham reserve centre forward, Martin Britt, another player who possessed an FA Youth Cup winner's medal. Britt was only twenty, a veteran of a mere twenty league appearances the first of which coincidentally was against Blackburn, and the scorer of just six goals. Just how this young man was supposed to save the club from the drop I will never know, and that is without the arthritic knee that, according to Wikipedia, West Ham declined to tell Rovers about. Britt's career at Ewood Park lasted precisely nine games without scoring a goal before the knee problem forced him to retire. Blackburn Rovers would not return to the top flight for another twenty-six years.

Jack Marshall's contract expired at the end of the season but for reasons known only to the board his services were retained on a weekly basis when he really should have been sacked, and even then it would have been overdue. The inevitable transfer of Rovers' most saleable asset, twenty-five-year old centre half Mike England, duly occurred when he moved to Tottenham for £95,000 and in very short order established himself as the best central defender in the country. However, although the transfer of England was inevitable the transfer of John Byrom to local rivals Bolton for £25,000 was not. Byrom had not sought a transfer and only moved at all because Bolton legend Nat Lofthouse, then the club's assistant trainer, personally persuaded him. Still aged only twenty-two when transferred to Bolton, his best years were in front of him. John Byrom gave Bolton ten years sterling service before returning to Blackburn in autumn 1976 when past his best. A brace against Burnley on Boxing Day 1976 was a stunning cameo reminder of the quality player that was casually elbowed out of the club into the arms of a rival more than a decade previously.

Within a couple of months of the 1966–67 season starting, the sheer folly of selling Byrom would become apparent. His replacement was Alan Gilliver, signed for £30,000 from Huddersfield, who in short order proved to be another crock like Martin Britt. On the face of it, twenty-two-year old Gilliver was a good signing. He had scored twenty-two goals in forty-five second division games for Huddersfield, a slightly better ratio than Byrom, but of course at a lower level. It became apparent once the competitive action started that Gilliver had a problem with his back and in the end he would be out of action for a year. He was never the same player and left Rovers in the summer of 1968, spending the rest of his career in the two lower divisions. Gilliver's place in soccer history is secured by the aftermath of his transfer. Not only were Huddersfield ordered to repay three-fifths of the transfer fee, the FA also determined that all players would henceforward have compulsory medicals before a transfer could be completed. In the close season Marshall also signed a new goalkeeper, John Barton, from Preston, and a driving midfield player, Barrie Hole, from Cardiff City. The playing staff was trimmed and departures on free transfers included goalkeepers Fred Else and Bobby Jones, and club stalwart Mick McGrath, my former primary school coach, who had made only one first team appearance in his last season at Ewood Park.

With Jack Marshall deciding that Rovers would now play 4-2-4, with six players that had been in the side that topped the league at Christmas 1963 still at Ewood Park, small boys like me believed that Rovers would bounce straight back. In the new formation Hole partnered Douglas in the engine room, and Ronnie Clayton moved back into a more defensive role. Five wins in the first seven games saw Rovers top of the table and we dared to dream. Then the wheels fell off. Despite the signing of England world cup squad member John Connelly from Manchester United in the teeth of opposition from two our first division neighbours, Burnley and Blackpool, only one of the next nine league games was won and that against Bury was only by virtue of a dubious last minute penalty. It was a period of utter chaos. Gilliver made his last appearance for a year in the same match. Martin Britt made his only appearance of the season and the final one of his injury wrecked career when Rovers were hammered 4-0 in the League Cup at Carlisle less than three weeks later. After seven goals in thirteen games, the manager decided he would no longer pick Andy McEvoy, who in 146 League and Cup games since being converted back to a striking role at the end of the 1962–63 season had scored ninety-five goals. McEvoy made only one further appearance for the club. At the end of that dismal run, George Jones, fed up at not being given a fair crack of the whip particularly since the injury to Gilliver, was sold back to Bury when he should have been in the first team. Somehow, Rovers managed to lose five strikers in as many months with Byrom the most grievous loss of all. In addition, centre half David Holt, who had broken into the first team towards the end of the previous season, decided to retire at the tender age of twenty-one! The supporters were bewildered as the season started to fall apart.

The response from the board was not to sack Marshall but to bring in former player Eddie Quigley as first team coach and assistant manager. Quigley had already built himself a reputation as coach at Bury and manager at Stockport. Presumably the board were minded to follow the lead of Burnley where an old school manager who just picked the best eleven was coupled with a bright young coach who would improve skills, offer tactical innovation and bring organisation on the field. Quigley's influence was felt almost immediately. Walter Joyce was moved from full back to midfield with a brief to nullify the opposition playmaker. The solution to the other problem position, centre back, the slot left open by Mike England's transfer, was found by switching Ronnie Clayton to the number 5 shirt. Under Quigley's influence Rovers now played 4-3-3 but, unlike the England international side, it was played with wingers. Defensively Rovers were much tighter but for the system to work it required a centre forward capable of scoring twenty goals a season as well as goals from elsewhere in the team. Frank Lord was brought in from Quigley's old club Stockport, but found the second division above his pay grade and scored only one goal in ten games before being sold to Chesterfield. In that season only eight goals were contributed from eight players who wore the number 9 shirt during the course of the campaign. That statistic and the chaotic period that followed the good start cost the club promotion. Rovers did get back into the race after Marshall finally resigned, probably unhappy at Quigley's increasing influence. There were of course no play-offs in those days. A vital fixture was lost to crude and physical promotion rivals Coventry on Easter Saturday, a game in which Mike Ferguson was sent off for retaliation. In the end they had too much to do and finished fourth.

The strong finish to 1966–67 encouraged a belief that 1967–68 would be better, but the events of summer filled fans with foreboding rather than optimism. First, the prolific but sadly disillusioned Andy McEvoy, a total pariah after Quigley's succession to the manager's chair despite continuing to bang in goals for the reserves who went on to win the Central League championship that season, was given a free transfer back to his native Ireland. Then the board played mind games with the fans by making it known that the club was trying to re-sign Fred Pickering, before pulling the plug on the deal. Two years later the board indulged in the same charade and Blackpool stepped in to sign him. Needless to say Pickering scored twenty goals for them in a promotion winning season. Rovers signed a goalkeeper, Adam Blacklaw from Burnley, and a centre back, John Coddington, from Huddersfield. Blacklaw was over thirty and Coddington had never played in the first division. Both these deals – and the Pickering non-deal – were representative of Rovers' reduced ambitions. The search for a centre forward continued and Quigley gave an extended run to Ben Anderson, who was converted from his normal role as a central defender. Anderson had played the last four games of the previous season in the central striking position and played there a further nine times early in the 1967–68 season. A return of five goals in thirteen games left the jury out but Eddie Quigley abandoned the experiment in favour of the returning Gilliver. Quigley also moved Clayton to his normal position, having signed a centre back, but after appearing in the first fifteen games Clayton would appear in only eight of the remaining twenty-seven. Bryan Douglas did not appear until the twelfth game of the season and only appeared six times in all. Eamonn Rogers, a promising young Irishman, soon established himself in the Douglas role. Quigley also abandoned using Joyce in the spoiling midfield position after four games and reverted to 4-2-4. The board were up to their old tricks and after only four games sold winger Mike Harrison to Plymouth, further reducing the depth of the squad and the profile of experience. The board had tried to sell Harrison to neighbours Burnley the previous season, presumably believing that the signing of Connelly gave them scope, but the deal collapsed when Burnley refused to give Harrison a signing on fee. Harrison was still only twenty-seven and his reliability from the penalty spot would be sorely missed. According to Harry Berry, one of the club's two main chroniclers, five penalties in all were missed that season, including four in succession in the league, three of them costing points. By contrast, Harrison missed only one out of thirteen in his Rovers' career.

After a good start that saw Rovers win six of their opening nine games and go top of the table, only five of the next twenty were won as Rovers gradually fell away. Four straight wins revived hopes briefly but a home defeat to QPR snuffed those out with eight games still remaining. Amidst the debris of another disappointing season, Rovers signed another centre forward, Don Martin from

Northampton. Martin had played in the first division and when joining Rovers had scored a respectable twelve goals in twenty-seven games for a club propping up the table. His first fifteen games for Rovers yielded five goals. Martin played for Rovers until 1975, and was much loved by the fans not least for his role in the third division championship winning side of 1974–75, but my own view is that he was more effective alongside a big traditional number 9 rather than leading the line himself. Fourteen goals from the number 9 shirt were still not enough and an even more telling statistic was that the club's top league goal scorer was winger Mike Ferguson with eight goals in thirty-nine appearances.

The following season was a disaster, mitigated only by a good start that saw Rovers go top of the table in early October after thirteen matches. Typically, Rovers were then beaten at home by bottom of the table Carlisle. Up to then only two games had been lost but in the remaining twenty-nine games, only seven were won and sixteen were lost. The collapse was at its most spectacular in the last third of the season when only one of the last fourteen games was won, and all of the last six were lost. Blackburn finished fourth from bottom in division two, their lowest ever league position. Even young optimistic fans like me knew what to expect after the board betrayed supporters again even before the 1968–69 season had started. During the summer, to the horror of younger fans like me, our hero and crowd favourite Mike Ferguson was sold to Aston Villa. It was unbelievable. The directors were clearly gambling that seventeen-year-old Stuart Metcalfe, who had made his debut late in the previous season, could fill the role. Metcalfe started thirty-eight games in 1968–69 and went on to become a club legend, but the truth was he had to play every week as there was no option. It was a huge challenge for the Blackburn born teenager at this stage of his career. To make matters worse, after just seven games, Rovers sold dynamic midfielder Barrie Hole, also to Aston Villa. The hole (no pun intended) could not be filled. Moving Eamonn Rogers back into that slot necessitated either bringing in David "Spider" Helliwell, surely the slightest player ever to wear the shirt, or recalling the aging and injury prone Douglas.

The other alternative, initially preferred, was recalling George Sharples directly into Hole's old position, but sadly he sustained a career ending injury at Derby. Ferguson was massively missed and the folly of relying on an unbalanced and wafer thin squad was cruelly laid bare. As far as the centre forward slot was concerned, Gilliver departed pre-season to third division Rotherham in exchange for Les Chappell having scored just nine goals in thirty-six league and cup games. Chappell made just seven appearances without scoring. Rovers signed yet another centre forward for whom the second division was above his pay grade. Jim Fryatt, bought from Stockport County, scored just three goals in twenty-four league games. Just seven goals came from the wearer of the number nine shirt in forty-two league games. Rogers, Connelly and Martin were joint top scorers with ten goals each. The board even attempted to sell Keith Newton, Rovers' last remaining top class player to Nottingham Forest, but mercifully he turned down the move. At the end of the season, two of Rovers' greatest ever players, Ronnie Clayton and Bryan Douglas, both of whom had been peripheral figures in their final two seasons, retired. Their testimonial games were joyous occasions, something increasingly rare as the club's decline continued.

Prior to the start of the 1969–70 season the board did spend some money and three new faces were brought in, although sadly they did not include Pickering, or indeed include a striker at all. Allan Hunter, a centre back was signed from Oldham. Two years later he was transferred to Ipswich where he spent the rest of his career and won an FA Cup winners medal in 1977–78. Ken Knighton, a powerhouse midfielder, joined from Preston, which filled a desperate need. The board also acknowledged the need for another winger and signed Brian Hill from Huddersfield, a move which was not a success. Amazingly, Rovers looked like getting promotion. After beating neighbours Preston 4-2 on 13 December, Rovers led the table by three points having won fourteen and lost only five of the twenty-four fixtures played.

Three weeks later the season was in tatters. Firstly, the board decided to sell Keith Newton to first division leaders Everton for £80,000. Surely this could have waited until the end of the season, depending on whether or not promotion was achieved. Then Quigley tried to re-sign Barrie Hole. The main issue between Quigley and the player during Hole's spell at the Rovers 1966–68 had been the latter's need for time to visit his family who remained in Wales. Needless to say, Hole remained at Aston Villa before moving to his home town of Swansea at the end of the season. Quigley then decided to move Eamonn Rogers to right back for the Boxing Day trip to Hull, having experimented with the move earlier for one game. Rogers refused to play, although he did consent to play at right back at home to Portsmouth the following day. Both matches were lost 0-3 and, with it, the league leadership. On the first Saturday of the New Year Blackburn faced Swindon in a televised FA Cup tie. Rogers was now left out as were two other players for a different breach of discipline. I cannot recall accurately whether it related to breach of a curfew or a refusal to train on New Year's Day. What it all amounted to was that Quigley, although yet again badly let down by the directors, had lost control of the dressing room. Rogers did not have a straightforward reputation, but he was the club's playmaker and although he should certainly have played where he was told in line with his contract, asking him to play right back was plain daft. Quigley would not have asked Bryan Douglas to play full back, so why ask Rogers. Also, the previous season Rovers had signed full back cover in the guise of Frank Kopel from Manchester United, presumably in anticipation of Newton's aborted move to Nottingham Forest going through. Kopel had deputised competently for Newton for five games earlier in the season. For whatever reason, he did not play again that season after Boxing Day. The season simply fell apart as ten of the remaining eighteen games were lost. Don Martin scored thirteen goals from forty-one games in the number 9 shirt. The only bit of good news was the signing of goalkeeper Roger Jones from Bournemouth to take over what had become another problem position. He would prove to be an excellent signing, giving six years high class service before getting a deserved shot at first division football with Newcastle. Utility player Freddie Goodwin was also signed from Stockport.

The summer of 1970 was relatively quiet. Connelly and Coddington were given free transfers. Rovers shopped again in the bargain basement for Alex Russell of Southport and Tony Parkes from non-league Buxton. Parkes, signed originally as a striker, would go on to be a club legend as player, coach, and frequent caretaker manager in his thirty-five years at the club. However, his first season was unremarkable with just one goal in twelve appearances. Rovers obtained Brian Conlon, a central striker from Norwich in a straight swap deal for Malcolm Darling. He scored precisely six goals in thirty games, only two of them when playing centre forward. Indeed, only eight goals were scored all season by the various wearers of the number 9 shirt. Disaster struck with an injury to Don Martin in the third game of the season. He would appear in only four more games in 1970–71. The new signing jinx struck again when left winger Jimmy Kerr bought from Bury for around £60,000, played only eleven games before sustaining a career ending knee injury. Only one of the opening thirteen games resulted in victory. The board swapped the duties of Eddie Quigley and Johnny Carey. Quigley was relieved of team responsibilities and became Administrative Manager and Carey resumed the job he had carried out so successfully between 1953 and 1958. Unfortunately, there was no second coming. Carey gave youth its chance, but it was too much to ask of young players to make up for the deficiencies in a light weight and underperforming squad. To cap it all, the board sold midfield dynamo Ken Knighton to Hull City for £60,000 with just twelve games left, of which only one was won.

Just when it seemed all hope was extinguished, Rovers re-signed Fred Pickering for a small fee from Blackpool. The search for a centre forward had turned full circle and the biggest league crowd of the season, a mere 10,458, came to see the hero's return. Sadly, Fred was not the player he was and scored only two goals in eleven games and missed a vital penalty against Millwall as Rovers drifted inexorably towards the third division. By the end of the season the place was like a morgue. A total of six wins in the season remains to this day the worst in the club's history. Only two league attendances exceeded 10,000. Ronnie Clayton's testimonial and two friendly matches against Burnley and Manchester United all attracted gates better than at any league game. All that can be said is that, unlike our neighbours, division three was the lowest the club sank. Indeed, the quality of director actually began to improve and Bill Bancroft at thirty-nine, became the club's youngest ever chairman part way through that awful season. Men of the calibre of Derrick Keighley, David Brown, Edgar Pickering and Bill Fox would join the board and would somehow not merely keep the club afloat but also competitive in the second division during the 1980s, the decade that almost forgot football as hooliganism and recession came close to driving ordinary supporters out of the decrepit grounds altogether.

Both Eddie Quigley and Johnny Carey were sacked by Bill Bancroft. Few fans attached any blame to Carey and as I recall there were few calls for Quigley's head before he was switched to an administrative role part way through the 1970 –71 season. I have recently been reading Neil Warnock's autobiography "The Gaffer", and no doubt he would be impressed by the fans' restraint, which would certainly not happen now. Although Neil Warnock has developed into a pantomime villain, and in some ways has become as much of a caricature of the manager as the late John Bond, his record of seven promotions is testament to his ability and he has been perhaps unfortunate in never getting a job in the top flight that was ever anything more than a battle for survival without resources. Where I take issue with Neil Warnock and managers like him is the attitude to fans, who pay their hard earned cash to be entertained and have the temerity to criticise the manager fiercely when they are not. In terms of the knowledge needed to criticise, football is the closest thing to school. We all attended school, but only a few of us did a stint as teachers. Nevertheless, every schoolboy and schoolgirl past and present could tell you eloquently who were the good and the bad teachers, who could motivate, who commanded respect and who really knew their subject. Football is very similar. Those of us who love the game may have played at no higher a level than the school team or Sunday pub football, but at even at those levels we knew who could coach, who could organise and galvanise, and who among our colleagues on the pitch did not put in a shift. Fans are acute observers of the game. They can read players' body language, they know when one up front is not working, and when defensive organisation is a shambles. A fan does not need to know the intricacies of the diamond formation to know when the manager is getting nothing out of the players, or worse still, is out of his depth. It should also be remembered that the average manager is just that – average.

For every top manager like Sir Alex Ferguson, Jose Mourinho, or Arsene Wenger, there is Steve Kean, Roy Keane and Paulo Di Canio on the other side of the coin, getting found out sooner or later. There are many lesser known names, remembered without affection and sometimes with loathing only by the supporters of the clubs unfortunate enough to be mismanaged by some delusional clown who imagined himself to be the next Brian Clough. After his departure, Eddie Quigley was critical of the board's failure to support his ambitions for the club, and he was right to be critical. Nevertheless, Eddie Quigley had no special talent as a manager. He was Mr Average, and Mr Average cannot afford to alienate key players who cannot be replaced if they leave and are an awkward presence in the dressing room if they stay. The departure of Mike Ferguson cannot be laid at the door of the boardroom, although they were perfectly happy to accept the transfer fee. Quigley drove Mike Ferguson out of the club just as he did Barry Hole later the same year. From his retirement in his native Burnley, Ferguson has recently confirmed on social media that he loathed Eddie Quigley. Eamonn Rogers outlasted the manager and regained his place as a Darwen End favourite, but team spirit under Quigley was never the same again. An above average manager may still have failed to gain promotion, particularly when you consider the nature of the club's board, but he would not have wasted the talents of Andy McEvoy, Mike Ferguson and Eamonn Rogers.

The next four seasons were spent in division three with local derbies against the likes of Southport, Oldham and Rochdale. Some of the opposition at this level, most notably Southport, played what Bill Shankly called alehouse football. Games against teams like this were a grim reminder of how far the club had fallen. Ken Furphy joined as manager from Watford. Promotion was nearly achieved in his second season and, inevitably, Furphy's ability already evidenced by his successes at Workington and Watford, led a bigger club to come calling late in 1973 when Sheffield United lured him away. His replacement, Gordon Lee, recruited from Port Vale guided Rovers back up in his first and only full season before he too moved on to a bigger job, this time at Newcastle. He was replaced by Jim Smith who at the age of thirty-four was then the club's youngest ever manager. The first season back in division two was a difficult one. Both regular full backs Mick Heaton and Andy Burgin were forced to retire with career ending injuries. Smith allowed surprisingly allowed crowd favourite Don Martin to leave and the remaining strikers found the second division above their pay grade. Gordon Lee came calling before the transfer deadline, no transfer window in those days, and took Roger Jones and Graham Oates to Newcastle. Attendances fell from 12,651 in the promotion year to 10,489, and dropped again the following year to 10,130.

Nevertheless, Jim Smith showed what a fine manager he would become putting together a side that would challenge for promotion in 1977-78. He was simply excellent in the transfer market bringing in veteran left winger David Wagstaffe in from Wolves, and two younger men in Glenn Keeley from Newcastle, and Noel Brotherston from Tottenham, signed in 1976 and 1977 respectively. Both men would remain at the club until 1987. Keeley, a robust centre back affectionately known as "Killer", formed a decade long central defensive partnership with Derek Fazackerley and captained the Full Members Cup winning side of 1987. Brotherston, a right winger, played for Northern Ireland in the 1982 World Cup. Smith also brought back John Byrom for a swansong in 1976-77. Byrom was not prolific with five goals in fifteen games, but his sense of occasion did not desert him when he scored both Rovers' goals against Burnley on Boxing Day. The signing of John Radford, "double" winner at Arsenal in 1970-71, just before Smith's departure was less successful. Smith retained the spine of Lee's team with Fazackerley, Stuart Metcalfe and Tony Parkes, all still only in their mid-twenties, continuing as first team regulars. Jim Smith also blooded young players. Paul Bradshaw replaced Jones in goal and Kevin Hurd and John Bailey rapidly became automatic choices. All three would move on for big fees, in Bradshaw's case early in the 1977-78 season when Wolves came calling with a £150,000 fee, the largest Rovers had ever received.

Goalkeeper became a problem position again but the real handicap to a sustained promotion bid was attendances. The problem was common to most clubs outside the leading handful with changing leisure habits, hooliganism, and growing unemployment all cited as reasons for a steep decline that would become steeper still in the next decade. At Blackburn there was an additional factor; the trust between supporters and the board had been damaged almost irreparably in the previous decade. The average of 12,227 (which would not be exceeded until 1991–92) was still well short of what was needed to keep the club on an even keel. Nothing would convince the critical mass of lost supporters that the club were serious about returning to the first division. The events of the next decade when Rovers became known as the "nearly men" would only reinforce that point of view. The club's directors were firmly and unfairly saddled with the disastrous reputation of the 1960's boardroom. Jim Smith departed for Birmingham in early March 1978 and was replaced by Jim Iley at the beginning of April. The promotion challenge fell away as only two points were taken from the last eight games and Rovers finished a distant fifth.

The 1978 –79 season was a disaster culminating in a second relegation to the third tier. The average attendance plummeted to 8,640. The new manager quickly lost the confidence of the players, supporters, the local press and the board. The sale of David Wagstaffe was particularly resented by the fans and when loan player David Gregory, three goals in five games elected to join third division Bury, average attendance 3,782, instead, the fans were up in arms. Unlike the relegations of 1965–66 and 1970–71 the board responded swiftly, but having failed to persuade Jimmy Armfield to take over as manager settled for an internal promotion and gave the job to John Pickering who was unable to keep the club up. When Leeds came calling before the deadline with a £350,000 bid for Kevin Hird, then a record fee received by Rovers, there was no choice but to sell. The board were able to provide some funds for the manager. The most important deals were the club record £80,000 spent on the mercurial Duncan McKenzie and £40,000 on Mick Rathbone who would remain at the club for eight years, but there was no miracle. The 1978–79 season marked the breakthrough of another club legend, Simon Garner. Strangely enough both Garner and Derek Fazackerley who holds the club record for appearances, 596 league games 1971–87, could have left the club in 1979. Fazackerley turned down a move to Oldham in March 1979, and Garner a move to Halifax in the autumn of that year. Oldham offered what would have been a club record £60,000 fee, very attractive to the Blackburn board, and fourth division strugglers Halifax, average attendance 1,821 in 1978–79, conjured up £40,000 to try and sign Simon Garner who was out of favour at the time. Thank God for old-fashioned loyalty.

At the end of the season Pickering was sacked and John Bailey moved to Everton for a much needed £300,000. Howard Kendall at just thirty-three years old was installed as player manager. At Christmas, Rovers were marooned in mid-table but then everything came together. Kendall found his striking partnership when Garner was recalled to the side alongside Andy Crawford and became an automatic choice for eleven years on his way to becoming the club's record scorer. McKenzie, operating well below his true pay grade excelled in a free role and terrorised third division defences. Metcalfe ceased to be a regular but the two other survivors from Rovers' first relegation to this level in 1970–71, Fazackerley and Parkes, continued to deliver. A run of fourteen wins in fifteen games, the other drawn, pushed Rovers right into the heart of the promotion race, eventually finishing runners up. The club also reached the fifth round of the FA Cup, knocking out first division Coventry on the way, sweet revenge for 1967.

During the season of joy when Blackburn won the third division title in their centenary year I became a part-time supporter, as in October 1974, I became a student at Madeley College of Education in Staffordshire. From having missed less than a handful of home matches in ten years, I missed that many before the Christmas holiday.

However, my mother would post me a copy of Saturday night's sports paper so that I could read the in-depth match reports and the weekly column by the Evening Telegraph's Rovers correspondent. Indeed, she continued to send me the Last Sports until publication ceased. A move to Kings Lynn to take up a teaching post at the end of my studies reduced my attendance at Ewood Park to an occasional treat. I attended just four home games in the 1979–80 season, two of those in the FA Cup. After that I did not attend another home game until 1989, which is why the detailed narrative of my love affair with Blackburn Rovers ends in 1980. Before the start of the next campaign my girlfriend moved in with me and we began to save for our own home. Trips to the north to watch football were now a luxury that could not be afforded. We moved to Staffordshire when I joined the prison service and I worked alternate weekends. By then I had lost the football watching habit and any thoughts of reinstating it were soon put on the back burner by fatherhood. I have to admit, shamefully, that I was not at Wembley when Rovers won the Full Members Cup in 1987. It was divorce that brought me back to Ewood Park, as I could combine taking my daughter to see her grandparents in Blackburn with a home game.

Between 1975 and 1992 Blackburn Rovers spent sixteen seasons in division two, twelve of them in succession, and one season, 1979–80, in division three. I was not there to share personally the agonies of the '80s when Rovers challenged for promotion six times in ten seasons, missing out once on goal difference, 1980–81 after which Howard Kendall departed for Everton, once by a single point in 1984–85, and then at the end of the decade missing out three years in succession in the play-offs, which had been introduced in 1987. In one other season Rovers scraped clear of relegation in the last game, and of course there was the one joyous occasion when Rovers did triumph, the Full Members Cup win over first division Charlton in 1987. The competition lasted only five years during the period English clubs were banned from Europe. The big teams did not take it seriously and neither did BBC or ITV as the match was not televised. However, 25,000 Blackburn fans present at Wembley that day did not care. On the basis that I was not there, it is not my place to write in detail about the trials and tribulations of the 1980s. The search for a centre forward continued although Rovers were lucky enough to have striker Simon Garner who between 1978 –79 and 1991–92 scored a club record 168 league goals from 476 games, plus another twenty-two in cup competitions and play off matches. Although Garner did spend a couple of seasons in the number 9 shirt, he was much better partnered with a traditional centre forward. Just when he had found a strike partner capable of twenty goals a season, David Speedie, he lost his place to then record signing Mike Newell. Other than Garner himself who did it twice, Speedie was the only Blackburn player to score twenty or more league goals in a season since Andy McEvoy and John Byrom in 1964–65 until the great Alan Shearer arrived, when Blackburn reached the premiership for its inaugural season, 1992–93. It tells its own story. Finally, in 2014–15 for the first time in fifty years, Rovers could boast two strikers who hit the twenty-goal mark in league games in the same season, Jordan Rhodes and Rudy Gestede.

When I finally did attend another game it almost felt like I had never been gone. There had been alterations to the main stand because of a fire and the Riverside Stand – which had overlooked the back section of the Riverside Terrace – had been condemned and demolished but otherwise it looked and sounded like the same faded cathedral where I used to worship and sing hymns of praise to our heroes every fortnight in the company of fellow members of the faithful gathered in congregation. My first game at Ewood Park was Bill Eckersley's testimonial match in 1961. My father knew both Bill Eckersley and Bryan Douglas and was close friends with Douglas's brother Jimmy, who lived just a couple of streets away. I would guess if Eckersley's son, also Bill, is still alive, that he can be found to this day playing snooker in Ewood Working Men's Club where my father was once a member. My father took me to my first league game, against Burnley in the same 1961–62 season. His shift work prevented me from becoming a regular until my tenth birthday in December 1962, when was I allowed to cross the busy Bolton Road alone and attend home matches unaccompanied. My mother was more worried about the road than she was about the crowd at the match. I was hooked and the terraces became a second home. By the time I returned in 1989 after a very long sabbatical, Heysel and Hillsborough had happened and the terraces were living on borrowed time. My memories of and thoughts about the terrace culture can be found in the next chapter.

Postscripts to appeal to soccer anoraks:

At the time of writing (August 2015) Blackburn Rovers have been involved in six on the pitch occurrences that are notable for being the last occasion they occurred in our game.

- In 1965 Rovers participated in the last ever Christmas Day fixture when they lost 4-2 at Blackpool. The last full programme of Christmas Day fixtures was played in 1959 when coincidentally Rovers also met Blackpool.
- Between a 2-2 draw at Old Trafford with Manchester United on 6 November, 1965, and a 0-0 draw at Charlton on 30 August, 1966, Blackburn Rovers went thirty League games without a draw. The closest sequence since, twenty-nine league matches, was achieved by Carlisle United in 2014–15.
- On 14 September, 1966, in a League Cup tie against Barrow, played in torrential rain in front of just 4,655 spectators, saw the last occasion when a penalty kick was converted indirectly in English football when Bryan

Douglas played the penalty forward to his right for Mike Ferguson to run on and slot the ball into the far corner past former Rovers' keeper Fred Else. I don't actually know if there is a previous occurrence, so it may have been a unique feat at the time. Two Arsenal players attempted the same feat in a premier league game in 2005 but made a mess of it. The only other instance I can find involves Johann Cruyff in a Dutch League game in 1982. Cruyff passed that penalty to a colleague who, unlike Ferguson, passed it back to the kicker for him to score. The footage of Cruyff's goal can be seen on you tube. Although it is not conclusive, my view is that Cruyff was offside when the ball was played back to him.

- On 21 September, 1968, in front of just 7,736 spectators in a second division game between Blackburn Rovers and Sheffield United, also played in torrential rain, the only goal was scored when Rovers forward Don Martin shoulder charged visiting keeper Alan Hodgkinson over the line with the ball. This was the last occasion when a goal of this nature was allowed by a referee in an English league game. By 1968 shoulder charging the goalkeeper was considered to be dangerous play by virtually all referees. In the modern game it would be a straight red card.

- On 14 May, 1977, England's World Cup winning captain Bobby Moore played his last league game, for Fulham, at Ewood Park. A mere 9,306 spectators witnessed the last domestic competitive appearance of a soccer legend.

- On 6 September, 2000, Blackburn's David Dunn became the last player to score a hat trick of penalties in a competitive game between two league clubs when he achieved the feat in a 6-0 League Cup victory against Rochdale. 12,977 people saw the game.

Blackburn Rovers have also been involved in one notable first when David Wagstaff achieved the unwanted distinction of being the very first player in the football league to receive a red card when playing for Blackburn Rovers at Leyton Orient on 2 October, 1976. Just 5,082 fans were at the game.

And finally...one for real anoraks, Blackburn is the only town to boast two FA Cup winning clubs, Blackburn Rovers (six times) including a hat trick 1884–86 for which Rovers were awarded a unique commemorative shield still displayed in the boardroom to this day, and Blackburn Olympic once. Olympic who won the cup in 1883 were formed in 1878 and disbanded just eleven years later after it was decided that Rovers rather than Olympic would join the new professional football league in 1888. Their former ground is now part of the site of my old school, St Mary's College.

Chapter Eight

The Terrace Culture

On 9 October, 1965, two twelve-year-old boys stood together on the terraces at a football match between deadly rivals Burnley and Blackburn Rovers at Turf Moor, the home of Burnley Football Club. Those two twelve-year-old boys were Bryan Snape, friend and classmate at St Mary's College, Blackburn, and of course myself. I travelled on the bus from my home near Ewood Park and Bryan similarly from his home in Withnell, near Chorley. We met at Blackburn bus station, each wearing our club scarves, and caught the bus to Burnley. We walked to the ground together, paid at the turnstiles together, and for half the game stood together. I changed ends for the first half. After the match, we travelled back to Blackburn together on the bus. Our fellow passengers were a mixture of Rovers and Burnley fans. Back in Blackburn we parted until Monday. For me it was a great day as Rovers won 4-1. It was a surprise as Rovers were bottom of division one, having won only one game all season and Burnley were sitting proudly at the top of the table. For those readers used to the modern names division one pre 1992 equates to the premier league.

To younger fans, particularly those of Blackburn and Burnley, that day must seem like another planet, and it is inconceivable that it will be repeated in my lifetime. Apart from a bit of firework throwing, the occasion was trouble free. Football hooliganism, which began to grow from the mid-1960s, and the sheer bitterness of Blackburn versus Burnley "derby" clashes has long since put paid to any notion of peaceful interaction on match days. Since the 1965–66 season Rovers and Burnley have played in the same division in only eight of the forty-nine subsequent league seasons. This must be a huge relief for Lancashire

Police for whom policing the game is one of the most challenging police operations faced by any senior officer. It is the most hate filled "derby" in the land rivalled only by West Ham versus Millwall, Cardiff versus Swansea and Portsmouth versus Southampton, games which like the cotton derby have in more recent times been played only very infrequently. To attend a Rovers-Burnley derby game at your opponents' ground fans must purchase their coach ticket and match ticket together. Independent travel is not permitted. Your coach will have a police escort for the whole of the ten-mile journey and, if you are lucky, it will not be stoned and the windows smashed by a welcoming committee. After the game you will be detained inside the ground for an hour before boarding the return coach which has been parked in a sterile cage. The return journey will once again be an escorted running of the gauntlet until you reach the motorway. Kick-off time is usually lunchtime on a Sunday, sometimes lunchtime on a Saturday. Pubs will be closed in whichever town is hosting the match. Not even marches by the English Defence League are subjected to this level of security. At the ground there will be blocks of seats out of use to create a "no-man's land" between rival supporters. There is no question of these games being played on bank holidays as they used to be.

These extreme precautions were introduced in the 2000–01 season when the clubs met for the first time in eighteen seasons. The last occasion the two clubs had met was on Easter Monday in 1983 at Ewood Park. Blackburn won the game with two penalties converted by record goal scorer and all time fans' idol Simon Garner, both scored at the end where the visiting fans were standing. Although fans could no longer get at each other on the terraces, the game was marred by the worst hooliganism ever seen at Ewood Park as Burnley fans rioted and some climbed the pillars that supported the roof at the Darwen End, ripping off slates and hurling them on the pitch causing the game to be temporarily halted. Police were forced to risk life and limb to rescue the staff working in the snack bar in one corner of the terrace. At the end of the season Burnley were relegated, and as has been said, for eighteen seasons the clubs went their separate ways. Absence certainly did not make the heart grow fonder and the resentment of Burnley fans only grew as Blackburn gained a benefactor in Jack Walker, who bankrolled the team that won the Premiership in 1994–95 while Burnley continued to languish in the lower divisions. When the clubs finally met again, in the second tier in December 2000, Lancashire Police were determined to prevent any repeat of the rioting. As it turned out the game, which Blackburn won 2-0, passed peacefully but Burnley fans, angered at being denied a punch up with their hated rivals, instead rioted in the streets near the ground smashing the windows of Asian owned shops, thus revealing the seedy racist underbelly of a town in which the BNP was notably active in the first decade of the twenty-first century. I ought to mention in fairness that the National Front, an older now defunct Fascist party, had been active in Blackburn in the 1970s and its breakaway group, the National Party, had succeeded in electing two councillors in Blackburn in 1976. My old friend Bryan Snape, a Burnley season ticket holder to this day, refuses on principal to travel to the away fixture under these conditions and I have to say I agree with him. Having lived away (sometimes very far away) from Blackburn for over forty years, I did not attend any "derby" games after 1979 until March of 2013 when I made the fairly short journey from my home in Huddersfield. All I can say is that Ewood Park was truly a cauldron of hate. Despite the fact that the match kicked off at 12.30 on a Sunday, a good number of fans in the Blackburn End were clearly drunk as skunks. The singing and chanting from rival fans was rarely less than obscene and laced with heartfelt vitriol, as normally sane and rational people took collective leave of their senses and brought back the atmosphere of menace and foreboding at football grounds that had been unfashionable since Hillsborough disaster of 1989, which finally brought football to its nadir and ushered in a more tolerant family friendly climate in the modern all-seated stadia that followed in its wake, albeit at eye-wateringly premium prices.

The return fixture in 1965–66 was played on New Year's Day, and this time Burnley were the victors by a 2-0 margin. Bryan and I did not travel together, not least because I lived barely 300 yards from Ewood Park, nor did we meet at the match. The game passed without trouble on the terraces despite fans sharing the away end in the first half. The only incident was a one man pitch invasion in the second half when a home fan attempted to assault Burnley goalkeeper Adam Blacklaw. Modern football fans will be unfamiliar with grounds where it was possible for supporters to change ends and therefore, always stand behind the goal that their team was attacking. Not all grounds were like this, but of those grounds I visited in this era supporters could also change ends at Burnley, Bury, Huddersfield, Hull, Rotherham, Carlisle and Torquay. I am advised that of the major first division grounds it was possible to change ends at Tottenham. No doubt older readers in different parts of the country can identify other grounds where a mass migration at half time was possible. For major matches at Ewood Park the captains even tossed up several minutes before the start to facilitate changing of ends before the match if necessary. Typically, Blackburn's noisiest fans gathered behind the Darwen End goal and visiting fans behind the Blackburn End goal. Traditionally Rovers did and, still do, prefer to attack the Darwen End (now renamed the Bryan Douglas Darwen End) in the first half and indeed it was considered bad luck to play to the Blackburn End (now the Ronnie Clayton Blackburn End) first, so most of the time there was only one migration. The Blackburn vs Manchester United fixture in 1964–65 attracted over 30,000 fans, the best attendance of the season. And at half time around one third of those supporters changed ends in an orderly manner, one set of fans round the top of the Riverside End, the other set round the bottom of the Riverside on the walkway just behind the perimeter wall. Modern fans may also not be aware that boys could sit on benches at the front of the perimeter wall on the running track round the pitch, just about as close to the action as you could get. I don't know exactly when this privilege was withdrawn and it was not always available at major matches, but pictorial evidence suggests it was last permitted early in the 1966–67 season. Given that tough tackling full backs could in those days legally carry out tackles that took man and ball out together and dump them on the running track, safety was not guaranteed, but then safety was not a word on everyone's lips in 1966. The modern reader may also have noted that two twelve years old boys were readily permitted by their parents to travel unsupervised to a major football match. Those modern parents who want to rule all risk out of their offspring's lives, other than getting fat sitting in front of a computer screen all day, should take note.

At football grounds, the age of innocence came to end within a few short years. There has always been a terrace culture but mass singing was relatively unusual until around 1963 when supporters on Liverpool's famous Kop End adopted Gerry and the Pacemakers number one single "You'll Never Walk Alone" as the club anthem. It was adopted at roughly the same time by Glasgow Celtic supporters who stood on the Jungle End of their ground. Within a few years, the song could be heard on most English football grounds but, apart from Liverpool, it is now rarely heard. As a measure of how things changed Manchester United fans devised their own version: "You'll Never Walk Again". It would be remiss of me not to mention Norwich, West Ham or Portsmouth, which did have club songs that were sung by fans. Indeed, "On the Ball City", the Norwich anthem is believed to be the oldest football song in the world dating back to the 1890s. "I'm forever blowing bubbles" was apparently adopted by West Ham supporters in the 1920s. By contrast to the two verses and a chorus of the Norwich song, the "Pompey chimes", as they are known, are composed of just three words, "Play up Pompey", repeated continuously. Rhythmic clapping in the form of the clubs name followed by a "cha, cha, cha" beat with the hands was imported from Brazil after the 1962 World Cup. Just pre-dating "You'll Never Walk Alone" was Tottenham Hotspur fans' rendition of "Glory, Glory, Alleluia" heard on television during Tottenham's European football campaigns in 1961–62 and 1962–63. It was television that gave the stimulus to the new terrace culture.

Firstly, it has to be remembered just how little televised football there was until 1964. There was the FA Cup final shown live on both channels (there were only two and ITV had only been in existence since 1955), and very little else. Other than the Manchester United-Real Madrid European Cup clash in 1958, the rare live coverage of European or international football was restricted to the second half only. Even this first ever competitive match between two of the planet's top clubs was shown in full only in the Granada (north-west region). The rest of the country had to make do with just the second half. As far as recorded highlights were concerned, there were snippets on the newsreels at the cinema and from the mid-fifties onwards highlights of the home international championship, usually shown late at night on either BBC or ITV. There were also occasional highlights of the earlier rounds of the FA Cup. As these internationals, including the then eagerly awaited annual meeting of England and Scotland, were played at the same time as a full league program there was no question of live coverage. There was an abortive attempt to televise live league football in 1960–61 when the second half of a match between Blackpool and Bolton was screened live, but this experiment was soon spiked by club chairman who believed that televised league football would adversely affect attendances, which were starting to fall after the post-war boom. The odd representative match was also televised and, for some reason, the annual match between sides representing the old north and south sections of the third division played at Accrington Stanley's ground in October 1955 found its way on to the small screen. However, it is also important to remember that television ownership was still a minority pursuit in 1955 as only one third of households possessed one and not all of them could receive ITV. By 1962, when the World Cup was played in Chile, that had grown to around three quarters of households and by August 1964, when Match of the Day began, that number had grown again to about eighty per cent. Put bluntly, if you wanted a regular fix of football in the early '60s you had to attend in person, just as your forefathers had done since the football league was founded in 1888.

Satellite coverage in the summer of 1962 was still primitive (this was just before the launch of Telstar) but nevertheless it was the first world cup broadcast to a mass audience and it introduced Brazilian style chanting into our homes and grounds. Match of the Day began in August 1964 and in its first season was available only to the 20,000 BBC Two subscribers, but by the start of the next season it had transferred to BBC One. It brought the swaying singing masses of Liverpool's Spion Kop terrace into our homes and ignited the new terrace culture. Singing became the norm at football matches, not the exception, and supporters competed to out-sing each other at matches. The BBC even ran a "Kop Choir" competition during the 1969–70 campaign, which strangely was won by Rotherham United supporters. They hadn't seemed so noisy or original when we visited two years earlier. The early repertoire of songs was not vast. As well as the ubiquitous "You'll Never Walk Alone", there were renditions of traditional African American gospel songs, "We Shall Not Be Moved" and "When the Saints Go Marching In", which for clubs other than Southampton would see the word Saints changed to blues, reds or whites in accordance with the club colours. Also popular was "Mammy", a song usually associated with black American entertainer Al Jolson (substitute name of favourite player and walk a million miles for one of his goals as opposed to smiles). Another familiar terrace song was Daisy (Daisy, Daisy, give me your answer do, I'm sure you know the rest). The last line became "on a bicycle made for 2-4-6-8 who do we appreciate, R-O-V-E-R-S" or whichever club it was. Liverpool supporters also popularized the nursery rhyme "The Farmer's in his den", heard nationwide at the 1965 FA Cup Final as "ee ay addio, we won the cup". The 1966 hit song "Guantanamera" is still spawning new terrace songs to this very day

It all sounds very innocent, but a harder edge came swiftly. To the tune of "My Bonny lies over the Ocean" came a charming little ditty much loved by both Blackburn and Burnley fans from around 1965 onwards and still sung occasionally to this day. It goes:

"If I had the wings of an angel, the dirty black arse of a crow, I'd fly over Burnley tomorrow and shit on the bastards below. Shit on, oh shit on, oh shit on the bastards below."

The tribute song to Eddie Cochrane "Just like Eddie" by Heinz was also given some new words:

"Whenever you're dull, whenever you're blue, whenever the Rovers are playing, in league or cup we fight like fuck, to keep the blue flag flying."

Even Auld Lang Syne got a makeover and became "Go home you bums, go home".

1966 was a good year for new songs. The Jim Reeves song, "Distant Drums" rapidly became "Distant Bums" with much finger pointing at opposing fans. There were two versions:

"I hear the sound of distant bums, over there, over there. And if they come, we shall not run, over there, over there."

The alternative version had as its second line: "And do they smell, like fucking hell, over there, over there."

The Beatles "(We all live in a) Yellow Submarine" also from that year became "We all piss in a tangerine pot" whenever Blackpool were the opposition. For whatever reason, Blackpool was held in particular contempt.

The song "We'll support you evermore" also had an alternative version again accompanied by much finger pointing as the massed ranks sang, "You're not fit to wipe my arse."

In more recent times, the intermittent resumption of Rovers vs Burnley fixtures has generated some new songs. Followers of the soap, Emmerdale, will be familiar with the large extended Dingle family. Steve Halliwell, who has played Zak Dingle for two decades, originates from Burnley and so Burnley are now referred to as the Dingles, caricatured as a family reared on incest. This has generated a couple of new songs: "Down on your sister, you're going down on your sister" sung to the tune of "Guantanamera" and the marginally more polite "Fuck off, go and shag your mum", sung to the tune of "Go West", which has been almost as prolific as "Guantanamera" in spawning terrace songs, many of which are unsuitable for family listening. I should add that Burnley fans have some equally crude songs and chants about Blackburn, whom they call Bastard Rovers.

Prior to the attack on the Burnley goalkeeper on New Year's Day 1966, hooliganism at Ewood Park was defined as throwing toilet rolls on to the pitch at the start of a game or to celebrate a goal. I have to admit that as small boys we raided the outdoor toilets at the nearby St Bartholomew's School (now demolished) and stole all the toilet rolls to throw on the pitch. Disgraceful...and the club's board and the local paper used to get upset about it. The directors had rather more to get upset about in the dreadful 1965–66 season that saw Rovers relegated and angry fans staging sit-down protests, also hurling stones through the windows of the Nuttall Street stand in the hope of finding the boardroom. In that same season as Match of the Day came to BBC One, ITV also began televising highlights on Sunday afternoons. It was impossible not to notice that Manchester United fans were standing on what were traditional home terraces during away games, although they did not try their luck at Everton or Liverpool. In May 1966 Manchester United came to Ewood Park, just five days after an incident where a number of Blackpool supporters were chased out of Ewood Park at half time. Five thousand United fans invaded and ensconced themselves on the Darwen End. To use the hooligan parlance that soon became common, they "took" the Darwen End, a feat not repeated until Bolton fans took it in 1970. The atmosphere was very different to the corresponding match barely a year earlier. There was an air of intimidation mixed with triumphalism and it had an immediate impact on Rovers hard core behind the goal support.

There have been numerous tomes written about soccer hooliganism by a range of people from eminent sociologists, writing in impenetrable jargon, to former and still practicing hooligans with varying degrees of literacy. In the worst of the books written by hooligans the home end is never taken, a beating is always because of being massively outnumbered, the police are total dimwits, and, of course, they are always the hardest firm in the business with their local rivals being the softest. In this genre, testosterone is always in inverse proportion to IQ. I doubt I can add much that is new. The '60s were a time of social ferment and the availability of regular, reasonably well paid work to teenagers fresh out of school only served to enhance the freedom that young people were seizing with both hands. The last national serviceman had been discharged in 1963 and there were no wars to harness the aggressive instincts of young men. It can probably be argued that the soccer terraces became a substitute battlefield and, at club level, local tribalism substituted for the conflict of nations. Another ingredient to add to the mix was a distinctive youth culture, first noticeable a decade earlier with the teddy boys but now manifesting itself in the conflicts between mods and rockers, the latter also known as greasers. How many of them actually owned a motor bike I do not know, but Blackburn was undeniably a greaser town and, at the height of their power, hundreds of leather jacketed greasers, who kept up their denims with studded belts, gathered behind the Darwen End goal at Ewood Park, and a good number of them regularly attended away games. One of those greasers known to this day as "Birdie", who can justifiably be labelled Rovers most fanatical fan, actually featured on BBC's The One Show earlier this year (2015) as part of the television station's presentation of the draw for the fifth round of the FA Cup. He was not a man to be messed with in the early days of terrace confrontation. As Grammar School boys, we did not consider it sensible to walk too close to the Queen Victoria statue at the old bus station as this was a noted greaser gathering point and they had no time for boys in blazers. After Manchester United, Blackburn were one of the first clubs to have a significant hooligan following and became much feared until the inevitable happened, that much bigger towns and cities caught up and the greasers grew up and became family men, turning out for a fight only on set-piece occasions, such as when league clashes with Burnley resumed in 1976–77.

Rovers began 1966–67 in the second division. There would be no clashes with Burnley, but local Derbies were resumed with Bolton, Preston and Bury. As I recall, there was also a friendly at Blackpool. My fourteenth birthday fell partway through the season and at this stage I was not allowed out of Lancashire to watch football so these were the only away games I saw and Rovers fans were intent on proving themselves top dogs on the terraces, invading the home ends at all of our local rivals. They did not dare try their luck at Ewood Park. Blackburn's hooligan following made back page headlines on the opening day of the 1967–68 season after clashes with home fans at Millwall, then the most feared supporters in football, who had hooligans before hooliganism was fashionable, a reputation they would embellish in years to come. Oddly enough, home games with Millwall in this era passed without incident on the terraces, although there was fighting outside the ground in the 1968–69 season. Blackburn fans typically serenaded Millwall fans with their own version of the Christmas Carol, Noel. The new words were "Millwall, Millwall, you are the kings of sweet fuck all", although I wouldn't go as far as claiming that the song originated at Blackburn. This season I was actually allowed out of Lancashire and, at the end of September 1967, I ventured on the coach with a group of school friends to Huddersfield. Rovers were sitting on top of the table and took a large following with the greasers leading the way into the Cowshed, the home terrace. At half time we changed ends and, after Huddersfield scored their second goal, the greasers decided they had seen enough and charged back round to the home end, planting themselves in the centre of the terrace singing and chanting defiantly. Our little group of Grammar School boys just stood there open mouthed...and stayed where we were. In what was a very wet autumn, with many matches postponed, it was a welcome relief for football starved fans to go to Preston in mid-November where a huge following invaded Preston's Kop and celebrated a 5-3 victory. The scariest place I went to that season was Derby, where a handful of us paid into the wrong part of the ground and got separated from the Rovers support. We had to melt away quietly. I was even stupid enough to join the greasers on Aston Villa's vast Holte End. It would be ridiculous to suggest that 150 supporters took it, but hooliganism had yet to take off at Aston Villa so we got away with our wild celebrations at Rovers' winning goal. Blackpool was invaded on Easter Monday, memorable only for the very first time I got drunk. Fortunately, I had sobered up before arriving home. A visit to Rotherham rounded off my travelling season.

Early in the 1968–69 season, Blackburn's hooligan following moved from the back pages to the front when ammonia was thrown over rival supporters at Blackpool's Bloomfield Road ground. Blackpool's ground had just the one large terrace behind the goal, the Spion Kop. The other end was seats with only a small standing area at the front. Consequently, Blackpool's home end housed visiting fans, whether they liked it or not, and it is fair to say that they did not. It must have been a nightmare for the police who could do little other than form a line between rival fans and somehow try to keep them apart. Eventually, for an FA Cup tie with Manchester United, the visitors were allocated the entire Kop End despite it constituting more than half the ground's capacity. As for the ammonia, it was smuggled in under a blue and white top hat and to add to the chaos Blackburn scored the winning goal to go top of the table less than a minute after the "bomb" was thrown. It was mayhem. After coaches were held for three hours in Ripon, following hooliganism during a refreshment stop on the way back from Middlesbrough, my father put his foot down and that was the end of away trips for the rest of that season. There were two other major outbreaks of hooliganism involving Blackburn fans that season and the first occurred when Portsmouth brought a large following for a fourth round FA Cup tie. The visiting fans simply did not seem to understand the concept of changing ends at half time. They found out the hard way as the greasers smashed their way into the back of the away end and police had to intervene to break up the fighting. Towards the end of the season, Bolton fans were stupid enough to gather on the Darwen End before the match. They were sent scattering and some even climbed out of the turnstiles before police could intervene. Their day would come. The season itself was a disaster as attendances slumped and Rovers finished fourth from bottom in division two, the lowest ever league finish in the club's history.

During the summer of '69 (which for me was not quite as exciting as that eulogized by Bryan Adams) I worked in a factory for nine weeks and early on in the new football season got a job at Ewood Park, walking around the perimeter selling crisps and popcorn. This money would bankroll my away trips, starting in August with a trip to Stockport for a League Cup tie, which passed off without incident, but introduced me to the latest youth culture which had finally reached the North – skinheads. A small group of them stood in their Manchester City colours on the open terrace behind the goal. No one took any real notice of them, but the cropped hair style and Doc Martin boots gave them a seriously intimidating look. Blackpool and Preston were also visited early in the season with the natives taking increased exception to Blackburn fans taking the piss at their grounds. Sheffield United fans were even less happy when a couple of dozen greasers invaded their Kop and they were fairly swiftly ejected. The vast majority of Rovers' 4,000 strong following had done the sensible thing and used the designated away end. The game ended in 4-0 hammering which probably encouraged home fans to leave us alone while we waited nervously in a side street for the coaches to arrive.

However, a visit to Carlisle in November was like a trip to a bygone age. The home team were due to meet first division West Bromwich shortly in a League Cup semi-final and supporters needed vouchers in order to purchase tickets for the game, which was expected to be a sell-out. In those days, before segregation, the vouchers were handed out to all fans paying at the turnstiles meaning that our following of around 1,000 supporters were in possession of a precious commodity that the home fans were content to ask for politely. As I recall, Rovers won 1-0 to stay top of the table and the day passed off peacefully. My second last away trip of the season was to Hull on Boxing Day, a ground I had first visited early in the previous season. Rovers were top of the table and took a large following. I could not work out why a tough seafaring city like Hull didn't have a firm and offered no opposition to the home end being taken. Defeat at Hull was the start of a major slump as promotion dreams faded away. I went to one more away game, at Bolton on Easter Monday. As was the custom, we arrived early and planted ourselves in the middle of the home terrace, the Lever End, a line of police positioned to our right as we looked down from the back. Bolton's police had a reputation for accepting no nonsense. Suddenly, just before the players came out on to the pitch, hundreds of home fans marched towards the police line, singing, chanting and gesturing. Nothing happened, but it was the first I had ever felt intimidated at Bolton and a sure sign that the balance of power was shifting. At the end of the game it was time to melt away quietly. Over the next few years Bolton would develop into one of the most feared hooligan firms outside the top division.

The first large skinhead following visited Blackburn in October 1969. They were from Leicester and although they were not able to capture the central part of the Darwen End, home to the toughest greasers, they were not ejected from the home end either. Blackburn's dominance of rival supporters in division two ended decisively in the 1970–71 season as crowds declined and the team was relegated. The Darwen End was taken by skinhead mobs from Bolton, Leicester, Sunderland and Sheffield United. Even regrouping at the other end was not a safe option as large mobs of visiting hooligans took advantage of the ability to change ends. Only Hull City fans were swiftly seen off, but it would not be long before their humiliations came to an end and Hull became a fearsome place to visit. I went to only two away games that season; the League Cup tie at Bolton and a seriously scary trip to Everton in the FA Cup. It would be my last away trip for four years, until going to Port Vale in 1975 to see Rovers clinch the third division title in their centenary season. Back at Ewood Park, the tradition of changing ends was terminated abruptly after the visit of Burnley for a "friendly" match in January after both sides had been knocked out of the FA Cup and therefore had a vacant Saturday. Burnley fans arrived early and ensconced themselves on the home end and police prevented Rovers fans from completing a march from the away end to confront them. That seemed to put an end to it, but with fifteen minutes left and the gates open, the greasers left the ground but instead of dispersing raced up Nuttall Street, burst on to the Darwen End through the open gates and sent the Burnley fans scattering. After that incident the club switched the home terrace to the Blackburn End and away supporters were given the Darwen End. It is fair to say that home fans were not initially happy at the loss of the traditional end. However, the Blackburn End did have a cantilever cover and so there were no pillars to obstruct the view.

Nevertheless, early in the 1971–72 season, I took the decision to join the more mature fans on the Riverside End, the large side terrace, and watched all my football from there until my girlfriend joined me in King's Lynn in 1980, when trying to do the grown up thing and save money for our future put an end to long trips back to Blackburn. The decision to switch to the respectable fans' terrace made sense. Although I had never fancied the skinhead uniform anyway, the truth was that I was not cut out to be a bovver boy. More to the point, I was more frightened of being arrested and having to face my father rather than being battered. As for being a greaser, had I ever been able to afford a leather jacket my father would have surely frog-marched me back to the shop to return the offending garment. My adolescent rebellion, as far as football was concerned, amounted to no more than joining in with obscene songs and chants and running behind the greasers only when the odds were in their favour, which for three or four years they were. For a couple of hours every fortnight, plus the occasional away game, I was released from the constraints of being simultaneously a respectable working-class lad and studious Grammar School boy. I could swear to my heart's content and utter the most dreadful obscenities unheard and safe from being chastised by my father and my schoolmasters. Only once did I get in trouble at school regarding my behaviour at a football match. This occurred when the Head of PE reprimanded me the following day for joining a sit-down protest on the terraces against our terminally useless board of directors, sometime towards the end of the 1965–66 season.

Segregation was enforced more or less successfully and infiltration at Ewood Park by either home or away supporters, unlike at other grounds particularly in London, was very rare. Hooliganism on the terraces at Ewood Park became almost a thing of the past, which was why the 1983 incident involving Burnley fans was such a shock, but the police still had to deal with problems outside. Like many grounds Ewood Park was more than a mile from both of the two nearest railway stations, with numerous ambush points and the coach park was across a main road. Not until ground rebuilding under Rovers' benefactor Jack Walker was completed in 1994 was it possible to provide secure parking facilities for visiting fans. The home hooligans enjoyed a built in advantage as regards potential ambushes, in that the Blackburn End was nearer than the visitors' terrace to the coach park and railway stations. The new arrangements were not ideal for me as my home was towards Darwen, so avoiding visiting fans could be quite difficult as it was no longer possible to exit the ground behind them. More sophisticated policing, whereby visiting fans were held in the ground for a period after high profile matches, was still a good many years away.

The trip to Port Vale in 1975 was a simple journey that only involved me taking a bus from Madeley College, where I was a student, into Newcastle-Under-Lyme and picking up a connection into Burslem, the part of Stoke-On-Trent where Port Vale actually play. Rovers had a massive following for a critical match and there was no attempt to invade the home end, which appeared to be protected by just a few dozen locals. A 4-1 victory made our day and left Rovers only having to avoid defeat by the highly improbable margin of 21-0 in their last match to take the Division Three title. I had no difficulty negotiating public transport safely back to the campus. I attended only three more away league games in the rest of the decade, all at Burnley when there was a three-year resumption of hostilities commencing in 1976–77. The home game on Boxing Day was drawn but the return fixture was an accurate narrative of what the terraces were now like as places to watch high profile football matches. Burnley had only recently introduced segregation and the arrangements involved placing a single line of railings about six feet high down the middle of the Long Side terrace, Burnley's home end (more accurately side) since the Cricket Field End had been converted to seats some years earlier.

At least at Ewood Park and many other grounds where hooligans were at opposite ends of the ground, supporters who had no interest in the tribal aspects of the fixture were safe, at least until they left the ground. The railings offered no protection against darts, marbles, ball-bearings and other potentially lethal missiles that were easily exchanged above and through the barrier. It was virtually impossible for police to make arrests and those protecting the barrier would have the dubious pleasure of going off duty with their uniforms covered in spittle. The next visit was on Boxing Day 1977, when there was a full house of just over 27,000 supporters in the ground, around 6,000 of them from Blackburn. Sensibly, Burnley had now created an eight-yard wide no man's land protected not just by two sets of railings but also a mesh fence reaching up to the roof to prevent exchanges of missiles. This arrangement was much safer, although it did not prevent Celtic fans from partially breaching the barriers during an Anglo-Scottish Cup tie in 1978. None of this prevented the running battles that took place outside the ground, which were repeated in Blackburn when the return fixture was played on Easter Saturday.

Disturbances at football matches in the UK were not a new phenomenon. Sectarian violence had scarred Celtic-Rangers games in Scotland almost from the start of Scottish League football. In Northern Ireland leading Catholic club Belfast Celtic withdrew from the Irish

League after three of their players were attacked by rioting supporters during an away game at Linfield in 1948. In England sectarian violence of this nature at football matches was not a feature and crowds were generally good humoured with the most obvious exception being Millwall, whose ground was closed by the FA in 1929 after missiles were thrown, in 1934 after crowd disturbances, and again in 1947 following pitch invasions. The modern hooligan era began in the mid-sixties, but was initially confined to a few clubs. Manchester United brought end-taking to the TV screen in 1965–66, but it was also being practiced by Millwall, a club whose support was similar in size to that of Blackburn, who were promoted from Division Three that year. Everton fans specialised in throwing missiles and wrecking trains. Their neighbours and rivals, Liverpool, whose fans were also known train wreckers, had a loveable public image rather like the Beatles, but in practice were a mean bunch of hombres who loved nothing better than confrontations with high profile opponents such as Leeds, Manchester United, and Manchester City, who returned to the top division in 1966. Blackburn's greasers were simply the first aboard the bandwagon started by Millwall and the leading big city clubs in the north. By the end of the decade most clubs could boast a hooligan firm and confrontation on the terraces became the norm whenever fans could get at each other, although in these early years there was far more posturing than fighting.

Hooliganism was accelerated by the greater ability of fans to travel. The first motorways opened in the 1960s and made possible long distance return journeys by coach on the same day. Additionally, Saturday morning factory work became less common. As a consequence, workers were not restricted to attending matches no more than an hour's travelling time from home. The impact of these developments was not immediate. I can recall in the 1965–66 season midland clubs such as Aston Villa and Nottingham Forest brought virtually no supporters at all.

Fans from London clubs were only sighted for the FA Cup clashes with Arsenal and West Ham. In the second division the following year the only club south of Coventry that I can remember bringing any sort of following was Millwall, and even their numbers were small. As a result, many matches passed without any crowd trouble at all. The willingness to travel as opposed to ability was also related to performance on the pitch. Fans were less keen to travel long journeys to watch a poor side than they would later become. When skinheads became the dominant youth culture on the terraces, this would start to change, as they were less concerned with performance on the pitch than they were on the terraces. The ability to travel, combined with the glamour lent to big clubs by TV exposure, also brought about another unwelcome development as younger supporters began to follow major clubs outside their own locality. When I started at Grammar School, anyone in my year or above who went to football supported Blackburn or Burnley, with the single sole exception of one boy who watched Darwen in the Lancashire Combination. Five years later, I knew boys who travelled not only to super glamorous Manchester United, but also to Liverpool, Everton, Manchester City and Leeds. This is a sad trend, to perceived glamour clubs, that persists to this day. Finding an allegiance outside the home town was also attractive to the professional hooligans who were spawned by the skinhead cult. There was simply more agro to be had as crowds were bigger and high profile games more frequent. The older greasers were true football fans for whom their home town team came first and they would never have dreamed of changing their allegiance. They preferred to lapse like Catholics, rather than hang their leather jackets in another soccer cathedral on a Saturday afternoon.

The first death on the terraces occurred on the Spion Kop End at Blackpool during a match against Bolton in 1973–74 when a fan was fatally stabbed. It would not be the last on the road to what was "annus horribilis", 1985.

In the space of a few short weeks, there were four major incidents, three of them down to hooliganism. Second only in ferocity to the Scottish Cup Final riot of 1980, when Celtic and Rangers fans invaded the pitch to get at each other, Millwall fans rioted on the terraces at Luton during a televised FA Cup game. Remarkably no one was killed, but a fifteen-year-old boy did lose his life during crowd violence at the Birmingham-Leeds game on the final day of the season. Overshadowing the tragedy in Birmingham was a disaster on the same day that was wholly unconnected with football hooliganism; the fire at Bradford City's Valley Parade ground which claimed the lives of fifty-six supporters. The wooden stand under which the fire broke was almost literally a tip. I never attended a match at Bradford, but I did attend games at Derby's Baseball Ground in 1967 and 1977, which can only be described as a complete and utter dump. These two events led to an enquiry into safety at sports grounds led by Judge Popplewell and subsequent legislation. Fortunately for football Popplewell's recommendations for supporters to hold club membership before being admitted to a ground and for a ban on away supporters were not implemented, although Luton's chairman, David Evans, who became a Tory MP in 1987, unilaterally implemented a membership scheme and ban on away fans at Luton for the start of the 1986–87 season that was only rescinded in 1990 after Evans had stepped down.

The worst hooligan event of all came just eighteen days after events at Birmingham and Bradford, when thirty-nine spectators died when a wall collapsed at Belgium's decrepit Heysel Stadium, trying to flee after Liverpool fans breached a flimsy barrier and attacked fans of their opponents, Juventus, prior to the start of the European Cup Final, which remarkably was still played as officials judged it safer to go ahead. As a consequence, English clubs were banned from European competition for five years, and Liverpool, a club which as with the city's most famous products, the Beatles, had an image that seemed to give them immunity from criticism, for a minimum of six. Heysel destroyed that reputation overnight. You would have thought that events would have brought people to their senses, but in fact hooliganism continued unabated for the rest of the decade and particularly disfigured England's international games which were now the only opportunity for hooligans to travel abroad.

Hooliganism should not be thought of solely as a British disease, although sadly it does appear that as well as the game itself we both invented and exported it. Most major European countries have a hooligan problem and it spread not just to countries where the inhabitants are stereotypically perceived to be volatile, such as Italy and Greece, but also to countries the Netherlands and Poland, whose hooligans are feared throughout Europe. As we have seen at major international and club tournaments, there is nothing Dutch hooligans like more than to prove themselves in battle against the English and the Germans. I was quite shocked on a visit to Holland in 2000 to discover that stadiums were still fenced, caged and penned as they had been in England a decade earlier. Our coach trip visited the small town of Volendam and we had the chance to look at its small sub 7,000 capacity stadium which hosted games in the Dutch second tier. It was as though this quiet, respectable, Catholic town metamorphosed into a warzone on Saturday afternoons. It seems as though our export is permanent as hooliganism abroad is now a much greater problem than it is in the UK.

The catalyst for change was the Hillsborough disaster of April 1989, when ninety-six Liverpool supporters died of crush injuries on the Leppings Lane terrace at the ground, where Liverpool were meeting Nottingham Forest in an FA Cup semi-final. Hillsborough was one of small number of neutral grounds used for semi-finals. Let me be clear that the deaths did not occur as a result of hooliganism on the day. The deaths occurred as a consequence of a police decision not to delay the kick off and instead open the gates to allow in around 5,000 fans who were still waiting outside, including an unknown number who did not have tickets. Unfortunately, most of them were admitted by default into the two central pens. The Leppings Lane terrace, like others up and down the country that housed visiting fans, was divided into smaller pens with a high fence at the front protecting the playing area. The construction of pens and fences were a direct consequence of hooliganism. The subdividing of terraces into pens was supposed to improve control and make arrests easier. Unfortunately, when they became overcrowded, there was no room for fans to spread sideways and no escape route on to the pitch. In short, they were a disaster waiting to happen. In hindsight the most glaring omission from the Popplewell report was a recommendation to dismantle the fences and discontinue the pens so fixed was the establishment mind-set that football supporters were animals who must be caged. I am a great believer that the sty makes the pig rather than vice-versa. Our decrepit football grounds, that in part resembled zoos, were as much a part of the problem as the moronic element that patronised them. It is often forgotten that 22,000 Nottingham Forest fans massed on the Spion Kop End at Hillsborough (the traditional home end for Sheffield Wednesday supporters) stood on that terrace in perfect safety despite the fences at the front for the very reason that the terrace was not divided into pens.

Within a short space of time Hillsborough put an end to standing on the terraces at major matches as all clubs in the top two divisions were required to convert to all-seated stadia. At the time of writing, only Brentford of the forty-four clubs in the top two divisions still has standing areas. They were promoted only last year (2014) and have three years in which to convert to all-seated accommodation. Such has been the rate of change that only five of the twenty-four clubs in the third tier still have terraces, although fourteen remain in the fourth tier. Hooliganism has been on the retreat since Hillsborough, but there are still sporadic outbreaks and, as mentioned earlier, there are a small number of high profile fixtures, mainly local "derbies" that have a capacity for disorder on an industrial scale without the sort of police precautions that are now standard for Blackburn-Burnley matches. The modern all-seated stadia that we now take for granted are undoubtedly safer, undoubtedly more comfortable and family friendly, and undoubtedly much easier in terms of crowd control. Blackburn Rovers has its benefactor, Jack Walker, to thank for the modern stadium at a completely rebuilt Ewood Park. Yet there is still a feeling that the baby of the terrace culture has been thrown out with the bathwater of hooliganism. At many grounds, large groups of fans refuse to sit and instead stand in front of their seats, and despite threats by club officials there is seemingly nothing they can do to prevent it. Sitting down inhibits singing. Without singing you have long periods of eerie silence when top class football is supposed to be played to a cacophony of noise. In Germany, where fans have real power, all major clubs have safe standing areas, affordable ticket prices and fantastic match day atmospheres. They are true community clubs. In the UK the metropolitan elite which runs our country and affects to have adopted football has no intention of giving the game back to the working people that it holds in contempt. I believe that the persistence of obscene chanting is actually a continuing gesture of proletarian defiance aimed at the "prawn sandwich brigade", as they were infamously labelled by former Manchester United Captain, Roy Keane. I do not expect to see the return of standing terraces in my lifetime, and more is the pity.

Finally, apart obviously from hooliganism, the one part of the old terrace culture I am glad to see the back of is racism. It would be dishonest to argue that it did not exist independently of hooliganism. The rare appearance of a black player in the mid-sixties would provoke a chorus of "ee ay addio, they've got a wog". At this time black and Asian migrants were struggling for acceptance in traditional white working-class communities and the same lack of tolerance and assumptions of white superiority manifested themselves on the terraces. Young black men did gain acceptance into skinhead gangs where they were known as spades. However, none of this inhibited the wholesale abuse of black players, which became par for the course as the numbers appearing in the league grew. West Bromwich Albion was perhaps the leading club in terms of employing black players in the late '70s. The manager, Ron Atkinson, nicknamed his three black players "The Three Degrees" after the American singing trio. In 2015, I doubt whether this would be considered politically correct. Only when virtually all clubs had black players on their books did the banana throwing and the hurling of racist abuse disappear. I have to admit that my own team, Blackburn Rovers, was probably one of the last in the football league to select a black player in the first team, when Howard Gayle made his club debut in August 1987. The mercurial Gayle who reminded older supporters of Mike Ferguson swiftly established himself as a crowd favourite and, as at other clubs and in society at large, familiarity bred tolerance and gradually eradicated contempt. Indeed the crudest and longest lasting racism was most in evidence when the England team played. There was a hard core of England supporters that refused to count goals scored by black players as well as giving the dog's abuse to Johnny foreigner, particularly if he was black. This hard core far right element remains as a minority to this day, but now contents itself with singing anti-IRA songs now that crude racist chanting is thankfully no longer tolerated at our grounds.

Very finally, it is also fair to say that the exponential growth of the premier league brand, funded by the SKY TV billions, has had a major positive impact on racism because the leading English clubs pay the highest salaries in the world and can attract the very best from anywhere in the world to the delight of supporters. If anything, our national game is now too cosmopolitan with English born players struggling to find starting places at leading clubs, with the obvious detrimental effect on the England team and its international standing. There is nothing like the law of unintended consequences.

Chapter Nine

The World of Work

Like most young people of my generation, the first experience of the discipline of paid work was the paper round. Eighteen shillings a week was a princely sum compared to the four shillings a week I could squeeze out of my father as pocket money. The newsagent, Mr Stockdale, was therefore my first boss. You could take on a paper round at the age of thirteen, but were not permitted to do the Sunday deliveries for which the newsagent had to make other arrangements. Being a paper boy entailed being up for work before 6.30am, more than an hour before it was necessary to get up for school and, more pertinently, more than an hour before my mother usually got up, unless she was woken by a restless baby. Quite rightly my parents took no responsibility for me getting up in time for the paper round, so this was my introduction to that most important of adult disciplines, being able to get out of bed, and get to work on time. If you missed your round, you didn't get paid and someone else grabbed a bonus round, albeit having to put up with complaints about late delivery. Local householders were distinctly unhappy if their paper did not arrive at the same time every day, and those who working day began at 8.00 or even 7.30am, expected it to be delivered before they left home for their own daily toil. Strictly speaking, we were not allowed to start deliveries until 7.00, but the convention was that we began at 6.45am. It wasn't a long round, it took about thirty minutes, and all the house numbers were marked on the daily papers by the newsagent who had been up since 5.00. So our life was easy by comparison. There was also an evening round delivering the Lancashire Evening Telegraph straight after school. This was a pain in the backside on a Saturday when it meant leaving Ewood Park a few minutes before the end of the game to be at the paper shop for 4.30pm. It was tolerable as Rovers drifted inexorably towards relegation in the spring of 1966, but much less tolerable when the new season began in August. The evening round had to go and when I was fifteen and eligible there was no question of a Saturday job in a shop. On a Saturday during the football season there was also the "sports pink" to deliver around 6pm.

I got my first factory job in the summer of 1968 when I was fifteen years old. During the Wakes' weeks many factories closed for production but carried out essential maintenance. Depending on your luck, you could be assisting a tradesman, washing down walls or doing a spot of fence painting. Along with a school friend, I was employed for two weeks in a factory in the Bastwell district of Blackburn. I don't remember a great deal about it, but I do remember perching on a ladder, which itself was perched on a cotton bail, complete with brush and pail washing down walls. Whether modern health and safety legislation would now permit such methods for what it calls "working at height" is another matter. I suspect not. The other striking memory was the lack of natural light and the coolness of the environment, even in summer. In due course, I would learn that the relative coolness was an illusion fostered by the machinery having its annual rest. The pay was the princely sum of seven pounds per week, worth £110.99 today. Direct comparisons are difficult as the modern fifteen-year old is restricted to a five-hour day in school holidays, may not work in factories or on building sites, and is not covered by minimum wage legislation. Back in the summer of 1968, around two-thirds of my fifteen-year-old contemporaries were joining the labour force permanently, the lucky ones as apprentices although they may not have thought so at the time. Grammar School boys like me were only playing at it.

I got a rather more representative taste of the working-class adult world the following summer when I worked at Redmayne and Isherwood's for nine weeks. The factory formerly known as Ewood Mill, which to this day is the name of the bus stop just by it although the mill has long since ceased business, dealt with cotton waste products and did not shut down during the wakes weeks. It was barely a five-minute walk from home. The pay was 5s 6d per hour (27 and a half pence in decimal currency) which translated into eleven pounds for a forty-hour week. Inflation means that it is worth £166.59 today. The current minimum wage for a sixteen-year old is £3.79 per hour, which translates into £151.60 per week for forty hours, so I guess our generation were ahead of the game for unskilled work, which in those days was plentiful, particularly as a sixteen-year old on a permanent contract with that firm got an extra £1.40 per week, £21.20 at current values when price inflation is calculated, making a total equivalence of £187.79 per week, almost twenty-four per cent better than the current minimum wage. The normal factory hours were from 7.30am to 5.30pm Monday to Thursday, and 7.30 to 11.30am on Friday. Factory legislation also permitted sixteen-year olds to do eight hours overtime per week, which by coincidence was what was available, four hours on a Friday afternoon and again on a Saturday morning when we had the luxury of starting at 8.00am. Paul Bury joined me there for a summer job and, indeed, eventually went back after he changed his mind about entering the sixth form.

At Friday lunchtime we felt very grown up when the foreman invited us to join other members of the workforce in the pub. We were, of course, underage but no one seemed to mind and it is fair to say that the laws against under-age drinking went largely unenforced in 1969. Provided you looked reasonably close to eighteen and behaved yourself in the pub, you could expect to be left alone. In any case our foreman ensured that we only had two pints. There was also an important legislative difference. The landlord could not be prosecuted if he reasonably believed that the customer was old enough, unlike the current law where the burden is placed squarely on the licensee (and also on bar staff), to ensure that the customer is old enough to purchase alcohol. The work itself appeared to consist of unloading wagons and moving bags of cotton waste on hand trucks to designated locations in the mill and doing the job in reverse if a wagon was taking goods out. There was no manufacturing carried out, this having ceased a few years earlier under previous owners. The dirtiest job was actually sorting bags of cotton waste and it is perhaps significant that this job was done primarily by the two Pakistani members of the workforce. A job Paul and I got seemingly every Friday afternoon was sweeping the loading bay. We even got to try our hands at driving a forklift truck, not very successfully in my case. As I have said before, this was before the Health and Safety at Work Act and a modern employer could expect to be prosecuted in fairly swiftly. Workplace tearooms would also not get past modern health and safety demands. They were shrouded in tobacco smoke at break times. The notion that areas where people ate their food would be smoke free had not even reached conception. For many young workers, the smoke shrouded tearoom merely replicated the home, if on a smaller scale.

Unlike the previous summer where the workforce was largely absent, we were fully integrated and as such took our place at the foot of the pecking order. The oldest worker was seventy-nine years old and boasted that he could still lift the bath towel in the air. Another veteran worker, who boasted of spreading his seed far and wide, referred to us as his spunk drops. We learned many new words and phrases for sexual activity and were the butt of good natured teasing by the working men. Indeed we probably escaped lightly. Apprentices in industry could expect to be sent for a long stand, which is about as harmless as it gets, but apprentice mechanics were initiated by having their balls greased. Police cadets, and for that matter police women, had the station stamp imprinted on their bare backsides. Initiation ceremonies of this nature would now be considered as sexual assaults and I would guess that these practices have largely died out. You had the privilege of calling adult co-workers by their first name, but it did not pay to give too much cheek. Cocky teenagers could expect a clip round the ear or a kick up the arse if they pushed their luck with adult work colleagues. I saw one cocky young man, who thought he was a hard case because he had done time, chinned by a printer at another factory where I worked. You were expected to know your place and were reminded firmly if you forgot. As for the bosses, as boys we had virtually no contact with them but the tannoy asking for Mr John or Mr David to return to the office told you the correct form of address for the Isherwood brothers.

The money I earned paid for another rite of passage, the first holiday with the lads and more to the point without the parents. Although I have no doubt that generally speaking our working-class upbringing was much stricter than it has been for subsequent generations, there was no issue about four sixteen-year old boys taking themselves off on an overnight coach to Torquay and disappearing for a week. Effectively, it was disappearing. There were of course no mobile phones and as we intended to find a hotel on arrival, which mercifully we did, there was no contact number available to our parents until we were able and chose to supply one. Modern sixteen-year olds may be indulged in ways inconceivable to my generation, but modern parents would be very reluctant to allow their offspring to simply clear off as we did. In reality, we were pretty sensible. We avoided drinking at lunchtimes and apart from the last night did not get legless. It probably helped that licensing hours were restricted in those days. We did go to a club on one of the nights. As I recall, the girls were not much impressed and neither were our pockets with the price of drinks. I also paid my first visit to the races at Newton Abbot, so beginning a lifelong love affair with the sport. As with the consumption of alcohol, we were not supposed to bet but the bookmakers did not seem to mind. Looking back, it was all very innocent whereas although the modern teenager may embark on this rite of passage a couple of years later, theirs is likely to be on a Greek island where the holiday reps appear to encourage industrial drinking and reckless promiscuity.

I returned to school in September 1969 with a few quid still in my pocket after the holiday in Torquay. Although I would not have normally considered Saturday work an opportunity to earn money, working at Blackburn Rovers on match days could not be turned down. Along with a handful of lads of a similar age, I dressed in a white coat and carried a tray of crisps, popcorn and sweets around the perimeter wall of Ewood Park and sometimes on to the terraces themselves. The boss was a bloke named Brian Dixon who, if he thought you were taking the piss out of him, used to say "My name's Dixon, not Dick." The usual pay, including commission, was £1.50 for a couple of hours work combined with all important free entry into the ground. The downside was that you could be under the stand refilling your tray when a goal was scored or a penalty awarded. You got to walk out to sell your wares via the players' tunnel and walk back the same way, the closest I would ever get to every boy's childhood dream of entering the hallowed portals. A white coat was a poor substitute for the iconic blue and white halved shirt, but it allowed me to look for myself on TV when the cameras came. Sadly, the ITV footage of the Blackburn versus Swindon FA Cup tie in January 1970, where there was a close-up of me, no longer survives. There was one scary episode, when Brian Dixon took Paul Bury and myself to work at a League Cup tie between Manchester City and Liverpool at the old Maine Road ground. Despite being only sixteen, we were given the job of running a bottle bar behind the away end. At half time the visiting Liverpool fans stole a considerable amount of beer and some of the takings before the police intervened and shut the bar. Brian took us for a pint afterwards and we put it down to experience. Looking back, there wasn't a hope in hell that scores of Scousers would wait patiently for us to pour beer, as we were not supposed to hand them the bottles for all the reasons that are obvious.

The following summer, 1970, gave me my first experience of the public sector, the railway then being a nationalised industry. Discipline had once been very strict on the railway but in this era the unions ruled. My father got me a job at Accrington locomotive sheds where he was then based. I can't remember the pay and don't remember the work being hard, but I do remember it being dirty. The Diesel Motor Units, or DMUs, came into this particular part of the shed for maintenance. The remaining contents of the toilet tanks were flushed into a long stone pit beneath the rolling stock. Once the units had been moved our job (there were two of us) was to clean the pit. This involved inserting a metal tube into a hosepipe, narrow end facing outwards, secured by a jubilee clip. This turned it into a high pressure hose which we used to drive the human waste down the pit and into a drain. We then scrubbed the pit with a stiff brush and disinfectant. Some days there would be very little to do. We saw little of the foreman and even less of the electrician who regularly slipped off to the bookies in the afternoon. His great ambition was to own his own betting shop, something he realised when he got the opportunity for voluntary redundancy when Accrington shed closed. My father transferred to Blackburn, but the electrician ploughed his cash into a betting shop. Sadly, it all ended in tears when he got cleaned out within a few months, being the exception to the rule that you never see a poor bookmaker.

After my final and not very successful year at school had finished in the summer of 1971, it was time for me to enter the real world of permanent employment. At this stage of my life I had simply had enough of education and wanted to earn a living. Asking my father for pocket money at the age of eighteen felt demeaning, particularly as I was now old enough to vote, the age criteria having been reduced from twenty-one to eighteen in 1968. I wanted no more deferred gratification. The stage of being a boarder in the parental home is an essential step towards adulthood for those who do not go into higher education after leaving school. Those unfortunate enough to have to return to the parental home after graduation are forced to go through a stage they not unreasonably hoped to miss out. Those who left school at fifteen or sixteen usually went through a phase where they handed over their pay and got pocket money back, before graduating to boarder status usually at around eighteen. The upside of this arrangement, particularly for poorly paid apprentices, was that they did not have to worry about budgeting for their own clothes. The obvious downside was that this arrangement indicated the continuation of childhood in the home. In the fullness of time I would come to understand that boarding in the parental home was but a small step up on the ladder. It was still their home and their rules. In any event, there is nothing particularly adult about treating the parental home as an inexpensive hotel with laundry facilities and an on-site bank that does not charge interest.

Between leaving school in 1971 and leaving the town to become a student teacher in 1974, I worked at four different firms, only one of which is still in business. After failing to get a job in the council offices, I did a stint as a management trainee in a plumber's merchants in the town. If memory serves, I spent around six months on the trade counters before moving into the office where for the most part I took orders over the phone and then passed them over to the trade counters to be made up and loaded on to the company lorries for delivery. My routine paperwork was mainly calculating draft invoices which then went to someone else for checking. As I was salaried, rather than paid weekly, going into the office was a perk as we started half an hour later. The firm was a family firm that had been taken over by a larger group whose top bosses were rarely seen in Blackburn. Superficially, it was friendly and informal with everyone on first name terms. The culture was paternalistic and there was no trade union presence. In reality, there was no motivation, no team ethic and an atmosphere of bitchiness and backbiting. Looking back, this was a company in cruise control, living off its former glories and slowly declining customer base.

When I started at the company, the Sales Director, a man in his early fifties, did not drive although he did eventually pass his test. *Whoever has heard of a Sales Director who couldn't drive?* Even after he passed his test, I can't recall him ever going out to see customers and support the company's small team of travelling representatives. Instead, he spent the entire week bitching to anyone who would listen about the incompetence and laziness of the sales reps, until Friday afternoon came when he was all sweetness and light when the reps came in for the weekly meeting. The Finance Director was a miser who borrowed his older brother's OAP pass to get into football matches at senior citizen rate. At a time when I didn't particularly think about the future, I was under no illusion that there was no future for me in this company. I had clearly been earmarked to replace an older member of the office staff when he retired and I duly took over his desk. Beyond him the next retirement below director level was twenty years away. It was truly dead man's shoes and the pay was absolutely awful, £900 per year when I left totally de-motivated (not difficult in those days) in the summer of 1973. The chance of me ever moving up to a management job, even assuming that I would ever become sufficiently interested in baths, toilets and copper tubing to get one, was remote at this firm. I'm under no illusion that they missed me any more than I missed them. I can only presume that they went out of business when Mrs Thatcher put a bomb under British industry and commerce in the next decade.

My next job was at a plumber's and builder's merchants in another part of town. It was another local family firm, albeit larger, that had been taken over by a bigger outfit. The pay was much better, £1,200 per year plus paid overtime on alternate Saturday mornings. This firm was less friendly and more business focussed. The drivers were unionised but the office staff were not. I was employed as an assistant buyer in the building department, so was back right at the foot of the learning curve. The buyer was also the assistant sales manager, so I was quickly dubbed the assistant to the assistant. I had tried to get a job at this particular company two years earlier and had not been disappointed when they didn't hire me. Perhaps I should have trusted my instincts and given this company a wide berth, rather than just looking at the bottom line. I lasted about three months and never once had a one-to-one discussion with either the buyer or the sales manager about my work or my future with the company until they told me I didn't have one. To this day I have no idea why they employed me as they clearly had no intention of investing a minute of anyone's time in my training and development. As I can find no record of the company in the modern directory of plumbers and builders merchants in Blackburn, I can only presume this was another company that did not survive the winds of change that blew across the industrial landscape in the next decade.

After that it was back to the factory floor. The last thing I fancied was yet another stint in a plumber's or builder's merchants. On the Monday following my departure from the old job, I started work at India Mill, Darwen, one of the town's few surviving cotton factories. It eventually closed in 1991. The department I worked in dyed cloth and my usual job, as I remember it, was standing under a machine that simultaneously filled from above a row of about ten cardboard boxes. Once a box was full, you cut the line, sealed the box and moved it to a collection point, and then as swiftly as possible put another empty box under the line, before it started to pile up on the floor. If you did not line up the box exactly, the line of cloth would flop out of one the sides of the box on to the floor. It always paid to have a supply of open boxes to save precious seconds and avoid getting behind. During production life could be quite frantic, if several boxes threatened to fill at the same time. Mercifully, the machine was not noisy and neither was production continuous. The foreman in this department wore a suit rather than overalls, I think he was actually a management trainee, and I recognised him straight away as someone who had been the music room prefect at my school when I was in the second year (year eight in modern speak). As I recall, he was mysteriously and suddenly expelled. He gave no impression of knowing me, although he obviously knew where I had been to school and, therefore, that I must have had some idea of the reason for his removal. As it turned out, work colleagues were more than happy to voice their views about the foreman's sexuality, which relieved me of what I feared might have been the burden of keeping my mouth shut in order to keep my job. At India Mills I was paid by the hour and collected a wage packet every week, rather than a monthly payment into a bank account. In 1973, this was nature's way of telling you that you were working class, although many blue collar workers earned more than their office based colleagues who were salaried and had what was called staff status, a significant class distinction at work when blue collar workers were still sometimes referred to as "hands". Thus, gentility at clerical and junior management levels came at a price, although not when you were sick as sick pay usually came only with staff status. As I recall, my pay was 54p per hour, which worked out as a weekly pay packet without overtime of £21.60 per week, which fitted somewhere between my two earlier jobs. That figure equates to £254.92 today, just a couple of pounds above the minimum wage for forty hours at 2014–15 rates for an adult.

However, his presence, and that of two former primary school classmates at India Mills, was a sharp reminder of what had happened to the boy most likely to succeed more than nine years since we had gone our separate ways in July 1964. The geeky eleven-year old with the pudding basin haircut, and a love of encyclopaedias, was an unskilled labourer, a mill hand, whereas the boy who had stood much closer to the back than to the front when we were lined up in the order in which we had finished in the twice yearly examinations, was now a time served electrician. I guess he must have savoured the moment. It is hard to convey just how important the distinction between skilled and unskilled labour in British industry was at this time. I would like to think he has been gainfully employed for all of the intervening four decades, but I wouldn't want to bet on it given the employment traumas that Blackburn with Darwen would face in the 1980s. The other lad with whom I had played alongside in the primary school football team was an unskilled factory hand like me. No doubt his life has been harder. I had already started to think about a different future and encounters like this made it all the more imperative.

As was often the case in the British workplace where management was weak, a powerful individual with no ranking at all could wield disproportionate influence. I remember this being particularly so in the prison service where surly cashiers dictated when they would hand over expenses claims, rather than the office manager in the days before self-certified claims and direct payment into bank accounts. India Mills was my first encounter with this type of individual, in this case the dyer, which I think was a semi-skilled role. He was a stocky former miner in his late fifties who presumed to call the works manager by his first name. Overtime was limited to working through lunch on weekdays and four hours on Saturday morning. This particular individual determined which days the machinery ran through the lunch break, which always seemed to coincide with days where he could sit in the tearoom for an hour. We continued to graft, he didn't...but still got time and a half. I put up with shovelling down a sandwich with one hand and working with the other for a while and then rebelled and rejected the overtime, which required management to get a volunteer from somewhere else in the mill. He then told me that there would be no more

Saturday morning overtime for me, like I gave a damn. I think what really upset him, was me joining him in the tearoom and watching him not work while he was being paid. The embarrassment was too much and he would disappear, ostentatiously on some fictional work related mission, fooling no one but his lazy self. The foreman knew exactly what was going on, but needless to say did nothing.

What really hit me was the three-day week introduced by Edward Heath's Conservative government at the beginning of January 1974 in response to the miners' overtime ban that had begun in November and which was escalated to a full strike in February as a consequence of the government's failure to give ground over a pay dispute. The three-day week lasted from 1 January until 6 March, 1974. Factories and offices either worked Monday, Tuesday and Wednesday, or Thursday, Friday and Saturday. Extensions of the working day were not permitted. Only essential services such as the police, transport, hospitals and prisons (and also newspapers) were exempt as the government sought to eke out its remaining coal stocks. The television went off at 10.30pm. In 1974, coal fired power stations generated around eighty per cent of our electricity. Four decades on it is barely half that and still declining, and now all of the coal is imported. Importing coal in 1974, as a means of counteracting the overtime ban and subsequent strike, was not an option as not one bag could conceivably have been unloaded by at Britain's docks. The 1974 miners' strike marked the zenith of the power of organised labour in the UK; although it did not feel like that in the cotton trade where the power of trade unions had long been weak and thus pay had substantially fallen behind inflation compared to workers with more industrial muscle. At India Mill our working days were Monday, Tuesday and Wednesday, so at least I would not miss any Rovers home games, although as it turned out three of Blackburn's home games during the three day week were switched to Sundays, when production was not permitted, with significantly improved attendances. The first professional league game played on a Sunday was between Millwall and Fulham on 20 January, 1974, although permission was given for FA cup ties to take place a fortnight earlier. There is nothing quite like the law of unintended consequences and it was the three-day week, which broke the taboo on Sunday football and signalled an eventual end to the nonsense of having to buy a programme in order to be admitted rather than pay directly at the turnstiles as a means of getting round the law. Cricket clubs had been doing this for more than a decade and televised one day Sunday cricket had begun in 1969, but our national game and the coverage it generated was of a very different order. The prospect of profanities and brawls on the terraces horrified those who believed in the sanctity of Sunday in a way that cricket could never do. It took until 1981 before the situation was regularised and admission to Sunday sporting events fell into line with every other day of the week.

The first two weeks of the three-day week were the worst. We had to register as unemployed in order to receive unemployment benefit for the other two days, but the first three days of unemployment did not attract any benefit. Thus, we had no benefit in the first week and only one day in the second, until the situation regularised in the third week. I understood the concept of three waiting days (raised to seven two years ago) in that it discouraged people who might get a new job swiftly from signing on and therefore supported the work ethic. However, our unemployment was caused directly by the government reducing the power available to industry and there was no realistic prospect of getting work on the other two days. It was a petty and mean attack on working people caught up, through no fault of their own, in a standoff between a government bent on pay restraint and a trade union bent on being an exception. Obviously, I cannot prove it but I do believe it cost the Heath government a small number of vital working-class votes at the general election held on 28

February, 1974, the last occasion an outgoing government won more votes but elected less MPs than the narrowly victorious main opposition party.

As a railwayman, my father was not affected by the three-day week in the course of his work, but like everyone else he was affected by domestic power restrictions. A daily timetable of power cuts was published in local papers so we knew pretty accurately when we would be without power. Fortunately, we had enough coal so heating one main room caused no difficulty and only put us back two years to where we had been before finally getting central heating in 1972. Lighting was provided via paraffin lamps and in the absence of the television there was the alternative of a battery powered transistor radio. Water could be boiled over the fire to produce boiling water for hot drinks so it was all survivable. It was eerily dark without street lighting, but at least the pubs were open serving customers by candlelight. Those pubs who had gone over to electric pumps must have regretted it as they were not able to serve draft beer during the power cut, which could last up to four hours. Obviously a pie and peas supper was out of the question as well.

Initially, it was not clear how the deadlock between the government and the National Union of Mineworkers might be broken, but on 7 February, 1974, with three-day working now into its sixth week, the Prime Minister responded to the miners' vote to upgrade the dispute to an all-out strike on 9 February by calling a general election, scheduled for 28 February, asking the question: "Who governs?" While we knew that a Labour victory would end the three-day week as there would certainly be a settlement, no one really knew what a decisive victory for the Conservative would mean, except that it would be ugly and leave scars on the body politic that would take years to heal. For those of a revolutionary persuasion, it was a potential opportunity for the forces of organised labour to reverse the humiliation of the 1926 General Strike and defeat the hated capitalist enemy in a pitched, industrial battle, despite the fact that the mines were publicly owned. For those of the polar opposite persuasion, a decisive win at the polls would free up the Prime Minister to use troops and then use the law to destroy trade union power. As I recall, the atmosphere was febrile and the press exceptionally partisan. It felt as though there was a great deal at stake. For myself, I wanted our tribe to win. February 1974 would be the occasion of my first vote in a general election, having been just a few months to young in 1970. In those far off days the Labour party still was the working man's party rather than the party which despises the working class that it has become, overlaid with a disdain about working people that even the most lordly Tories of my youth could never match. My allegiance was clear, as was my view that capturing parliament was what mattered, not capturing the streets.

The opinion polls had forecast a Conservative victory, but in the end it was their leader Edward Heath who vacated 10 Downing Street to be replaced by the returning Harold Wilson at the head of a minority Labour government. The Conservatives actually won more votes than the Labour opposition, but it was Labour who just led in terms of seats, 301 to 297, but still 17 short of a majority in what was then a 635 seat House of Commons. Edward Heath attempted to form a coalition with the Liberal party, which had 14 MPs, at the time led by the charismatic Jeremy Thorpe, but negotiations broke down and finally four days after the election he accepted the inevitable and resigned, his gamble having failed. The Daily Mirror dubbed Edward Heath "the squatter at number 10". With the benefit of hindsight, it is hard to believe that Heath offered Thorpe the post of Home Secretary, given that Thorpe's one time penchant for rough trade was an open secret in the House of Commons and it is inconceivable that Heath had not at some point been brought up to date on Thorpe's activities by MI5, in the unlikely event of him being unaware of the latter's proclivities.

I still have a February 1974 copy of Private Eye, which published during the campaign an article about Thorpe's relationship with Norman Scott, nearly five years before the public learned of it when Thorpe, along with others, was accused of conspiracy to murder Scott in order to prevent his allegations of a homosexual relationship with Thorpe from finally reaching the public domain. Looking back, it appears that Thorpe was acquitted thanks to the combination of an almost wholly biased judge and a star struck jury who believed that a gentleman of Thorpe's standing was incapable of such caddish behaviour. Only now are we starting to learn that behaviour far worse than Thorpe's was covered up by the establishment. The significance of the Thorpe affair itself is much debated but, if nothing else, it marks the beginning of a process as the electorate became a little less credulous about their leaders moving across the spectrum to a position whereby politicians are sometimes regarded with outright contempt rendering deference stone dead.

The new government quickly settled the dispute, on the miners' terms, in the first week and also announced the end of the three-day week. We could all get back to normal, or as normal as was possible with rampant inflation, which at times exceeded thirty per cent and no obvious end to the spiral. I decided to move on and handed in my notice at India Mill, Darwen, taking a job at India Mill, Blackburn, the home of Graham and Brown's wallpaper factory. Graham and Brown, founded in 1946 by Harold Graham and Henry Brown are very much still in business and very much still a family firm, supplying high end products all over the world. I gather the firm now has around 650 employees, so it has grown significantly. This would be my last full-time job before heading off into higher education seven months later. I can't recall the hourly rate, but I do recall there were plenty of hours as the firm strove to catch up on production and compete in its market places. The trade union, which I think was simply called the Wallpaper Workers Union, now a part of

Unite the country's largest trade union, reached an agreement with management about the hours of work needed and thus we worked 7.00am to 6.00pm Monday to Thursday, 7.00am to 4.30pm on a Friday, and for those willing to volunteer from 7.00am to 1.00pm on a Saturday, which was time and a half. I can't remember the pay rate for the compulsory weekday overtime, but I do recall that the minimum 53.5-hour week equalled good money. There were no issues here about whether or not the machines ran through the lunch period; they did and we were given a paid half-hour break, which was covered internally. The other perks were free transport to work and a production bonus if targets were hit. We also got two free pairs of overalls, which the company laundered on our behalf.

The work itself was monotonous. Unlike my previous job in the cotton factory, the printing machines ran almost continuously and rarely broke down. This was the production line in the raw. On a daily basis I would carry out the same set of physical actions around 2,300 times a day. Each of the printing machines which were arranged in a long line in the factory, which I think was a weaving shed in a former incarnation, was manned by a printer, a backtenter, and a winder. The printer was a skilled man responsible for the process of pattern making on the wallpaper. Tenting (or tending) was an industrial word for observing a process or watching items. He was the eyes and ears of the printer. A tenter (or tender) would have been classed as semi-skilled, and was also responsible for ensuring that the huge reels of paper, on which patterns were printed, were feeding continuously into the printing machines. The winder, also known as the reelerman, simply turned a handle to a fixed maximum and reeled paper into the guillotine with one hand, then chopped the roll and caught it simultaneously with the other, under the guillotine, before stacking it on a truck. I was employed as a winder and every working day my machine produced about 2,300 rolls of wallpaper. I was fortunate. At 4.5 rolls of paper per minute, mine was one of the slower machines, and you could allow the paper to build a little while you had a smoke. You couldn't allow it to get heavy or the paper would tear under the weight of paper on top as you wound it in. Re-threading the paper through your guillotine was a pain in the arse and the foreman took a dim view if production was interrupted through laziness or carelessness. If you needed the toilet, then the guy on the next machine had to cover for you, although during the morning and afternoon tea breaks the backtenter covered for you after he had first taken his own break.

This was a very masculine world. Outside of the office staff and the canteen, I can recall only one female employee on the shop floor, and she was the quality controller, known to all as QC, and we considered her to be management. As well as production line workers, there were other employees that you would expect to find in an enterprise of this nature; warehousemen, drivers, and other skilled tradesmen needed for maintenance work. I don't recall it being intensely noisy, but you noticed the difference when production ceased for cleaning part way through Friday afternoon. The winders tended to be the younger end of the workforce and after Easter I recall there was a small influx of sixteen-year-old school leavers, about to begin a life of toil at the foot of the working-class pecking order. For those that remained unskilled, which would be most of them, this would be their place for the next fifty years. What seemed a king's ransom to a sixteen-year old fresh out of school, would not seem so much ten years later when he wanted to purchase his first home and start a family, always assuming that he had dodged the ravages of the great recession of the early 1980s. Of course, all this was in the future and although unemployment was rising there were still jobs in industry for all who wanted them.

Nevertheless, the citizens of Blackburn were worried about the future and a minority saw Blackburn's Pakistani community in a very jaundiced light as the jobs market gradually tightened. Asians, principally from Pakistan, had begun coming to Blackburn as well as other industrial towns and cities in the early sixties, in the days when there was a labour shortage rather than a glut and were happy to take the worst jobs. They were not exactly made welcome, but exclusion from the workplace depended on local markets and the ability of trade unions to operate a colour bar. The modern reader might well be surprised to discover that it was not unusual for management and trade unions to have local agreements about the numbers of black faces permitted at the particular depot or enterprise. In what was left of the cotton industry (the reader should refer back to Chapter One for employment figures in the cotton industry at various points during the twentieth century), white male workers had been able to get out fairly easily in favour of better paid work elsewhere. Thus, even in a declining industry, there were labour shortages which were filled by migrants. Indeed, by the end of the 1970s, four fifths of jobs in what was left of the cotton trade were filled by Asians, without arousing too much resentment. They were welcome to those jobs, if not exactly welcome in British society. The grim irony for the migrants was that they and their families would be the principal sufferers when the industry finally expired. For the most, racism was based on a very different assumption rather than perceived unfair competition; one in which incomers were inferiors by virtue of the colour of their skin and were civilised only on the basis that their homelands had once been fortunate enough to be part of the mighty British empire presided over by enlightened, incorruptible and paternalistic colonial officials. This was a view common across both the class structure and political spectrum. Racist language was common at work, as indeed it was in the gentlemen's clubs of London. Twenty-five years is a long time if you are enduring discrimination on a daily basis but, looking back to 1974 and where we were, it is close to astonishing how much attitudes to racism had changed by the end of the century and the extent to which derogatory racist language had become utterly unacceptable. Although the fascist fringe is still with us in the form of the BNP, it is no longer possible for its leaders to stand on public platforms as John Kingsley Read did in the mid-seventies and tell his audience that he would not talk about immigrants, but rather he would "talk about wogs, coons and niggers", and not be arrested and treated as a social pariah. There is still work to do, the extent of which is the subject of fierce debate, but there are genuine grounds for believing that a colour blind society is possible in my lifetime, and I am now sixty-three. Back in 1974, the National Front obtained over four per cent of the vote in Blackburn in the two general elections with the aforesaid Kingsley Read as candidate. After an internal split Kingsley Read emerged as leader of the National Party, and along with a colleague succeeded in being elected to the town council in 1976. Mercifully, it proved to be a short lived triumph, but it sent a shock wave through society as none of these people were considered remotely electable and it brought the town into temporary disrepute.

Chapter Ten

Growing Away

Late in 1973 I bumped into David Baxter who had been two years younger than me at school and had left in the summer of that year. We had not particularly been friends as people mixed largely within their own year. Instead, we were acquainted by dint of using the same church on Sunday, at least until somewhere approaching my fifteenth birthday when I rebelled yet again, this time successfully against being packed off to church every Sunday by my mother who hadn't herself attended Mass in living memory. Over a pint we compared notes. He was having a gap year before going up to Oxford in October 1974. If memory serves, he was destined for Oriel College. At the time, he had a white collar job with the local authority. I had attempted to get a clerical post with Lancashire County Council two years earlier, but without success. I can't say it was their loss. The upshot of the conversation was that I made contact with my old school and arranged to have a second crack at "A" level History in the summer of 1974. They were kind enough to loan me some books and to pay for the examination entry. This time I didn't waste their money and attained a comfortable "C" grade. As it turned out I did not need the second "A" level to secure a place at Madeley College of Education, but the real value is that it got me studying again as I had not touched a book since finishing revision for my "A" levels some two and a half years earlier. I had given up on education and, over two years, had drifted from white collar work to the factory floor. The chance meeting was the catalyst for changing direction, or rather returning to the direction ordained for me when I passed the 11 plus, joining one of the professions rather than simply having an occupation. The dormant ambition to become a teacher was brought back to life. To achieve that it was necessary for me to break away from Blackburn, although it would not necessarily preclude a return. As the comedian Jim Davidson succinctly put it, I had tried being working class and found I didn't like it.

Unless you were a day student, higher education necessarily involved leaving both the parental home and the home town to strike out elsewhere. In 1974 the nearest Universities and Colleges of Education were in Manchester some twenty-four miles away. It never occurred to me to travel daily as that would only prolong my permanent residence in the parental home. I had discovered that there was nothing grown up about living at home and paying board. I was ready to move on and not just to the next street. During my childhood it was the norm, as it had been for generations for young people, on marriage to settle close to the parental home sometimes even in the same street. One boy I recall actually lived next door to his grandparents. Thus, family support was always close by. Virtually all had left school at the earliest opportunity and experience of life outside these closed communities was limited to war service for the older generation and conscription for the generation above me. In the case of those who did national service, that experience was exclusively male. Working-class access to higher education had a significant effect on working-class kinship, although it was not the only factor involved in dispersing extended families that had been settled for generations. Cheap emigration to Australia at a mere ten pounds for passage played a part. The period of social change that emancipated young people from their parents was possibly the most significant factor of all. Young people who had money in their pocket, as a result of full employment that both increased opportunity and bid up wages, were able to strike out on their own away from parental restraints. Education was not the only driver. Nevertheless, it is significant in my own family that the three of four siblings who attended Grammar School were the ones who left Blackburn, in all of our cases permanently, except to visit our parents, now both deceased.

I found myself in an obscure village in Staffordshire quite by chance. The application form for a place at a College of Education, as teacher training colleges had been renamed, was similar to that for a place at university in that you listed five choices in order of preference. As my old school was supplying the reference, I had to place the two Catholic colleges, one based at Horsforth, a suburb of Leeds, and the other in Twickenham, West London, first and second on the form. Beyond those, I had never heard of any of the other establishments and put Madeley third on the list largely because it was far enough from my home town to be away from it, but close enough to get back to quickly if there were to be a family emergency or more likely an important football match at Ewood Park. Madeley was a twenty-minute bus ride to Crewe railway station. It was an arbitrary decision to put Madeley just in front of Crewe and Alsager College on the form. I can't remember what establishment filled the fifth and final space on the list. The only strategy involved was to reject interviews at the two Catholic establishments and have my application forms passed down the line. I did not want or need the Catholic teacher's certificate and indeed was horrified at the thought of being expected to teach Catholic dogma to impressionable children. It would have been an exercise in gross hypocrisy, given that I did not attend Mass, to take the sacraments or accept the restrictions on my private life that the church sought to impose. Equally, the memories of the humiliations suffered at the hands of the Sisters of the Passion were simply too fresh. I could not be part of a regime that humiliated small children in the name of a supposedly gracious and benign God. Even though my already very articulate nine year old sister told me that the Sisters of the Passion no longer treated their charges in this way, the psychological wounds were still raw when exposed to the light. I should stress that I attach no blame to the Marist fathers and hope that they would forgive what for me was a necessary deceit.

Having already postponed the interview once, I pitched up at Madeley sometime towards the end of July. I can remember getting off the bus one stop too early as it turned out and seeing a modern residential estate to my right and five four-storey halls of residence to my left. The halls looked out at right angles to the college playing fields. As I was early I took a walk around, continued past the fork in the road and noted two pubs and a very large pond that was the centre piece of the village. Behind the pond was another estate on which miners, who worked at the nearby Silverdale colliery, lived. This was the gritty part of rural Staffordshire. On this first walk I did not go as far as the atmospheric parish churchyard. Turning back I followed the road, this time taking the fork passing a few shops, a bank, and on the other side of the road, a working men's club. The village had passed its inspection. Shortly after I walked past the club, I found the main entrance to the College. I only remember bits and pieces about the interview process. There were three or four other people there and we were conducted to a classroom to do some English tests. In the fullness of time I was ushered into the office of the admissions tutor, Walter Read. His opening question was, "Mr Laxton, are you superb?" For the uninitiated Laxton's "superb" are an apple first bred in Bedfordshire by Thomas Laxton in 1897. The family business continued until it was sold in 1957 and the original orchards were built over. There is still a surviving orchard in Bedford. As far as I am aware, my family is not related to Thomas Laxton and his heirs. I said something to the effect that if he offered me a place then he would have the pleasure of finding out for himself. We briefly discussed my desire to teach and what I had been doing over the last three years. I was offered a place there and then and went off to the nearest pub, The Bridge, for a celebratory pint, prior to heading back to Blackburn to celebrate a friend's twenty-first birthday. I did not really take in the information about the first year halls of residence being ten miles away, nor did I take in his comments about the accommodation being less than modern. I didn't care. I was about to start a new chapter in life. From returning to work in August after the summer fortnight, I had precisely nine weeks left to work in the wallpaper factory.

It was now time to apply for a student grant. Since 1962 students in higher education, defined as those studying for degrees and/or teaching qualifications in universities, polytechnics and colleges of education, were entitled to claim a mandatory grant from their home local authority to cover living costs for up to a maximum of four years, subject to a parental means test. Student loans were advocated only by right wing extremists who looked to the USA for their economic gurus. Unfortunately, their time would come. As I had worked for three years since leaving school, I was classed as an independent student and therefore my parent's income was disregarded. Tuition fees were paid by the local authority. During vacations, students could claim social security benefits. In fact, for me it got better. Having worked for three years, I had a contribution record and could claim unemployment benefit enhanced by earnings related payments when I signed on. In practice, I signed on only at Christmas and Easter when, other than the Christmas post or cash in hand bar jobs, no employer in Blackburn was interested in taking on someone just for a couple of weeks. It was student heaven.

In the fullness of time, all these perks disappeared. Earnings related benefit was one of the first things abolished by Mrs Thatcher and most students lost the right to claim benefits altogether. Student loans were also introduced to replace grants, also under Mrs Thatcher in 1989. Tuition fees were introduced in 1998 and in a fairly short space of time have been hiked from £1,000 p.a., to £9,000 p.a. I have no hesitation in defending the old system. It was not as expensive as it sounds, as only sixteen per cent of people in the 18–21 age group were in higher education, compared to around forty-three per cent today. The system allowed students to concentrate on learning rather than being forced to juggle studies with part-time jobs just to survive. The old system had its faults, not least the means testing which disadvantaged those students whose parents either could not or would not provide financial support, but it did not lumber young people with massive debts that some will never be able to repay. As a nation, we could easily afford a generous system of student support by the very simple solution of radically slashing the number of people in higher education and taking universities back to their proper elite academic function. The comprehensive university is a contradiction in terms. Many young people would be far better suited by apprenticeships, sandwich courses and learning on the job. They would be earning money three years earlier, rather than wasting those years at a university no one has heard of running up massive debts acquired in the pursuit of a third class honours degree in media studies. Anyway, rant over. In due course, my grant was confirmed although needless to say Lancashire County Council was unable to pay it on time.

A formal letter from Madeley College confirming my place and room in the halls of residence arrived in due course, along with a document called the Code of Community Living which included the elliptical sentence, "students must sleep in their own rooms". The envelope also contained a welcome letter from students in the year above me complete with nicknames of the authors and useful information about hall fees to cover such things as communal TV and newspapers, and also that the power points took only old-fashioned two pin plugs, which still didn't set any alarm bells ringing as we hadn't yet been rewired at home. The remainder of the summer passed more or less in a blur, notable only for hope to spring in the hearts of all true Blackburn Rovers supporters as the team got off to a good start in its fourth consecutive season of third division football. 1974–75 was the club's centenary season, so the return to full membership of the football league (third and fourth division clubs only had associate member status) at the end of that season was a source of considerable celebration. However, a return to the top flight, which as it turned out was as a founder member of the FA Premier League, had to wait until 1992. I can remember buying a few books and some stationery, as well as a modest restock of the wardrobe, and of course, there was a valedictory drinking session finishing up at the local Mecca where overpriced, bland and bloating keg beer was served until 2am. My friends confidently predicted that I would be thrown out before Christmas. Being asked to leave the local Mecca due to gross intoxication only seemed to confirm their opinion.

Sunday 6 October, 1974, dawned bright and sunny and thankfully my hangover wasn't too bad. My instructions were that students travelling by train would be picked up at Stafford station. Accompanied by a very large and heavy trunk, my father drove me to Blackburn railway station. I can recall arriving at Stafford early and meeting up with some fellow new students in the station café. Berend Wallace whose main subject was German, would be in the same hall of residence as me. Public school educated and well-travelled, he seemed rather more sophisticated than me, as well as being a couple of years older. At least I would not be the only one three years older than everyone else in my year. In fact, although the intake was obviously dominated by eighteen-year-old students fresh out of school, there was actually a significant group that was two or more years older bringing different life experiences with them to the campus. More new students, including a pretty blonde from Maghull, Merseyside, by the name of Jill Sutter, joined us before eventually a minibus arrived and we were driven around ten miles through the Staffordshire countryside to Nelson Hall, about four miles from the nearest town, Eccleshall.

Nelson Hall came as a surprise and, to some of my

more cosseted fellow students, a rude shock. Instead of modern halls of residence, there were eleven single storey huts each shaped like an "H" with two long corridors of around twenty rooms on either side of a square common room. From the air, it would have looked like Long Kesh internment camp in Northern Ireland but crucially without the barbed wire, fences, and bomb proof gate-lodge. With the benefit of hindsight, my only surprise is that it did not become an open prison like Ford when the military had finished with it. During the War, Nelson Hall had been built originally to house munitions workers at the nearby ordnance factory in the hamlet of Cold Meece, known as ROF Swynnerton, taking its name from the larger village a couple of miles away. Later in the War, civilian workers gave way to American troops. After the War, it was decided that Nelson Hall would become a Teacher Training College. Teacher provision needed considerable expansion if life was to be breathed into the 1944 Education Act and so in 1949 the County of Stafford Training College opened its doors to the very first students, for the first few years exclusively female. The College Principal was Elizabeth Malloch. In due course, when Madeley College of Education, as teacher training establishments were renamed, opened in 1962 in another burst of expansion, Nelson Hall became an annex housing all first year students requiring residential places, and some second year students to act as mentors and make the newcomers feel at home. By the time Liz Malloch retired in 1970 the college had more than 1,200 students on the roll, including post graduates. By the standards of the time this was considered to be a large college.

The rooms were unusual in that they had two doors, although only one was in use. The reason was that during the War what was now an individual student room had actually been two rooms. The accommodation for munitions workers must have been positively monastic given that the student rooms were not much bigger than a prison cell. The walls were extremely thin and therefore lovemaking was private only in that those participating were not seen as opposed to being heard. Unlike the modern halls at the main campus, there were no wash basins in the rooms. The communal washrooms were divided into open cubicles and the bathrooms opposite the washbasins had stable doors rather than full length doors. Ten years later, when I was posted to Werrington House Detention Centre, having quit teaching and joined the Prison Service, I was reminded of Nelson Hall when I first saw the washing facilities. There were no showers and no urinals, but at least the toilet cubicles had full length doors. Just like a prison, they were equipped only with hard toilet paper. Having grown up in a house with an outside toilet, and without a bathroom until 1972, I did not find the accommodation excessively spartan. Since our toilet paper came courtesy of British Rail that also did not register as a significant discomfort. Just like home the central heating was wasteful, inefficient, and unfit for purpose on the coldest days of the winter. The bar area, known as the red room, reminded me of some of Blackburn's toughest pubs with its ancient slashed settees and peeling paintwork. All that was missing were the spittoons and sawdust. It was the perfect environment for Rugby Club circle games, which frequently involved someone getting naked standing in a hollowed out barrel being drenched by beer. It was not for the faint hearted or those from a sheltered background.

Nelson Hall would be my student home for two years. You either loved it or hated it. For students in the latter category, the first year could not pass quickly enough. Those in the former category had to enter a ballot to stay for a second year, if there were insufficient rooms available. For those who loved it, the isolated community catered for all their needs and there were a couple of pubs, both long since closed, within walking distance. All meals were provided and there was a bar, shop, and library as well as a gymnasium and sports fields. Female students outnumbered their male counterparts by two to one so there were no complaints on that front! The locals referred to Nelson Hall as the "brothel on the hill". One suspects they were simply jealous.

The first term passed in a blur and in mid-December I returned to Blackburn for the Christmas holiday. My friends were surprised that I had survived the first term and confidently predicted that next term's teaching practice would put an end to my stint in higher education. My good friend Brian Scott arranged for me to escort a young lady to the local Mecca that night, assuring me that it was all laid on. Well, she had been laid all right, about eight months earlier. As I recall, her interest in going to the Mecca was to confront the father. There's nothing like your friends when it comes to a welcome home prank. Our first teaching practice, given the rather more unthreatening title of Initial School Experience, was scheduled to begin about five days after our return from holiday. I can remember our tutor, Ron Young, handing out advice for the next four weeks. It was made clear to female students that trousers were largely unacceptable. As for the men, any student who refused an instruction by the Headmaster to get a haircut (male hair was very long in the 1970s) could expect to have the placement changed to Walsall, unpopular because it was a long journey, had more than its fair share of tough schools, and the locals spoke like Noddy Holder on speed. Eventually someone said: "Excuse me, Mr Young, what do we do about discipline?" Back came the not terribly reassuring reply that provided our lessons were well prepared and interesting all would be fine. Looking back, I can't believe he was really that casual but he may well have thought it was the best line to take in the circumstances, as he must have known that the one thing we all feared was being unable to keep discipline. I'm sure other tutors would have simply told war stories. I was sent with another student to a primary school in Oakengates, birthplace of Sir Gordon Richards, the first of only two jockeys ever to be knighted, and my first ever lesson went swimmingly for about two minutes, until one of my nine-year olds was sick. Nothing prepares you for this and just as panic was about to take over, a little boy called Kevin White said, "Please, Sir, I'm the sick monitor," and off he went to get the brush, pan and sawdust. You never forget a child's name after an incident like that. Clearly the school was a well-oiled machine. At the end of the practice, Ron Young had us write up accounts of our experiences. He had a sense of humour bypass at my account, which contained my observations on this and other gems of human interaction which in his view suggested I hadn't taken things seriously. Well, if he'd seen the hours I sweated on lesson preparation he may have taken a different view. My friends back in Blackburn now predicted my demise in the examinations. They were out of luck as there were none in the first year.

In the end I spent five years at Madeley College, four years for my academic work which brought me an Upper Second Class Honours Degree in History and Education from the University of Keele, and one sabbatical year as the college's last President of the Students' Union before Madeley was swallowed up by North Staffordshire Polytechnic, and became its teacher training annex. In many ways, Madeley became my home. I still made trips to Blackburn at Christmas and Easter, but in the last two summer vacations I took temporary jobs in Staffordshire rather than go back to Blackburn. Even the Christmas and Easter visits were shortened as I became a student activist and regularly attended the biennial National Union of Students conferences in Blackpool, a hotel always being preferable to going home and sharing a room with my younger brother. If I am honest, and my student room had not often been required for income generating conferences run by the college, my visits to Blackburn would have been both even shorter and less frequent. This was not because I was at war with my parents, those days had gone. I simply had a new life that was a gateway to one that was still to come.

In any event, the number of friends back home in Blackburn was thinning out. Some, like me, were in higher education in other parts of the country and some of those who had already completed it had moved on. Jan Gorak went so far as to leave the country, to lecture in America in 1979 and we have not seen each other since, although we did exchange the occasional letter for about seven years. Who writes letters now? Jan is now Professor of English at the University of Denver and a distinguished author. Marriage and fatherhood, not necessarily in that order, removed others from Fridays and Saturdays out with the lads. Paul Bury was first to go as early as 1973, although his work as a self-employed carpet fitter had already taken us out of each other's orbit. Brian Scott, who is my oldest friend, succumbed in 1976 and the third member of our regular drinking club, Frank Poulton, duly carried out his threat to get married when there was no one left to go boozing with a couple of years later. The three of us finally met up again along with our respective spouses, just after Christmas in 1992. By then, Frank Poulton was living and working in Bedfordshire. One last get together seemed to satisfy his curiosity, but over the next ten years I did continue to have the odd drink with Brian Scott when visiting Blackburn, which ceased when my by now widowed mother elected to move to Oxford to be close to my youngest sister in January 2003. We have not met since and it is high time we renewed a friendship that began in the autumn of 1962. Another good friend, Bryan Snape, joined Lancashire Police, one of those jobs which, like the prison service, gradually severs most of the connections with your old life. We would not meet again for thirty-four years. In those days there was no social media and if someone moved on without leaving a forwarding address, then the chances were you had lost touch. I was not quite the last to get married when my turn came in February 1982. My last visit to Blackburn as a bachelor was a very fleeting one for Christmas 1981 and my memory is that only two old mates out of what had once been a very wide circle of friends and acquaintances were still around, and one of those, like me, was doing his filial duty at the festive season. I could not wait to get back to my life in King's Lynn, where, coincidentally, one of my female cousins had also settled.

One of the pleasures of being a student was that it had the effect of extending adolescence but without the dependence on and the deference to one's parents, unless you were unlucky enough to be dependent on them to finance you through higher education, or actually preferred to live at home, and some people actually did. Colleges of Education were not like some university arts courses where the only fixed timetable commitment was a weekly tutorial. For the likes of us, lectures were compulsory, and most of the time methods were didactic, which for some of my fellow students who lacked confidence in their intellectual capacity came as a relief. Nevertheless, the timetable was not so full as to get in the way of long lie-ins, epic partying, and an active love life for those that sought one. Wednesday afternoons were free for students to play sport, engage in other recreational activities – which covers a broad spectrum – or simply sit and chill with friends. This last activity was known as festering. For me it was a new world. I had been used to the discipline of early starts for work and quite limited time off that certainly did not include midweek afternoons. Hard drinking had only been a weekend activity when there was no work to worry about in the morning. There was no question of taking young ladies home for some afternoon delight at any time of the week. A minority of students struggled with the freedom and every term a small number would have their courses terminated, not because they were academically out of their depth as the work was not that demanding, but because they had got so far behind as a consequence of not giving it priority over more pleasurable activities. Inevitably, teaching practice weeded out a few more, but in retrospect the failure rate was surprisingly low.

Other students struggled with the freedom in different ways. It was a sexually competitive environment where women outnumbered the men by two to one, fuelled by the presence of the greater number of alpha males made available by virtue of the physical education course. Sadly for some female students the testosterone generated was too much for them and, as a consequence, gained reputations as easy lays amongst the physical education students. In the mid-1970s, these things still mattered as the old double standard was alive and well, and some young women found themselves deeply unhappy as a consequence of not being emotionally able, or just as pertinently not allowed, to shag like the men. Finding a steady boyfriend who would not treat them like a piece of meat and help them recover their self-esteem then became a problem. Thankfully, later generations have become less judgemental and much more egalitarian about sexual ethics. Many students, including me, found their future spouse on campus and usually from a very different part of the country. Some are even still together! The relationships least likely to survive were those pre-existing when one half of the partnership left to enter higher education or alternatively both left the home location to attend different institutions. Suddenly, the old boyfriend or girlfriend could seem dreadfully dull and provincial and usually by the end of the first or second term a combination of distance and infidelity had put paid to the relationship. It was all part of growing away. Those in the few relationships that did survive achieved that only by putting college life in a compartment, not allowing the occasional taste of forbidden fruit to sour the partnership. It is best summed up as "don't ask, don't tell". One pre-existing couple I recall did find the answer. They attended Madeley together and unofficially shared a room for three years. Whether they are still together is not known to me, but you would hope that they are.

Nothing symbolises an extended adolescence more than involvement in student politics. It was a very black and white world, one of heroes and (pantomime) villains and nothing in between, devoid of humour, and replete with middle-class guilt. Just like white British blues artists ached to be black, so the well-heeled public school products ached to be working class. It is this combination of excessive earnestness and lack of self-awareness that often takes student politics into the realms of the absurd. Looking back, it was the posturing absurdity rather than the occasional public displays of extremism which excited the Daily Mail, which seemed to typify student politics. I notice that nothing has changed, with the current National Union of Students (NUS) executive refusing to condemn the murderous extremists who call themselves Islamic State (IS), on the basis that it might be perceived as Islamophobic! I just hope that as adult politicians they prove to be more grown up than my generation in power, though I am not hopeful.

Returning to the theme, one particular member of the NUS executive – who for obvious reasons shall remain nameless – after giving a speech at one of our general meetings about the evils amongst other things of sexism, reputedly then asked for a woman for the night. The story is believable if only because revolutionary consciousness amongst men had to be forcibly challenged by feminists to recognise a role for women beyond making the tea and providing sexual services on demand to the male revolutionary elite. On another occasion I can recall there was a mass walkout from the Park House Hotel in Blackpool after a barman referred to a female student as a "chick". A much smaller group, including me, elected to stay as the bar served excellent Boddington's bitter and was open until 4am. Some thirty-four years later an unknown MP of my generation, Labour's Kate Green, got her fifteen minutes of fame by successfully getting a beer called "top totty" removed from the House of Commons bars on the grounds that it was offensive and demeaning to women. The only effect of this synthetic row was that the publicity resulted in a doubling of orders of the beer across the country. The brewers, Slaters of Eccleshall, were delighted. How can anyone take seriously MPs who behave like student politicians during a major economic crisis and with major moral issues like the Libyan civil war and the continued operation of Guantanamo Bay to occupy their time?

There was more posturing on another occasion when conference was disrupted by students complaining that there would not be time to debate Gay Rights, which had joined Apartheid in South Africa and the destruction of Israel at the top of the list of causes important to student activists. I should add that opposition to apartheid was a cause I supported wholeheartedly, which made the rampant Anti-Semitism amongst student activists that much harder to stomach. Indeed one of the most passionate opponents of Israel as a Jewish state was himself a Jew. It stunned me that one man could loath his own people so much. However, I now realise that our ruling elite, many of whom were students in the 1970s, share this characteristic in their contempt for all things British. As for the Gay Rights debate, it was lost because of the serial disruption of conference by the same activists who were now protesting about the lost opportunity to demonstrate their egalitarian credentials. This was a world far away from the one I had known.

Working-class kids in Blackburn knew nothing nor cared nothing about gay rights and used rather more colourful expressions than gay. My father's preferred terminology was "brown hatter", which at fourteen years of age I was too embarrassed to ask him to explain. A stranger mentioning the subject of gay rights to a native of the town would have been directed to the Merchant's Hotel and told to watch his arse if he needed to use the toilet. The fact that the Merchants had an openly gay landlord who had received publicity in one of the Sunday tabloids, and was a relatively safe haven for gay men, was considered at the time to be progressive and tolerant. However, unlike NUS conferences Madeley College did not provide any challenge to the prejudices I had imbibed growing up. On the odd occasions Gay Rights resolutions came up they were voted down. Homosexuals were equated with paedophiles in the eyes of many of my fellow students and therefore had no place in the teaching profession. Here there was no division between middle- and working-class students. Opposition to Gay Rights united both the celibate until marriage members of the Christian Union with the aggressive heterosexuals of the Athletic Union, just about the only time they ever got in bed together. If there were any gay men or women, and there surely must have been, I never knowingly met any of them. Unlike Oxford, Bristol and Durham, this was an institute of higher education where people stayed firmly in the closet as it was the safest place. Madeley College was also almost exclusively white, unlike my home town, and it would be untruthful of me to say that there was not some casual racism amongst the student body, more as a product of ignorance and lack of contact with minority communities than malice or crude prejudice. For NUS activists, however, race was a defining issue.

Like most people who go into politics for any length of time, I and my fellow students wanted to change the world for the better. For the majority of student activists that entailed either the destruction of capitalism or at the very least permitting it only a subordinate and regulated role in the socialist society, that would come either through the revolution when the workers threw off their chains, or by electing a Labour government that actually carried out a socialist program. National conference actually continued until midnight on all but the last day. The bars in the winter gardens at Blackpool did a roaring trade and even sold beer in two pint mugs to thirsty students like myself, for whom sitting through hours of what passed for intellectual debate was simply too much. Nevertheless, there were some delegates who sat through every minute and regarded those who, like me, needed a break as politically unsound. During the early hours there would be caucuses of the various political groups, sometimes addressed by fraternal guest speakers and, sometimes, shows of solidarity in one of the big hotels with one oppressed group or another. I can recall on one occasion a group of female students demonstrating their solidarity with female Irish republican prisoners wearing just blankets. Just like it is not considered correct to ask a Scotsman what he wears under his kilt, it was not permitted to speculate what was worn under the blanket. It is fair to say that delegates took themselves as seriously as they did the issues they were debating. However, little of this got in the way of drinking until 4am, and for those with inexhaustible stamina nocturnal activities to follow until it was time to begin all over again at 9am promptly.

The political groupings did not match the world outside. The ruling clique was called the Broad Left, composed of Labour, Liberal and Communist students. Further to the left were various Trotskyite groups, prone to splitting and falling out over arcane interpretations of Marx and Lenin. Their designer scruffiness betrayed their independent school origins. A good rule of thumb regarding the left in the NUS was that the further left the political group, the further up the social scale were its adherents although obviously there were exceptions. To the right was the Federation of Conservative Students, although in their pre-Thatcherite incarnation they were more of a social democratic grouping and appeared right wing only when compared to the student left, which in all its guises was well to the left of Labour Prime Minister, James Callaghan. Student politicians, for the most part, represented themselves. Turnouts for policy making general meetings of student bodies were often very low, particularly where there were few halls of residence close by. Thus, the politically committed could take advantage of situations where there was either no quorum required for debate, or it was set so low as to be meaningless. Turnouts for elections could also be depressingly low. It has to be remembered that academic institutions were much smaller back in the 1970s and thus overall had a greater sense of community. It's just that most students chose other aspects of community life and were not bothered, even where institutions were of a manageable size, what sort of people ran the students union so long as a top act was booked for the Summer Ball, and the rugby club was properly funded. I suppose this is one area where student life and real life coincide, whereby a large body of the electorate chooses not to pick from, as they see it, the menu of posturing clowns placed in front of them.

As a society, we suffer from the lack of active participation in politics. In student unions it is contained and therefore relatively harmless, but when those student politicians refuse to grow up when they graduate to politics in the big wide world as happened with many of my generation, it can have a transformative effect for the worse. Modern political correctness is the direct descendant of the student politics of the 1970s. Diversity and environmentalism have replaced Christianity as the official faiths of the country. My generation of student politicians realised in the 1980s that if the workers' revolution could not occur when Mrs Thatcher was in power, and there were more than three million people unemployed (and that was just the official figures), then it never would. As a consequence, they made their accommodation with capitalism as we saw under Mr Blair, and adopted new gurus in post Marxist thinkers such as Gramsci, who preached the subversion of the institutions that sustained the state, and Marcuse, who advocated the control of language to express ideas so that freedom of speech applied only within the narrow confines of what was permitted by the ruling elite. We now have a political class that dominates the Labour and Liberal parties, and has succeeded in capturing key positions at the top of the Conservative Party. This class shares a broadly common outlook on key issues such as EU membership and the undesirability of the UK being self-governing, global warming, relations with the USA, the intrinsic nature of human rights, and multiculturalism as well as adopting socially revolutionary aspects of the radical feminist and gay rights movements. And still they wonder why UKIP has made such spectacular progress...I may have grown away but I consider that I still retain my very old Labour values. Sadly, there is no political party any more that represents working-class people and people like me who successfully aspired but retain a close affinity with their roots.

Returning to the narrative, my extended adolescence came to a formal end in the summer of 1979 when I was offered a post as a History teacher at Springwood High School in King's Lynn, Norfolk, where I spent the next four years of my life. I was now a salaried professional. Mercifully, we were paid on the nineteenth of the month, so there was not too long to wait for the first infusion, and of course it was handy being paid just before Christmas. Unlike the modern generation, I was fortunate enough to graduate free of debt and on arrival in Kings Lynn just under a fortnight before the start of term, all I needed to sustain me was an overdraft of £300 (just over £1,500 at today's values) plus £50 or so that I had in the bank. With this I was able to rent a room in a multi-occupational house at £52 per month plus deposit, upgrade my wardrobe and pay my other living costs, surviving with a little to spare until the first payday came around. If I hadn't still been a smoker (I gave up a year later) and a man who liked a couple of pints most nights (I still do) it would have been very comfortable. My starting salary was around £4k per year and I was able to pay off my overdraft by Christmas. In those years before teaching became an all graduate profession, those who like me were graduates started several points up the incremental scale. A twenty-one-year old with just the basic Certificate in Education would have received £3,231. The starting salary for a teacher in 2014–15 is £22,203 compared to the national average pay of around £27,000 in 2014, although averages are misleading as they are skewed by both London and higher earners. It should be remembered that only around one third of the working population earn or exceed the average salary. Median average pay (the pay earned by Mr or Mrs Midpoint of the working population) of £22,044 is a figure rather closer to the average worker's experience and even that figure is skewed upwards by the London effect. Where I live in Huddersfield, the median average pay is just £17,576 (April 2014 figure). The price of a pint of bitter in Kings Lynn when I arrived in August 1979 was just 36p. At today's values the price of a pint should be £1.81 if it had risen strictly in line with inflation. The current average price of a pint of beer in Norfolk is £3.40, which demonstrates beyond all doubt that the anti-alcohol lobby are lying through their teeth when they insist that alcohol has become cheaper. The price of a pint has also comfortably outstripped salary rises as well as price inflation since 1979. A packet of cigarettes could be bought for 58p in January 1979. The average price post the 2014 budget for a pack of twenty is £8.47, representing an increase of almost triple the rate of inflation over thirty-five years. At least no one pretends that cigarettes are cheap. As I have said, I gave up the following year.

If the truth be known, I lived like a student, albeit one with a salary, in my first year in Kings Lynn. I was one of seven tenants sharing a house in a pleasant part of Kings Lynn opposite The Walks, a tree lined parkland area that you cut through to go to the town centre. We shared a kitchen, bathroom and lounge and fortunately all the rooms had wash basins. My fellow flat sharers were mainly young professionals like myself, but there was one young woman who had left her violent husband and worked in a local factory. The landlord kept the central heating control under lock and key as he was paying the bills and as I recall, it got rather cold after nine o'clock in winter. There were two options; have an early night or go to the pub. I usually chose the latter and became a regular at the Woolpack at the top of Tennyson Road. The clientele was a mixture of locals and incomers and I joined three fellow teachers as regulars at the pub. Dave Robins, who taught at another comprehensive in the town, was best man at my first wedding and remains a good friend to this day. Weekends tended to start on Thursday and the beer would really flow on a Friday and Saturday as we got the working week out of our systems. After hours, we often adjourned across the road to one of the lad's houses complete with party sevens (remember them) to play Yahtzee, the world's best-selling dice game for (relatively) small stakes. I also started going to the races regularly at this time, mainly Newmarket, but also further afield when the opportunity arose. Trips always began with beer. Just before the guard blew his whistle the cry would go up of "fingers on rings" and as soon as the train began to move the ring pulls would be simultaneously ripped off the cans and a day of drinking and gambling would commence. I felt truly at home in Kings Lynn and it is only the career I have enjoyed subsequently that tempers my regret at leaving.

However, the following year my girlfriend came down to join me and we rented a three-bedroom home together on an estate at the rather steeper rate of £125 per month. This was the effective end of my bachelor life. Our new home was bang in the catchment area and some of my pupils were faintly scandalised that I lived with my girlfriend. It seems extraordinary looking back but even in 1980 cohabiting, now the norm rather than the exception, still had a whiff of immorality about it. I don't recall my parents commenting on the rare occasions I saw them in this period, but I doubt they wholly approved. My father would had to have admitted to his workmates in the pub that his eldest son was "living over the brush", as it was still known back home in Blackburn. Growing away allowed you to ignore your parent's values. We also began saving for our own home immediately, even though we hadn't yet discussed marriage. Nevertheless, the racing trips, darts matches and Thursday night down the Woolpack survived intact. In February 1982 we married and six months later bought our own home, a two-bedroom semi in the Chase area of the town, and crucially for me back within walking distance of the Woolpack. Just short of my thirtieth birthday I was now on the property ladder, burdened with a mortgage that wouldn't be repaid for twenty-five years or more, an unimaginable time when you are young. I had now become respectable and responsible in the same year. Having put down roots by investing in our own home, it seemed like the growing away process was complete. However, as I would find out, life is what happens to you when you are busy making other plans.

My first wife never settled in West Norfolk and wished to return to the North Staffordshire area. For her there would be no growing away. After our notice periods were served, we spent a short period renting before we bought a semi-detached home just a few doors away from her mother. Fast forward twenty years and she could be found just two doors away from her mother in Stoke-On-Trent where she remains to this day. Moving back to North Staffordshire was not without its complications and in the end it would entail me abandoning the teaching profession. I lay no claim to have been anything other than a classroom journeyman and harbour no illusions that I jettisoned a potentially glittering career. As a classroom teacher I was well suited to "A" level students at one end and Year Seven – as it is now called – at the other. I found youngsters who were uninterested in education frustrating and lacked the guile to avoid letting it show. Children pick up on that sort of thing very swiftly and in that environment teaching can become a war of attrition, rather than imparting knowledge and a love of searching for it. Insofar as I am remembered at all, I would imagine the memories will be very mixed, rather like my teaching. We had hoped that I might be able to move on promotion, as moving sideways usually entailed competing against cheaper probationers and there was also an unspoken presumption that such applications betrayed a lack of ambition. I discovered fairly swiftly that a B.Ed was not considered an appropriate qualification for a Head of

History. Without a B.A., I would need a Masters and duly applied to the University of Keele in Staffordshire for a place.

My application for an M.A. course was successful, but unfortunately grants for higher degrees were discretionary not mandatory. In the financial climate that pertained in 1983, it came as no great surprise that Staffordshire County Council would not fund my studies. I was forced to turn down the place and took a temporary job as a History teacher at a high school in Newcastle-Under-Lyme. In a climate where posts were contracting, Staffordshire gave preference to existing employees for redeployment to vacant positions. I was faced with the prospect of a string of temporary posts, mixed in with supply teaching, before at some unspecified date in the future I might secure a permanent contract. If we wanted to get back swiftly on the housing ladder and remain there, then the only option was a career change. In the end I opted to apply for the prison service rather than the Inland Revenue.

For a few years after leaving education I felt very guilty about walking away from a life I considered to be a vocation as well as a career. On and off, I toyed with the idea of returning to the profession. My curriculum vitae would have looked a good deal more attractive on the back of working with young offenders for three years, particularly as I had now acquired the skills to manage young people of low intelligence, zero motivation and poor attainment. In 1988 the penal establishment where I worked, HMYOI Werrington, became a juvenile establishment with a greater emphasis on the pastoral as opposed to the punitive. Five years earlier, while still teaching, I had not come to terms with the pastoral system as it had developed in large comprehensive schools. I wanted to be an educator, not a social worker. I harked back to how it was when I was school, not that many years ago when pastoral care was considered to be a matter for your parents, other than when a religious input was needed. The truth was I was still playing skiffle while the rest of the band had moved on to rock and roll. Dave Robins and I would have numerous conversations, over a pint, about the shortcomings of pastoral systems and senior colleagues who seemed to have an unerring knack of coinciding a meeting with some recalcitrant child's parents with a teaching commitment, resulting in junior staff like us being forced to cover. In time, Dave would make his accommodation and retire as a senior pastoral head. I'm sure I would have done the same had I stayed the course. Instead the prison service spotted a talent that a few years earlier I had denied having, and for two years until moving on as a result of promotion I had a very satisfying professional life. Taking promotion in the service put paid to any thoughts of leaving. That combined with a divorce made it financially unviable. In the end I would never return to the classroom and have not seriously considered it since I retired from the prison service. I'm under no illusions that I would be anything other than a dinosaur. The world of education has long moved on without me.

Those readers interested in a full account of my prison service career are directed to my memoirs entitled "26 Years behind Bars: The Recollections of a Prison Governor". As regards this chapter, I will confine my observations to those in tune with the main theme of this chapter. I joined as a prison officer and the lower ranks in those days were firmly working class, mostly secondary modern educated and consequently lacking in academic qualifications, but not necessarily ability. The Governor grades, by contrast, were almost all university educated, and those that were not middle class by birth were middle class by education. This occurred as a result of two separate streams of entry, abolished in 1987, that mirrored the system that still pertains in the armed forces; those who are destined to be officers and gentlemen on the one hand and those who are destined to be NCOs and private soldiers on the other. I applied twice unsuccessfully to be an Assistant Governor; once as an external candidate and after two years' service as an internal candidate. The majority of my new colleagues were ex-servicemen, the older ones usually former national servicemen, the younger ones former regulars. They brought the familiar values of working-class communities, loyalty, fraternity and patriotism with them, but also a downside of insularity and rigidity. These qualities combined made the Prison Officers Association a very formidable trade union.

In some ways I had come home, but in others I had encountered an alien world. Firstly, apart from open establishments and even these are screened from prying eyes by fences, prisons operate behind high walls. They are there to keep people in and the very presence of a prison in a community is a reminder of the fate that awaits the wrongdoer. What happens behind the walls is largely a mystery and what most people know about prisons is stilled gleaned from a forty-year-old sitcom, "Porridge". The work carried out by prison staff is physically and mentally isolating. It is easy to feel misunderstood, particularly because of the misinformation in the press and the propensity of a number of MPs who should know better to fire off cheap shots. Government policy over the last two decades has had the effect of isolating prisons further from the communities they serve. Secondly, although prison officer grades only comprise about half the staff of the service, they are its most visible presence, obviously because of the front line role with prisoners, but also because they wear uniform. In that sense they are closer to the military, still an important recruiting source, and to the police, but without the daily interaction with the public.

It was very hard to convince my father that I was not actually a policeman. On one particular occasion when I was able to combine a visit to Blackburn with a game at Ewood Park, I returned to my parent's home after the match to find him arguing with someone whose car he had deliberately blocked in. Out of the corner of my eye I spotted a police officer approaching. This was not just any police officer, he had three pips and carried a pace stick. This was clearly the match day commander, a chief inspector. The top man himself had come to sort out this dispute about inconsiderate parking. My father wanted to continue the argument and I told him he'd got the most senior officer on duty and it would be sensible to back down, which in fairly short order he did but not without audible comments regarding "your lot" and the side I had apparently chosen. This ambiguity in working-class families about their sons (and their daughters) joining the police and the prison service was not unusual. Although families would be pleased that you had a secure job with prospects, a pension, and a place to live, there was a residual view that you had joined those who when called upon had the job of oppressing the working class, as per the 1984–85 miners' strike. Joining a law enforcement agency was therefore another form of growing away.

With only one significant setback soon overcome, the 1990s were a decade of career success. At the beginning of 1990 I was a prison officer. By the end of the decade I had risen to be a Deputy Governor. I had become a junior Governor grade in 1995 and therefore swapped the uniform for a suit. There was no longer any ambiguity about my position in the class structure. I continued in the prison service until October 2010. The new decade was not one of comparable achievement. I passed the assessment centre, which made me eligible for in-charge appointments, but apart from a temporary in-charge appointment I was never substantively promoted. Thus, I was allowed to stand on the summit but not leave any record of me being there in the form of my name appearing on the Roll of past governors of that establishment. I did serve on the NEC of the Prison Governors Association. My father was a train driver who wore his 1955 ASLEF strike badge on his cap. Trade Unionism was in my blood and there was no question of growing away from that. It's a source of great pride to me that I was elected to serve on the NEC of my professional association and I treasure the Distinguished Life Membership that I was awarded on retirement.

Between 1991 and 2007, I moved home either alone or with a spouse seven times in pursuit of my career. As I have said, my first marriage did not survive and we separated in 1989, three years after the birth of our daughter, my only child. The downside side of this nomadic life, all subsidised by the service, which was once the norm for ambitious staff pursuing a career, was that it was difficult to put down any roots. Indeed, gradually you become rootless, the least comfortable aspect of growing away. It also makes things awkward when you are a parent without custody as I was. My marriage to the second Mrs Laxton in 1992 was very short. Our relationship began when we were working together at Bedford prison. Her main aim in life was to end her exile and get back to Wakefield, her home city. I was able to achieve that for her, but we swiftly went our separate ways. I met my third wife in 1995 and we are still together, now growing old together, having married in 2002. As a pair we have moved four times with my job, five if you count the first move in 1995, when we initially purchased separate homes. With retirement heaving into the view, possibly the most important decision of the rest of lives now had to be made, the one about the final move. Put simply, the question was where do we live? We elected to move back north from East Sussex to West Yorkshire, where we originally met and where my wife had friends that somehow she had held on to when loyally accompanying me around the country, always putting my career first. This allowed us to sell up and, with the help of my lump sum, buy our retirement home outright. The last thing we needed was paying even a small mortgage out of our pensions, especially as we intended to have plenty of holidays while we were still fit enough to enjoy them. This entailed downsizing our expectations from the three storey town house overlooking the marina at Newhaven, on which we were paying £1,000 a month for the privilege, and still owed a six figure sum. We bought an ordinary semi in an ordinary cul-de-sac in Huddersfield. Our neighbours are either retired people like ourselves, or ordinary working people doing ordinary jobs to maintain their families and provide for their futures. In short, the district where I now live is almost the mirror image of the respectable working-class district in which I grew up. There are fewer overalls and more white collars, but that simply reflects the changing demo-graphic of the workforce with the decline of manufacturing. In some respects life has come full circle.

Growing away is harder for my daughter's generation. She graduated from Swansea University in 2008 and spent a year working in Cardiff before going on a working trip to Australia in 2009. My daughter returned to England in 2010 at the height of the recession. The growing away process was dramatically reversed by the need to return to her mother's home in Stoke-On-Trent while she found work. I'm happy to report that she was soon gainfully employed and doing well at her company, but only recently has she been able to move back out of her mother's home. It's much harder for her generation. They are burdened with student debt, rents and house prices are much higher in relation to salaries than they were when I was her age, and opportunities are fewer and competition greater with more graduates on the job market. They can also look forward to working longer and to poorer pensions, although I doubt that is an immediate concern. Nevertheless, I would be surprised if my daughter does spend her life in Stoke-On-Trent. The urge to grow away is just temporarily dormant in her case, unless I am massively mistaken. Young people do not worry about becoming rootless as they look forward not back.

My last link with Blackburn is my brother and his family who live in the Ewood district where we grew up. He has lived in either Blackburn or neighbouring Darwen, now all joined together as Blackburn with Darwen, all his life unlike his three siblings. Our father used to say that he would only leave the family home in a box and indeed he did. I would guess that my brother will be the same, hopefully not until many more years have passed. My sisters live in West Wales and Oxfordshire respectively and are settled where they are. After our late mother moved to Oxford in 2003, I have visited the town only a handful of times at the most. My father's brother's family are no longer represented in the Blackburn and Darwen area. Uncle Allan, still going strong in his eighty-ninth year, now lives in Essex with his daughter, having moved there following the death of his wife, Aunt Clara. My cousin Nigel, Allan's eldest son, has lived in Australia for more than a quarter of a century. Realistically, I can't see him coming home. His younger brother, Mark, was last heard of living in Torquay. Cousin Pauline on my mother's side has lived in Canada for more than forty years. Her brother and sister have both lived in Canada for their entire adult lives.

So it remains to be seen if any of my brother's children keep our surname on the town's electoral roll or whether we die out as a local family and disappear from a borough where generations of Laxtons have lived since the industrial revolution, when one of our ancestors felt the need to grow away from rural Norfolk and take his chances in the cotton mills. Of course it is not something I shall live to see.